Palgrave Macmillan Studies in Banking and Financial Institutions

Series Editor
Philip Molyneux, Bangor University, Bangor, UK

The Palgrave Macmillan Studies in Banking and Financial Institutions series is international in orientation and includes studies of banking systems in particular countries or regions as well as contemporary themes such as Islamic Banking, Financial Exclusion, Mergers and Acquisitions, Risk Management, and IT in Banking. The books focus on research and practice and include up to date and innovative studies that cover issues which impact banking systems globally.

Felix I. Lessambo

Anti-Money Laundering, Counter Financing Terrorism and Cybersecurity in the Banking Industry

A Comparative Study within the G-20

palgrave
macmillan

Felix I. Lessambo
Fordham University
New Britain, CT, USA

ISSN 2523-336X   ISSN 2523-3378 (electronic)
Palgrave Macmillan Studies in Banking and Financial Institutions
ISBN 978-3-031-23483-5   ISBN 978-3-031-23484-2 (eBook)
https://doi.org/10.1007/978-3-031-23484-2

Cover illustration: Zoonar GmbH/Alamy Stock Photo

This Palgrave Macmillan imprint is published by the registered company Springer Nature Switzerland AG
The registered company address is: Gewerbestrasse 11, 6330 Cham, Switzerland

ACKNOWLEDGMENTS

Writing a book is always a challenge. However, writing a book on AML/CFT and Cybersecurity in the Banking Industry, a more daring intellectual exercise.

I would like to thank my astoundingly supportive friends who motivated me all along the project, knowing my dedication to the subject and thought I am more than able to complete this project: Dr. Marsha Gordon, Dr. Linda Sama, Dr. Lavern A. Wright, Dr. Lester Reid, Jordan Romine, Yanick Gil, and Jerry Izouele.

Last but not least, thank you to all the original readers of this book when it was in its infancy. Without your enthusiasm and encouragement, this book may have never been ready.

DISCLAIMER

While the author has made every effort to ensure that the information in this book is correct at the time of publication, he does not assume and hereby disclaims any liability to any party for any loss, damage, or disruption caused by errors or omissions, whether such errors or omissions result from negligence, accident, or any other cause.

This publication is designed to provide accurate and authoritative information with regard to the subject matter covered. It is sold on the understanding that the publisher is not engaged in rendering professional services. If professional advice or other expert assistance is needed, the services of a competent professional should be sought.

CONTENTS

1	**Money Laundering and Combating Finance Terrorism**	1
	1.1 General	1
	1.2 Money Laundering	2
	1.3 Money Laundering Cycle	2
	1.3.1 Placement	3
	1.3.2 Layering	3
	1.3.3 Integration	4
	1.4 Combating Financial Crimes	4
	1.5 International Money Laundering organizations	5
	1.5.1 Financial Action Task Force	5
	1.5.2 The Office of Foreign Assets Control	6
	1.5.3 The Financial Crimes Enforcement Network	6
	1.5.4 The Asia/Pacific Group on Money Laundering	7
	1.5.5 The Egmont Group of Financial Intelligence Units	7
	1.5.6 The International Association of Insurance Supervisors	8
	1.5.7 The Association of Certified Anti-Money Laundering Specialists	9
	1.5.8 ComplyAdvantage	9
	1.6 The Failure of the Current System	9
2	**The Cybersecurity Counteroffensive**	11

2.1	*General*		11
2.2	*History of Cybersecurity*		12
	2.2.1	*1920s*	12
	2.2.2	*1930s*	13
	2.2.3	*1940s: The Time Before Crime*	13
	2.2.4	*1950s: The Phone Phreaks*	13
	2.2.5	*1960s: All Quiet on the Western Front*	14
	2.2.6	*1970s: Computer Security Is Born*	14
	2.2.7	*1980s: From ARPANET to Internet*	15
	2.2.8	*1987: The Birth of Cybersecurity*	16
	2.2.9	*1990s: The World Goes Online*	17
	2.2.10	*2000s: Threats Diversify and Multiply*	19
	2.2.11	*2010s: The Next Generation*	20
2.3	*Types of Cyberattacks*		21
2.4	*Cybersecurity Risk vs. Traditional Risk*		28
	2.4.1	*Application Security*	28
	2.4.2	*Cloud Security*	28
	2.4.3	*Infrastructure Security*	29
	2.4.4	*Internet of Things (IoT) Security*	29
	2.4.5	*Network Security*	30
2.5	*Cybersecurity and the Banking Industry*		30
2.6	*International Cooperation*		31
3	**AML/CFT, Cybersecurity and International Organization**		**33**
3.1	*General*		33
3.2	*AML/CFT International Organizations*		33
	3.2.1	*The Financial Action Task Force on Money Laundering (FAFT)*	33
	3.2.2	*The International Money Laundering Information Network (IMoLIN)*	34
	3.2.3	*Financial Action Task Force on Money Laundering in Latin America (GAFILAT)*	36
3.3	*Cybersecurity in International Organizations*		36
	3.3.1	*The Council of Europe: Action Against Cybercrime*	37
	3.3.2	*International Criminal Police Organization (INTERPOL)*	40

	3.3.3	International Telecommunications Union (ITU)	41
	3.3.4	United Nations Office of Drugs and Crime (UNODC)	42
	3.3.5	The Organization of Economic Cooperation and Development (OECD)	43
	3.3.6	G8 24/7 Cybercrime Network	43
	3.3.7	The Internet Society (ISOC)	44
	3.3.8	The International Cyber Security Protection Alliance (ICSPA)	44
	3.3.9	International Association of Insurance Supervisors (IAIS)	45
	3.3.10	International Organization of Securities Commissions (IOSCO)	45
3.4	An International Strategy		46
3.5	Cybercrime Conventions		46
	3.5.1	The International Cybercrime Treaty	46
	3.5.2	The UNDOP International Treaty on Cybercrime	47
	3.5.3	African Union Convention on Cyberspace Security and Personal Data Protection	47

4 AML and Cybersecurity in Banking Industry: Challenges   49
4.1	Overview		49
4.2	AML and the Banking Industry		50
4.3	Cybersecurity in the Banking Industry		50
4.4	Core Cybersecurity Risks in the Banking		51
	4.4.1	The Compromising of Confidential data	51
	4.4.2	The Compromising of Data Availability or Systems	52
	4.4.3	The Compromising of Data Integrity	52
4.5	Ensuring Cyber Security in Banks		53

5 AML/CFT and Cyber Security Laws in the United States   57
5.1	General	57
5.2	AML/CFT Laws	57
5.3	AML/CFT Legislations	58

5.3.1   *The Bank Secrecy Act (aka the Financial
         Recordkeeping of Currency and Foreign
         Transactions Act of 1970*   58
5.3.2   *Money Laundering Control Act (1986)*   59
5.3.3   *Anti-Drug Abuse Act (1988)*   60
5.3.4   *Annunzio-Wylie Anti-money Laundering
         Act (1992)*   60
5.3.5   *Money Laundering Suppression Act (1994)*   61
5.3.6   *Money Laundering and Financial Crimes
         Strategy Act (1998)*   63
5.3.7   *Uniting and Strengthening America
         by Providing Appropriate Tools Required
         to Intercept and Obstruct Terrorism Act
         of 2001 (USA PATRIOT Act)*   65
5.3.8   *The USA Patriot Improvement
         and Reauthorization Act of 2005*   65
5.3.9   *The National Defense Authorization Act
         for Fiscal Year 2021 (NDAA)*   68
5.4   Cybersecurity Laws   68
5.4.1   *Comprehensive Crime Control Act of 1984*   69
5.4.2   *The Computer Fraud and Abuse Act of 1986*   69
5.4.3   *The Electronic Communications Privacy
         Act of 1986*   70
5.4.4   *The Health Insurance Portability
         and Accountability Act (HIPAA) of 1996*   70
5.4.5   *Intelligence Reform & Terrorism
         Prevention Act (2004)*   71
5.4.6   *The Cybersecurity Act of 2012*   71
5.4.7   *Cybersecurity Enhancement Act of 2014*   72
5.4.8   *The Infrastructure Security Services Act
         of 2015*   72
5.5   Federal Cybersecurity Laws in the Banking Industry   73
5.5.1   *Federal Cybersecurity Laws*   73
5.5.2   *Cybersecurity State Laws*   75
5.6   Federal Government Agencies   77
5.6.1   *Department of Justice–Division
         of Computer Crime & Intellectual
         Property Section (CCIPS)*   77
5.6.2   *U.S. Secret Service*   78

| | 5.6.3 | Immigration & Customs Enforcement (ICE) | 78 |

6   AML/CFT and Cybersecurity Laws in the European Union — 79
- 6.1   General — 79
- 6.2   AML/CFT in the EU — 80
  - 6.2.1   Fifth Anti-Money Laundering Directive — 80
  - 6.2.2   General Data Protection Regulation (GDPR) — 81
  - 6.2.3   The Second Payments Services Directive (PSD2) — 82
  - 6.2.4   Sixth Anti-Money Laundering Directive — 84
- 6.3   Cybersecurity in the EU — 86
  - 6.3.1   Budapest Convention on Cybercrime (2001) — 86
  - 6.3.2   EU Network and Information Security (NIS) Directive — 88
  - 6.3.3   Proposed EU General Data Protection Regulation — 88

7   AML/CFT and Cybersecurity Laws in Germany — 91
- 7.1   AML Laws in Germany — 91
- 7.2   Cybersecurity Laws — 93
- 7.3   Cybersecurity Laws and Regulations — 93
  - 7.3.1   Federal Data Protection Act (BDSG) — 93
- 7.4   Cybersecurity Laws in the Banking and Financial Sector — 96
  - 7.4.1   Comprehensive Information and Security System — 97
  - 7.4.2   Well-Established Information Network — 97
  - 7.4.3   Regular Controls — 97
  - 7.4.4   Employee Awareness — 98

8   AML/CFT and Cybersecurity Laws in France — 99
- 8.1   General — 99
- 8.2   AML/CFT Laws — 100
- 8.3   Cybersecurity — 104
  - 8.3.1   Cybersecurity Laws and Regulations — 104
  - 8.3.2   Cybersecurity in Banking — 106

9   AML/CFT and Cybersecurity Laws in Italy — 107
- 9.1   AML/CFT Laws — 107

9.2 AML/ CFT Legislations 108
9.3 Cybersecurity Laws and Regulations 108
   9.3.1 Prime Ministerial Decree of 17 February 108
   9.3.2 Italian Legislative Decree No. 65/2018 109
   9.3.3 Italian Legislative Decree No. 105/2019 109
   9.3.4 Italian Legislative Decree No. 82/2021 109
9.4 Cybersecurity in the Banking Industry 110

10 AML/CFT and Cybersecurity Laws in Spain 113
10.1 General 113
10.2 AML/CFT Laws 114
10.3 Cybersecurity Regulations 114
   10.3.1 Article 197 114
   10.3.2 Article 248 116
   10.3.3 Article 264 116
   10.3.4 Article 256 117
   10.3.5 Article 270 117
   10.3.6 Article 273 117
10.4 Cybersecurity in the Banking Industry 118

11 AML/CFT and Cybersecurity Laws in Switzerland 119
11.1 General 119
11.2 AML/CFT Laws 120
11.3 Cybersecurity Laws 121
11.4 Cybersecurity Laws in the Banking Industry 122

12 AML/CFT and Cybersecurity Laws in China 125
12.1 General 125
12.2 AML/CFT Laws 126
12.3 Cybersecurity Laws in China 127
   12.3.1 The Chinese Cybersecurity Law 127
   12.3.2 The "Cybersecurity Multi-Level Protection
       System 2.0" or "MLPS 2.0 128
   12.3.3 Cybersecurity Protection of Critical
       Information Infrastructure (GB/T
       39204-2020) 129
12.4 Cybersecurity in the Banking Industry 129

13 AML/CFT and Cybersecurity Laws in Japan 131
13.1 General 131
13.2 AML/CFT 131

13.3   Cybersecurity Laws   133
       13.3.1   The Basic Cybersecurity Act   133
       13.3.2   The Unauthorized Computer Access
                Prohibition Act   133
       13.3.3   The Specially Designated Secret Protection
                Act (Act no. 108 of 2013)   134
       13.3.4   The Basic Act on the Formation
                of an Advanced Information
                and Telecommunications Network Society   134
       13.3.5   The Act on Electronic Signatures
                and Certification Business   134
       13.3.6   The Act on the Protection of Personal
                Information (APPI)   135
13.4   Cybersecurity in the Banking Industry   135

14   AML/CFT and Cybersecurity Laws in India   137
14.1   General   137
14.2   AML/CFT Laws   137
       14.2.1   The Prevention of Money Laundering Act,
                2002   138
       14.2.2   The Conservation of Foreign Exchange
                and Prevention of Smuggling Activities
                Act, 1974   139
       14.2.3   The Benami Transactions (Prohibition)
                Act, 1988   139
       14.2.4   The Indian Penal Code, 1860 and Code
                of Criminal Procedure, 1973   139
       14.2.5   The Narcotic Drugs and Psychotropic
                Substances Act, 1985   140
14.3   Cybersecurity Laws   140
       14.3.1   The Information Technology Act of 2000
                (IT Act)   140
       14.3.2   The Information Technology (Reasonable
                Security Practices and Procedures
                and Sensitive Personal Data
                or Information) Rules—"Privacy
                Rules"   141
14.4   Cybersecurity in the Banking Industry   141

15   AML/CFT and Cybersecurity Laws in South Korea   143

15.1		*General*	143
15.2		*AML/CFT Laws*	143
	15.2.1	*The 1995 Act on Special Cases Concerning the Prevention of Illegal Trafficking in Narcotics, Psychotropic Substances and Hemp (ASPIT)*	144
	15.2.2	*The 2001 Proceeds of Crime Act (POCA)*	144
	15.2.3	*The Prohibition of Financing for Offences of Public Intimidation Act (PFOPIA)*	145
15.3		*Cybersecurity Laws*	145
	15.3.1	*Act on the Protection of Information and Communications Infrastructure Information and Communications Network Act*	145
	15.3.2	*Personal Information Protection Act (PIPA)*	146
15.4		*Cybersecurity in the Banking Industry*	146

16   AML/CFT and Cybersecurity Laws in Indonesia   147

16.1		*General*	147
16.2		*AML/CFT Laws*	147
	16.2.1	*Indonesia OJK Regulation No. 12/POJK.01/2017*	148
16.3		*Cybersecurity Laws*	148
	16.3.1	*Electronic Information and Transactions Law*	149
	16.3.2	*MoCI Regulation 20/2016*	149
	16.3.3	*GR 71/2019*	150
16.4		*Cybersecurity in the Banking Industry*	150

17   AML/CFT and Cybersecurity Law in the UK   151

17.1		*General*	151
17.2		*AML/CFT Laws*	152
	17.2.1	*The Economic Crime (Transparency and Enforcement) Act 2022 (ECA 2022)*	152
17.3		*Cybersecurity Laws*	153
	17.3.1	*Computer Misuse Act of 1990 (Amended in 2006)*	154
	17.3.2	*The UK Data Protection Act of 1998 (as Amended in 2018)*	154
17.4		*Cybersecurity in the Banking Industry*	155

| | 17.4.1 | *The NatWest Case* | 156 |
| | 17.4.2 | *The HSBC Bank Plc Case* | 156 |

18 AML/CFT and Cybersecurity Law in Canada **157**
18.1 *General* 157
18.2 *AML/CFT Laws* 158
18.3 *Cybersecurity in Canada* 159
    18.3.1 *Personal Information Protection &*
         Electronic Documents Act (PIPEDA) (2005) 160
18.4 *Cybersecurity Laws in the Banking Industry* 161

19 AML/CFT and Cybersecurity Law in Australia **163**
19.1 *General* 163
19.2 *AML/CFT Laws* 164
19.3 *Code* 164
    19.3.1 *The Anti-Money Laundering*
         and Counter-Terrorism Financing
         Act 2006 164
19.4 *Cybersecurity Laws* 165
    19.4.1 *Telecommunications (Interception*
         and Access) Act 1979 165
    19.4.2 *Privacy Act 1998 (Amended 2017)* 166
    19.4.3 *Assistance and Access Act (AA Act,*
         as Amended in 2018) 166
    19.4.4 *Consumer Data Right* 166
    19.4.5 *The Security of Critical Infrastructure Act*
         2018 (SOCI) (Amended in 2021) 167
    19.4.6 *The Consumer Privacy Protection Bill*
         (CPPA) (2022) 167
19.5 *Cybersecurity Laws in the Banking Industry* 168

20 AML/CFT and Cybersecurity Laws in Russia **169**
20.1 *General* 169
20.2 *AML/CFT Laws* 170
20.3 *Cybersecurity Laws* 170
    20.3.1 *The Federal Law No. 152-FZ Dated 27*
         July 2006 "On Personal Data" (the "Data
         Protection Law") 170
    20.3.2 *The Labor Code of the Russian Federation*
         (for Personal Data of Employees) 171

20.4 Cybersecurity in the Banking Industry   172

21 AML/CFT and Cybersecurity Laws in Turkey   173
    21.1 General   173
    21.2 AML/CFT Laws   173
        21.2.1 Law No. 5549 on the Prevention
                of the Laundering of the Proceeds of Crime   173
    21.3 Cybersecurity Laws   174
        21.3.1 The Constitution of the Turkish Republic   174
        21.3.2 The Data Protection Laws   175
        21.3.3 Internet Law No. 5651 of 2007   175
        21.3.4 Law on Electronic Communication No.
                5809 ("Law No. 5809")   176
        21.3.5 Turkish Criminal Code No. 5237   177
    21.4 Cybersecurity Laws in the Banking Industry   177
        21.4.1 Banking Law No. 5411   177

22 AML/CFT and Cybersecurity Laws in Brazil   179
    22.1 General   179
    22.2 AML/CFT Laws   179
        22.2.1 Law No. 12,683, of July 9, 2012 ('Law
                12,683/12')   180
    22.3 Cybersecurity Laws   180
    22.4 Cybersecurity in the Banking Industry   181

23 AML/CFT and Cybersecurity Laws in Mexico   183
    23.1 General   183
    23.2 AML/CFT Laws   184
    23.3 Cybersecurity Laws   185
        23.3.1 The Mexican Constitution   185
        23.3.2 The Data Protection Law   186
    23.4 Cybersecurity Laws in the Banking Industry   186

24 AML/CFT and Cybersecurity Laws in Argentina   189
    24.1 General   189
    24.2 AML/CFT Laws   189
        24.2.1 Resolution 30-E/2017 on AML/CFT   190
    24.3 Cybersecurity Laws   190
        24.3.1 Privacy and Data Protection   191
    24.4 Cybersecurity in the Banking Industry   192

25 AML/CFT and Cybersecurity Laws in Saudi Arabia   193
    25.1 General   193
    25.2 AML/CFT Laws   194
    25.3 Cybersecurity Laws   194
        25.3.1 The Anti-Cybercrimes Law of 2017   194
        25.3.2 The National Data Governance Interim
              Regulations of 2020   195
    25.4 Cybersecurity in the Banking Industry   195

26 AML/CFT and Cybersecurity Laws in South Africa   197
    26.1 General   197
    26.2 AML/ CFT Laws   198
        26.2.1 The Financial Intelligence Centre Act, No
              38 of 2001 (The FIC Act)   198
        26.2.2 The Prevention and Combatting of Corrupt
              Activities Act, 2004 (PRECCA)   198
        26.2.3 The Protection of Constitutional Democracy
              Against Terrorist and Related Activities
              Act, 2004 (Amended in 2021)   199
    26.3 Cybersecurity Laws   200
        26.3.1 The Protection of Personal Information Act
              4 of 2013   201
        26.3.2 The Cybercrimes and Cybersecurity Act
              (2021)   201
    26.4 Cybersecurity in the Banking Industry   201

27 AML/CFT Compliance and Audit   205
    27.1 General   205
    27.2 AML Compliance   207
    27.3 CFT Compliance   207
    27.4 AML/CFT Audit   208
        27.4.1 Internal AML/CFT Audit   208
        27.4.2 External AML/CFT Audit   209
    27.5 The AML/CFT Compliance Index (AML/CFT CI)   210
        27.5.1 Basel AML Index   211
        27.5.2 The Global Organized Crime Index   213

28 International and Regional Cooperation   215
    28.1 General   215

28.2   Cooperation and exchange of information
        in AML/CFT   216
        28.2.1   In the Authorization Process   216
        28.2.2   In the Ongoing Supervision   216
        28.2.3   Regarding Enforcement Actions   217
        28.2.4   Confidentiality Treatment   217
28.3   Cooperation and Exchange of Information
        in Cybersecurity   217
        28.3.1   The OECD Approach   218
        28.3.2   The International Telecommunications
                  Union (ITU)   218
        28.3.3   The European Union Agency for Network
                  and Information Security (ENISA)   219

Glossary of Terms   221

Bibliography   227

Index   231

Acronyms

ABA	Australian Bankers Association
AI	Artificial Intelligence
AML/CFT	Anti-Money Laundering/Countering the Financing of Terrorism
AMLD	Anti-Money Laundering Directive
BCBS	Basel Committee on Banking Supervision
BIS	Bank for International Settlements
CBA	Canadian Bankers Association
CCIPS	Computer Crime & Intellectual Property Section (US DoJ)
CFT	Counter Financing of Terrorism
COE	Council of Europe
DSP	Digital Service Provider
ECTF	Electronic Crime Task Force
ETF	Internet Engineering Task Force
EU	European Union
FATF	Financial Action Task Force
FFMS	Federal Financial Monitoring Services
FIU	Financial Intelligence Unit
FSI	Financial Secrecy Index
ICE	Immigration and Customs Enforcement
ICSPA	International Cyber Security Protection Alliance
IMF	International Monetary Fund
IO	Immediate Outcome (FATF)
ML/TF	Money Laundering/Terrorist Financing
NATO	North Atlantic Treaty Organization
NGO	Non-Governmental Organization
OECD	Organization for Economic Co-operation and Development

TI CPI   Transparency International Corruption Perceptions Index
UN   United Nations
US INCSR   United States State Department International Narcotics Control
            Strategy Report
US   United States
WEF   World Economic Forum
WJP   World Justice Project

LIST OF FIGURES

Fig. 1.1   Money laundering cycle   4
Fig. 1.2   UN-estimated global proceedings of crime (*Source*
            UN-estimated global proceeds of crime, 3.6% GDP)   10
Fig. 2.1   Percentage of organization hit by ransomware (*Source*
            Sophos)   12
Fig. 2.2   Evolution of U.S. cyber power (*Source* US GAO [2022]:
            The Evolution of U.S. Cyber power)   27
Fig. 2.3   Most cyber-secured countries (*Source* International
            Telecommunication Union 2017)   32
Fig. 5.1   Computer fraud & abuse/sentences   70
Fig. 5.2   Essential critical infrastructure workers   73
Fig. 6.1   Budapest convention on cybersecurity (*Source* CoE
            [2020])   87
Fig. 9.1   Italian national cybersecurity architecture   110
Fig. 11.1   Cybersecurity in banking and other financial industry   123
Fig. 27.1   Basel AML index (*Source* BIS [2020])   212
Fig. 27.2   BIS—Scaling & weighing indicators (*Source* BIS [2020]:
            Scaling and weighing indicators)   212
Fig. 27.3   Five worst countries in 2021 (*Source* BIS [2021])   213

CHAPTER 1

Money Laundering and Combating Finance Terrorism

1.1 GENERAL

UN Vienna 1988 Convention Article 3.1 describes Money Laundering as: "the conversion or transfer of property, knowing that such property is derived from any offense(s), for the purpose of concealing or disguising the illicit origin of the property or of assisting any person who is involved in such offense(s) to evade the legal consequences of his actions".[1] The estimated amount of money laundered globally in one year is 2–5% of global GDP, or $800 billion–$2 trillion in current U.S. dollars. Due to the clandestine nature of money laundering, it is, however, difficult to estimate the total amount of money that goes through the laundering cycle.[2] In the same vein, terrorists and terrorist organizations usually need to rely on money to sustain themselves and to carry out terrorist acts. Some criminals use the financial system to support terrorists or acts of terrorism. Terrorist financiers and other criminals use the formal financial system, new payment methods such as bitcoin and Ripple, traditional methods of value transfer such as hawala*, trade-based money laundering, and cash

---

[1] https://www.unodc.org/unodc/en/money-laundering/overview.html.

[2] https://www.unodc.org/unodc/en/money-laundering/overview.html.

© The Author(s), under exclusive license to Springer Nature Switzerland AG 2023
F. I. Lessambo, *Anti-Money Laundering, Counter Financing Terrorism and Cybersecurity in the Banking Industry*, Palgrave Macmillan Studies in Banking and Financial Institutions,
https://doi.org/10.1007/978-3-031-23484-2_1

couriers, particularly in countries with non-existent or weak national anti-money laundering/countering the financing of terrorism (AML/CFT) tools.[3] Within the UE alone, the combined value of anti-money laundering penalties in 2018 and 2019, mostly levied on banks, was $4.3 billion and $8.1 billion, respectively.[4]

1.2   MONEY LAUNDERING

Money laundering is a practice almost as old time itself. From as early as 2000 BCE, wealthy Chinese merchants would move their profits outside of China, as the government did not support commercial trading. They would then reinvest their smuggled funds into other enterprises, a technique still used today. The term "money laundering" has become more colloquial from the mafia's ownership of Laundromats in the United States in the 1920s and 1930s. Organized criminals were making so much money from extortion, prostitution, gambling, and bootlegging; they needed to show a legitimate source of the money by hiding its true origin. Money laundering has been a crime in the United States since 1986, making the country one of the first countries to criminalize money laundering conduct. Indeed, criminal activity has been associated with a number of bank failures around the globe, including the failure of the first Internet bank, the European Union Bank.[5]

1.3   MONEY LAUNDERING CYCLE

The process in which money is laundered has been subject to much debate. It has traditionally centered upon a three-stage model of placement, layering, and integration that forms the foundation of governments' understanding about the money laundering process.[6]

---

[3] https://www.state.gov/anti-money-laundering-and-countering-the-financing-of-terrorism/.

[4] C. Burns (2019): Analysis from Encompass Shows 2019 Set to be Year of Record AML Fines. https://bit.ly/34uu5gv.

[5] John McDowell (2001): The Consequences of Money Laundering and Financial Crime, Economic Perspectives: An Electronic Journal of the U.S. Department of State, Vol. 6, No. 2, May 2001.

[6] Paul Michael Gilmour (2022): Reexamining the Anti-money-laundering Framework: A Legal Critique and New Approach to Combating Money Laundering, Journal of

1.3.1 Placement

The first stage of money laundering is when the individual participating in criminal activity places cash proceeds into the financial system. This is done so that they can get rid of the cash that is derived from criminal sources. It can be unsafe for people to hold onto a large amount of cash at one time, so they may try to dump the cash somewhere that provides greater security. Placement is more than merely moving the illegal proceeds into bank account. This stage corresponds to the greatest degree of vulnerability for the criminal. Financial officials are on the lookout for suspicious transactions that are cash-based. One of the biggest challenges is to identify the evolving placement methods. Criminals and syndicates will try to come up with new methods of placements so as to defeat the AML/ATF regime.[7]

1.3.2 Layering

The next stage of money laundering attempts to separate the money from its original, illegal source. This step is called 'layering' because the layers of financial transactions camouflage the illegal proceeds owners and obscure the money trail.[8] This part of the process is often complicated. By moving the money quickly and to different areas, the money may be transformed so that it is not detected through audits. During this stage, the money may be transferred between multiple countries. Layering can involve electronic transactions such as wires and ACHs, paper transactions, and/or manual movement of the funds between countries using covert means. Those laundering the funds may also decide to use non-traditional financial systems. That is, money may take the form of various investments and move faster than the regulators can trace back.

Financial Crime, pp. 1–13, https://www.newswise.com/pdf_docs/164803893193015_Gilmour%202022.pdf.

[7] Mohd Yazid bin Zul Kepli, Maruf Adeniyi Nasir (2016): Money Laundering: Analysis on the Placement methods, International Journal of Business, Economics and Law, Vol. 11, No. 5, pp. 1–9.

[8] Alison S. Bachus (2004): From Drugs to Terrorism—The Focus Shifts in the International Fight Against Money Laundering After September 11, 2001 (2004), Arizona Journal of International & Comparative Law 844.

Fig. 1.1   Money laundering cycle

1.3.3   Integration

This is the final stage of the money laundering process. This involves the process to get the funds back to the criminal from what seems to be a reputable source. After placing and layering the cash into the financial system, the funds become integrated.[9] In this manner, the criminal can receive funds from their original illegal source in methods that do not draw attention to the situation. This may include receiving money from a business purchased by the funds, such as a restaurant, department store, car wash, or laundry business. The business may carefully follow all other regulations in order to avoid detection, such as carefully paying all employee and business taxes and filing tax returns on a timely basis (Fig. 1.1).

1.4   COMBATING FINANCIAL CRIMES

Although the primary motivation of terrorism is not financial gain, which stands in sharp contrast to most crime, terrorists still need to use the

---

[9] Michael J. Anderson and Tracey A. Anderson (2015): Anti-money Laundering: History and Current Developments, https://www.researchgate.net/publication/316526 702_Anti-Money_Laundering_History_and_Current_Developments.

financial infrastructure to mobilize and channel their funds.[10] Financial crime has been around since the invention of currency. Stricto sensu, the term "financial crime" refers to any kind of criminal conduct relating to money or to financial services or markets, including any offense involving: fraud or dishonesty, misconduct in, or misuse of information relating to, a financial market, handling the proceeds of crime, or the financing of terrorism.[11] The IMF defines financial crime as a subset of financial abuse, which refers to any non-violent crime that generally results in a financial loss, including financial fraud. It also includes a range of illegal activities such as money laundering and tax evasion.[12] Terrorist financing shares multiple characteristics with money laundering in terms of sources, techniques, adaptability, and risks implied. Both are criminal activities attempting to disguise the sources and destination of funds, change the form of funds, or move the funds to a place where they are less likely to attract attention.[13]

1.5 International Money Laundering Organizations

1.5.1 *Financial Action Task Force*

The Financial Action Task Force, also known by its French name, Groupe d'action financière, is an intergovernmental organization founded in 1989 on the initiative of the G7 to develop policies to combat money laundering. In 2001, its mandate was expanded to include terrorism financing. The FATF is the main independent intergovernmental body at a global

---

[10] Barry Johnston and Oana M. Nedelescu (2005): The Impact of Terrorism on Financial Markets, IMF—Monetary and Financial Systems Department, pp. 1–24, https://www.imf.org/external/pubs/ft/irb/2005/eng/02/index.pdf.

[11] Marius-Christian Frunza (2016): Introduction to the Theories and Varieties of Modern Crime in Financial Markets, Elsevier, https://www.sciencedirect.com/book/978 0128012215/introduction-to-the-theories-and-varieties-of-modern-crime-in-financial-mar kets.

[12] IMF (2001): Financial System Abuse, Financial Crime and Money Laundering—Background Paper, pp. 1–41, https://www.imf.org/external/np/ml/2001/eng/021201. pdf.

[13] Barry Johnston and Oana M. Nedelescu (2005): The Impact of Terrorism on Financial Markets, IMF—Monetary and Financial Systems Department, pp. 1–24, https://www.imf.org/external/pubs/ft/irb/2005/eng/02/index.pdf.

level with the purpose of protecting the international financial system by promoting and developing regulations to counteract crimes such as money laundering, proliferation of weapons of mass destruction, and terrorist financing.[14]

1.5.2   The Office of Foreign Assets Control

The Office of Foreign Assets Control is a financial intelligence and enforcement agency of the U.S. Treasury Department. It administers and enforces economic and trade sanctions in support of U.S. national security and foreign policy objectives. It also lists individuals, groups, and entities, such as terrorists and narcotics traffickers designated under programs that are not country-specific. In May 2019, the U.S. Department of the Treasury's Office of Foreign Assets Control (OFAC) issued a broad framework identifying what OFAC views as the essential elements of risk-based sanctions compliance. At the same time, OFAC announced that it would consider how well these elements have been incorporated when considering its enforcement response to sanctions violations. In general, non-U.S. financial institutions are required to comply with OFAC's requirements only when conducting business that has some connection to the United States.[15] The new framework recommends that all organizations review enforcement actions published by OFAC for purposes of reassessing and enhancing sanctions compliance.[16]

1.5.3   The Financial Crimes Enforcement Network

The U.S. Department of the Treasury established the Financial Crimes Enforcement Network in 1990 to provide a government-wide multi-source financial intelligence and analysis network. The organization's operation was broadened in 1994 to include regulatory responsibilities for administering the Bank Secrecy Act, one of the nation's most potent weapons for preventing corruption of the U.S. financial system. The

---

[14] Corina-Narcisa, Maria Nitu, Mircea Constantin Scheau (2021): Efficiency of Money Laundering Countermeasures: Case Studies from European Union Member States, Risks, Vol. 9, p. 120. https://doi.org/10.3390/risks9060120.

[15] Benjamin W. Hutten (2021): Compliance Lessons in Recent Office of Foreign Assets Control EEnforcement, Journal of Financial Compliance, Vol. 4, No. 3, pp. 210–221.

[16] Idem.

mission of the Financial Crimes Enforcement Network is to enhance U.S. national security, deter and detect criminal activity, and safeguard financial systems from abuse by promoting transparency in the U.S. and international financial systems.[17] The Financial Crimes Enforcement Network is a bureau of the United States Department of the Treasury that collects and analyzes information about financial transactions in order to combat domestic and international money laundering, terrorist financing, and other financial crimes.

1.5.4 *The Asia/Pacific Group on Money Laundering*

The Asia/Pacific Group on Money Laundering is a FATF style regional intergovernmental body, the members of which are committed to implement international standards against money laundering, the financing of terrorism, and financing the proliferation of weapons of mass destruction. It is an intergovernmental organization, consisting of 41 member jurisdictions. The objective of the APG is to ensure that individual members effectively implement the international standards against money laundering, terrorist financing, and proliferation financing related to weapons of mass destruction.[18]

1.5.5 *The Egmont Group of Financial Intelligence Units*

The Egmont Group of Financial Intelligence Units (FIUs) is an international network of FIUs. The Egmont Group is designed to improve communication, information sharing, and training coordination among its FIU members. Its goal is to provide a forum for members of FIUs to improve support to their respective governments in the fight against money laundering, terrorist financing, and other financial crimes. The Egmont Group supports its FIU members by helping them to expand and systematize the exchange of financial intelligence and information, improve expertise and capabilities of personnel, and enable secure communication with one another. Furthermore, the Egmont Group supports the efforts of other international stakeholders on anti-money laundering and combating the financing of terrorism (AML/CFT),

---

[17] https://www.fincen.gov/mission-fincen.

[18] http://www.apgml.org/.

including the United Nations Security Council, the Financial Action Task Force, and the G20 Finance Ministers.[19] The Egmont Group has eight Regional Groups for member FIUs. The Regional Groups provide an opportunity for FIUs to coordinate on regional issues and communicate with the Egmont Group. There are four Egmont Working Groups: Information Exchange; Membership, Support, and Compliance; Policy and Procedures; and Technical Assistance and Training. In 2018, the Egmont Group established the Egmont Centre of FIU Excellence & Leadership (ECOFEL) to provide specialized training, mentoring, coaching, and other support to FIUs. ECOFEL is funded by the U.S. Department of State/Bureau of International Narcotics and Law Enforcement Affairs, among other donors.[20]

1.5.6 The International Association of Insurance Supervisors

The International Association of Insurance Supervisors is a voluntary membership organization of insurance supervisors from over 190 jurisdictions, constituting 97% of the world's insurance premiums. It is the international standards-setting body for the insurance sector. The IAIS is committed to preventing the misuse of insurance companies for money laundering purposes by giving guidance to insurance supervisory authorities as well as, as appropriate, to the insurance industry and by strengthening cooperation between its members and with the industry.[21] The IAIS has sought closer relations with the FATF by applying for observer status in the FATF, submitted comments on the Consultation Paper regarding the review of the FATF Recommendations, and attended meetings of the FATF working group on the review of the Recommendations. By participating in the review, the IAIS wants to ensure that FATF Recommendations accurately reflect the unique nature of the insurance business.[22]

---

[19] https://www.fincen.gov/resources/international/egmont-group-financial-intelligence-units.

[20] https://www.fincen.gov/resources/international/egmont-group-financial-intelligence-units.

[21] BIS (2003): The Joint-Forum-Initiatives by the BCBS, IAIS and IOSCO to Combat Money Laundering and the Financing of Terrorism, pp. 1–10, https://www.bis.org/publ/joint05.pdf.

[22] BIS (2003): The Joint-Forum-Initiatives by the BCBS, IAIS and IOSCO to Combat Money Laundering and the Financing of Terrorism, pp. 1–10, https://www.bis.org/publ/joint05.pdf.

1.5.7   *The Association of Certified Anti-Money Laundering Specialists*

The Association of Certified Anti-Money Laundering Specialists is an organization that provides training and certification, runs conferences, and disseminates information on detection and prevention of money laundering. The association began in 2001. In 2010, membership was around 9,500; now, we have 26,000 members worldwide. About 60% are in North America. It is composed of both private- and public-sector members. They are as disparate as FBI agents and bank examiners, compliance officers, and consultants.

1.5.8   *ComplyAdvantage*

ComplyAdvantage, founded in 2014, is a RegTech company that provides anti-money laundering technology. The company uses artificial intelligence, machine learning, and natural language processing to help regulated organizations manage risk obligations and counteract financial crime. ComplyAdvantage uses machine learning to detect and analyze potential financial crime risks, and says its systems allow firms to do advanced due diligence on customers while reducing their reliance on manual checks.[23]

1.6   THE FAILURE OF THE CURRENT SYSTEM

Despite the efforts and tools used to fight against AML/CFT, the results are not still there. An extensive study within the European Union study estimated "criminal revenues from [a] selected number of illicit markets (heroin, cocaine, cannabis, ecstasy, amphetamines, ITTP [illicit tobacco trade], counterfeiting, and MTIC [VAT] fraud and cargo theft)" of "at least" €110 billion annually.[24] The study excluded "important illicit

---

[23] Nicholas Megaw (2021): Goldman bets on UK Anti-money Laundering Start-up, Financial Times, https://www.ft.com/content/24152e93-a465-4159-9018-486120 161d5a.

[24] Europol (2016): Does Crime Still Pay? Criminal Asset Recovery in the EU. The Hague: Europol, https://bit.ly/2jMSuca.

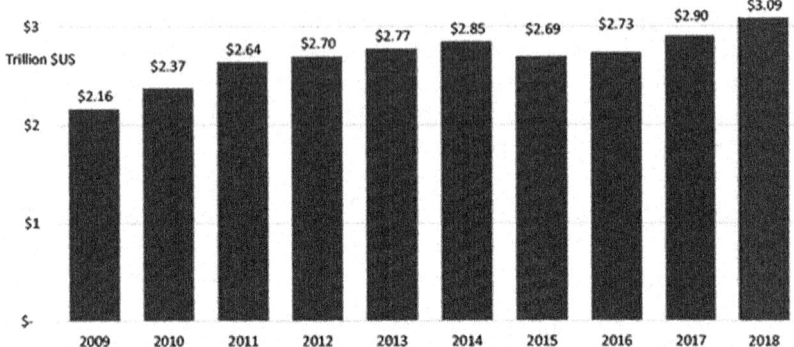

Fig. 1.2 UN-estimated global proceedings of crime (*Source* UN-estimated global proceeds of crime, 3.6% GDP)

markets, such as [human] trafficking...[and] extortion, illegal gambling and other types of fraud"[25] (Fig. 1.2).

[25] E. U. Savona and M. Riccardi (2015): From Illegal Markets to Legitimate Businesses: The Portfolio of Organized Crime in Europe. Trento, https://bit.ly/1Dli7W1.

CHAPTER 2

The Cybersecurity Counteroffensive

2.1 General

A country should have laws in place addressing criminal conduct—as provided in the country's criminal laws—directed against the confidentiality, integrity, and availability of computer systems and networks, as well as the data stored and processed on them, and criminal acts carried out through the instrumentality of such systems, networks, and data.[1] Consumers, governments, and businesses are all vulnerable as we are increasingly dependent on the Internet. Cybersecurity is important because it protects all categories of data from theft and damage. This includes sensitive data, personally identifiable information (PII), protected health information (PHI), personal information, intellectual property, data, and governmental and industry information systems. It is thus important that cybersecurity be fully integrated into the development of new processes from the start. Cybersecurity consists of all the technologies and practices that keep computer systems and electronic data safe. According to the Cyber Security & Infrastructure Security Agency (CISA), "Cyber security is the art of protecting networks, devices and data from unauthorized access or criminal use and the practice of ensuring

---

[1] World Bank (2017): World Bank Toolkit on Combating Cybercrime.

© The Author(s), under exclusive license to Springer Nature
Switzerland AG 2023
F. I. Lessambo, *Anti-Money Laundering, Counter Financing Terrorism
and Cybersecurity in the Banking Industry*, Palgrave Macmillan
Studies in Banking and Financial Institutions,
https://doi.org/10.1007/978-3-031-23484-2_2

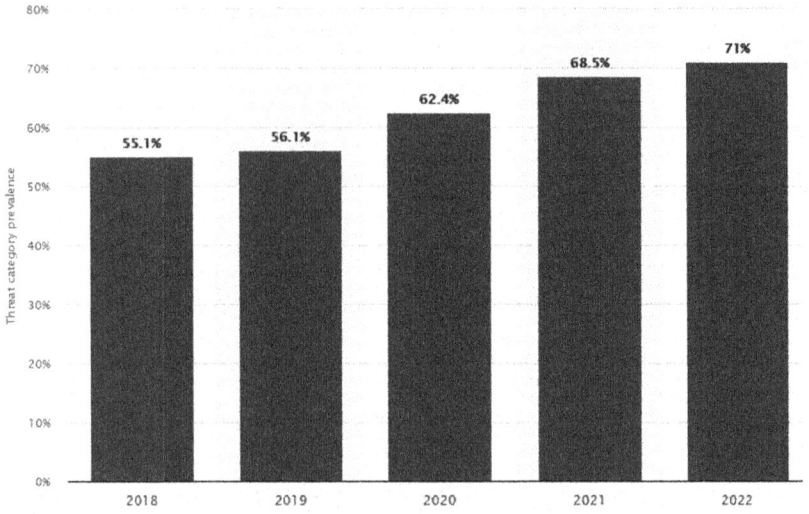

Fig. 2.1   Percentage of organization hit by ransomware (*Source* Sophos)

confidentiality, integrity and availability of information." According to the international research and advisory firm Gartner Inc., worldwide security spending will hit $170 billion by 2022, an 8% increase in just a year. According to "Cybersecurity Ventures", Cybersecurity threats are projected to reach a global cost of USD 10.5 trillion by 2025 (Fig. 2.1).

2.2   HISTORY OF CYBERSECURITY[2]

2.2.1   1920s

The German plugboard-equipped Enigma became Nazi Germany's principal crypto-system. The Enigma Machine was an electro-mechanical encryption device, which combined hardware and software (crude by today's standards, but nevertheless, they were algorithms in the form of rotors), with human operators for the purpose of manipulating information. In December 1932, it was "broken" by mathematician Marian Rejewski at the Polish General Staff's Cipher Bureau, using mathematical

---

[2] Katie Chadd (2020): The History of Cybercrime and Cybersecurity, 1940–2020.

permutation group theory combined with French-supplied intelligence material obtained from a German spy.[3] Alan Turing and his team were able to crack the Enigma Code by identifying a flaw in the way the code was generated. The flaw was that every letter was encrypted as a letter that was different than itself.

2.2.2   1930s

Interestingly, in the United States, the Navy was also the first military branch to adopt a device similar to the Enigma Machine, dubbed SIGABA, in the late 1930s. By the end of World War II, cipher machines were in widespread use.[4] Also in the late 1930s, another German inventor, by the name of Konrad Zuse, designed the first freely programmable mechanical computer, called the Z1.[5]

2.2.3   1940s: The Time Before Crime

For nearly two decades after the creation of the world's first digital computer in 1943, carrying out cyberattacks was tricky. Access to the giant electronic machines was limited to small numbers of people and they weren't networked—only a few people knew how to work them so the threat was almost non-existent. Interestingly, the theory underlying computer viruses was first made public in 1949 when computer pioneer John von Neumann speculated that computer programs could reproduce.

2.2.4   1950s: The Phone Phreaks

The technological and subcultural roots of hacking are as much related to early telephones as they are to computers. In the late 1950s, 'phone phreaking' emerged. The term captures several methods that 'phreaks'—people with a particular interest in the workings of phones—used to hijack the protocols that allowed telecoms engineers to work on the network

---

[3] Tony Sale, The Breaking of German Naval Enigma, Naval Enigma Index, accessed June 4, 2012, http://www.codesandciphers.org.uk/virtualbp/navenigma/navenig1.htm.

[4] Richard Pekelney: What Is The SIGABA-ECM Mark II and Why It Was Important? Crypto Machines, accessed June 4, 2012, last modified April 30, 2012, http://www.jproc.ca/crypto/ecm2.html.

[5] https://history.computer.org/pioneers/zuse.html.

remotely to make free calls and avoid long-distance tolls. Sadly for the phone companies, there was no way of stopping the phreaks, although the practice eventually died out in the 1980s. The phreaks had become a community, even issuing newsletters, and included technological trailblazers like Apple's founders Steve Wozniak and Steve Jobs. The mold was set for digital technology.

2.2.5   1960s: All Quiet on the Western Front

The first-ever reference to malicious hacking was in the Massachusetts Institute of Technology's student newspaper. Even by the mid-1960s, most computers were huge mainframes, locked away in secure temperature-controlled rooms. These machines were very costly, so access—even to programmers—remained limited. However, there were early forays into hacking by some of those with access, often students. At this stage, the attacks had no commercial or geopolitical benefits. Most hackers were curious mischief-makers or those who sought to improve existing systems by making them work more quickly or efficiently.

In 1967, IBM invited school kids to try out their new computer. After exploring the accessible parts of the system, the students worked to probe deeper, learning the system's language, and gaining access to other parts of the system. This was a valuable lesson to the company and they acknowledged their gratitude to "a number of high school students for their compulsion to bomb the system", which resulted in the development of defensive measures—and possibly the defensive mindset that would prove essential to developers from then on. Ethical hacking is still practiced today. As computers started to reduce in size and cost, many large companies invested in technologies to store and manage data and systems. Storing them under lock and key became redundant as more people needed access to them and passwords began to be used.

2.2.6   1970s: Computer Security Is Born

Cybersecurity began in 1972 with a research project on ARPANET (The Advanced Research Projects Agency Network), a precursor to the Internet. Researcher Bob Thomas created a computer program called Creeper that could move across ARPANET's network, leaving a breadcrumb trail wherever it went. It read: 'I'm the creeper, catch me if you can.' Ray Tomlinson—the inventor of email—wrote the program

Reaper, which chased and deleted Creeper. Reaper was not only the very first example of antivirus software, but it was also the first self-replicating program, making it the first-ever computer worm. Challenging the vulnerabilities in these emerging technologies became more important as more organizations were starting to use the telephone to create remote networks. Each piece of connected hardware presented a new 'entry point' and needed to be protected.

As reliance on computers increased and networking grew, it became clear to governments that security was essential, and unauthorized access to data and systems could be catastrophic. 1972–1974 witnessed a marked increase in discussions around computer security, mainly by academics in papers. Creating early computer security was undertaken by ESD and ARPA with the U.S. Air Force and other organizations that worked cooperatively to develop a design for a security kernel for the Honeywell Multics (HIS level 68) computer system. UCLA and the Stanford Research Institute worked on similar projects. ARPA's Protection Analysis project explored operating system security; identifying, where possible, automatable techniques for detecting vulnerabilities in software. By the mid-1970s, the concept of cybersecurity was maturing. In 1976, *Operating System Structures to Support Security and Reliable Software* stated:

> Security has become an important and challenging goal in the design of computer systems.

In 1979, 16-year-old Kevin Mitnick famously hacked into The Ark—the computer at the Digital Equipment Corporation used for developing operating systems—and made copies of the software. He was arrested and jailed for what would be the first of several cyberattacks he conducted over the next few decades. Today, he runs Mitnick Security Consulting.

2.2.7   1980s: From ARPANET to Internet

The 1980s brought an increase in high-profile attacks, including those at National CSS, AT&T, and Los Alamos National Laboratory. The movie War Games, in which a rogue computer program takes over nuclear missiles systems under the guise of a game, was released in 1983. This was the same year that the terms Trojan Horse and Computer Virus were first used.

At the time of the Cold War, the threat of cyber espionage evolved. In 1985, the U.S. Department of Defense published the Trusted Computer System Evaluation Criteria (aka The Orange Book) that provided guidance on:

- Assessing the degree of trust that can be placed in software that processes classified or other sensitive information.
- What security measures manufacturers needed to build into their commercial products?

Despite this, in 1986, German hacker Marcus Hess used an Internet gateway in Berkeley, CA, to piggyback onto the ARPANET. He hacked 400 military computers, including mainframes at the Pentagon, intending to sell information to the KGB.

Security started to be taken more seriously. Savvy users quickly learned to monitor the command.com file size, having noticed that an increase in size was the first sign of potential infection. Cybersecurity measures incorporated this thinking, and a sudden reduction in free operating memory remains a sign of attack to this day.

2.2.8   1987: The Birth of Cybersecurity

1987 was the birth year of commercial antivirus, although there are competing claims for the innovator of the first antivirus product.

- Andreas Lüning and Kai Figge released their first antivirus product for the Atari ST—which also saw the release of Ultimate Virus Killer (UVK).
- Three Czechoslovakians created the first version of NOD antivirus.
- In the U.S., John McAfee founded McAfee (now part of Intel Security) and released VirusScan.

Also in 1987:

- One of the earliest documented 'in the wild' virus removals was performed by German Bernd Fix when he neutralized the infamous Vienna virus—an early example of malware that spread and corrupted files.

• The encrypted Cascade virus, which infected .COM files, first appeared. A year later, Cascade caused a serious incident in IBM's Belgian office and served as the impetus for IBM's antivirus product development. Before this, any antivirus solutions developed at IBM had been intended for internal use only.

By 1988, many antivirus companies had been established around the world—including Avast, which was founded by Eduard Kučera and Pavel Baudiš in Prague, Czech Republic. Today, Avast has a team of more than 1,700 worldwide and stops around 1.5 billion attacks every month.

Early antivirus software consisted of simple scanners that performed context searches to detect unique virus code sequences. Many of these scanners also included 'immunizers' that modified programs to make viruses think the computer was already infected and not attack them. As the number of viruses increased into the hundreds, immunizers quickly became ineffective.

It was also becoming clear to antivirus companies that they could only react to existing attacks, and a lack of a universal and ubiquitous network (the Internet) made updates hard to deploy.

As the world slowly started to take notice of computer viruses, 1988 also witnessed the first electronic forum devoted to antivirus security—Virus-L—on the Usenet network. The decade also saw the birth of the antivirus press: UK-based Sophos-sponsored Virus Bulletin and Dr. Solomon's Virus Fax International. The decade closed with more additions to the cybersecurity market, including F-Prot, ThunderBYTE, and Norman Virus Control. In 1989, IBM finally commercialized their internal antivirus project and IBM Virscan for MS-DOS went on sale for $35.

2.2.9   1990s: The World Goes Online

The first polymorphic viruses were created (code that mutates while keeping the original algorithm intact to avoid detection).

British computer magazine *PC Today* released an edition with a free disk that 'accidentally' contained the Disk Killer virus, infecting tens of thousands of computers.

EICAR (European Institute for Computer Antivirus Research) was established.

Early antivirus was purely signature-based, comparing binaries on a system with a database of virus 'signatures.' This meant that early antivirus produced many false positives and used a lot of computational power—which frustrated users as productivity slowed.

As more antivirus scanners hit the market, cybercriminals were responding, and in 1992, the first anti-antivirus program appeared.

By 1996, many viruses used new techniques and innovative methods, including stealth capability, polymorphism, and 'macro viruses,' posing a new set of challenges for antivirus vendors who had to develop new detection and removal capabilities.

New virus and malware numbers exploded in the 1990s, from tens of thousands early in the decade growing to 5 million every year by 2007. By the mid-1990s, it was clear that cybersecurity had to be mass-produced to protect the public. One NASA researcher developed the first firewall program, modeling it on the physical structures that prevent the spread of actual fires in buildings.

The late 1990s were also marked by conflict and friction between antivirus developers:

- McAfee accused Dr. Solomon's of cheating so that testing of uninfected discs showed good speed results and the scan tests of virus collections showed good detection results. Dr. Solomon's filed suit in response.
- Taiwanese developer Trend Micro accused McAfee and Symantec of violating its patent on virus scan-checking technology via the Internet and electronic mail. Symantec then accused McAfee of using code from Symantec's Norton AntiVirus.

Heuristic detection also emerged as a new method to tackle the huge number of virus variants. Antivirus scanners started to use generic signatures—often containing non-contiguous code and using wildcard characters—to detect viruses even if the threat had been 'hidden' inside meaningless code. Toward the end of the 1990s, email was proliferating, and while it promised to revolutionize communication, it also opened up a new entry point for viruses.

In 1999, the Melissa virus was unleashed. It entered the user's computer via a Word document and then emailed copies of itself to the first 50 email addresses in Microsoft Outlook. It remains one of the fastest spreading viruses and the damage cost around $80 million to fix.

2.2.10   2000s: Threats Diversify and Multiply

With the Internet available in more homes and offices across the globe, cybercriminals had more devices and software vulnerabilities to exploit than ever before. And, as more and more data were being kept digitally, there was more to plunder.

In 2001, a new infection technique appeared: users no longer needed to download files—visiting an infected website was enough as bad actors replaced clean pages with infected ones or 'hid' malware on legitimate webpages. Instant messaging services also began to get attacked, and worms designed to propagate via IRC (Internet Chat Relay) channel also arrived.

The development of zero-day attacks, which make use of 'holes' in security measures for new software and applications, meant that antivirus was becoming less effective—you can't check code against existing attack signatures unless the virus already exists in the database. Computer magazine c't found that detection rates for zero-day threats had dropped from 40–50% in 2006 to only 20–30% in 2007.

As crime organizations started to heavily fund professional cyberattacks, the good guys were hot on their trail:

- 2000: the first open-source antivirus engine *OpenAntivirus Project* is made available.
- 2001: ClamAV is launched, the first-ever open-source antivirus engine to be commercialized.
- 2001: Avast launches free antivirus software, offering a fully-featured security solution to the masses. The initiative grew the Avast user base to more than 20 million in five years.

A key challenge of antivirus is that it can often slow a computer's performance. One solution to this was to move the software off the computer and into the cloud. In 2007, Panda Security combined cloud technology with threat intelligence in their antivirus product—an industry-first. McAfee Labs followed suit in 2008, adding cloud-based anti-malware functionality to VirusScan. The following year, the Anti-Malware Testing Standards Organization (AMTSO) was created and started working shortly after on a method of testing cloud products.

Another innovation in this decade was OS security—cybersecurity that's built into the operating system, providing an additional layer of protection. This often includes performing regular OS patch updates, installation of updated antivirus engines and software, firewalls, and secure accounts with user management.

With the proliferation of smartphones, antivirus was also developed for Android and Windows mobile.

2.2.11   2010s: The Next Generation

The 2010s saw many high-profile breaches and attacks starting to impact the national security of countries and cost businesses millions.

- 2012: Saudi hacker OXOMAR publishes the details of more than 400,000 credit cards online
- 2013: Former CIA employee for the U.S. Government Edward Snowden copied and leaked classified information from the National Security Agency (NSA)
- 2013–2014: Malicious hackers broke into Yahoo, compromising the accounts and personal information of its 3 billion users. Yahoo was subsequently fined $35 million for failing to disclose the news
- 2017: WannaCry ransomware infects 230,000 computers in one day
- 2019: Multiple DDoS attacks forced New Zealand's stock market to temporarily shut down

The increasing connectedness and the ongoing digitization of many aspects of life continued to offer cybercriminals new opportunities to exploit. Cybersecurity tailored specifically to the needs of businesses became more prominent, and in 2011, Avast launched its first business product.

As cybersecurity developed to tackle the expanding range of attack types, criminals responded with their own innovations: multi-vector attacks and social engineering. Attackers were becoming smarter and antivirus was forced to shift away from signature-based methods of detection to 'next generation' innovations.

Next-gen cybersecurity uses different approaches to increase detection of new and unprecedented threats, while also reducing the number of false positives. It typically involves:

- Multi-factor authentication (MFA)
- Network Behavioral Analysis (NBA)—identifying malicious files based on behavioral deviations or anomalies
- Threat intelligence and update automation
- Real-time protection—also referred to as on-access scanning, background guard, resident shield and auto-protect
- Sandboxing—creating an isolated test environment where you can execute a suspicious file or URL
- Forensics—replaying attacks to help security teams better mitigate future breaches
- Back-up and mirroring
- Web application firewalls (WAF)—protecting against cross-site forgery, cross-site-scripting (XSS), file inclusion, and SQL injection.

2.3 Types of Cyberattacks

Cyberattacks come in different forms and variants. Below are the most commonly forms:

- Denial of service

  A method of attack from a single source that denies system access to legitimate users by overwhelming the target computer with messages and blocking legitimate traffic. It can prevent a system from being able to exchange data with other systems or use the Internet. The main goal of this attack is to make the target Internet service unavailable to other users, or, at least, to degrade the quality and speed of the service. In general, DoS attacks are targeted on web servers to prevent users from accessing web content. The primary targets of DoS attacks include web, mail, database, file, and domain system servers, and remote access services. Attacks can also block traffic on the target internal networks.[6]

- Distributed denial of service

  A variant of the denial-of-service attack that uses a coordinated attack from a distributed system of computers rather than from a single source. It often makes use of worms to spread to multiple computers that can then attack the target. Distributed denial-of-service (DDoS) attacks can put the communication networks in instability by throwing malicious traffic and requests in bulk over the network.[7] DDoS attacks on the Internet can be launched using two techniques. In the first technique, the attacker sends some malicious packets to the victim to confuse a protocol or an application running on it (i.e., vulnerability attack. The second technique essentially includes the network/transport-level/application-level flooding attacks, in which an attacker to do one or both of the following: (i) interrupt a legitimate user's connectivity by exhausting bandwidth, network resources, or router processing capacity or (ii) disrupt services of a legitimate user's connectivity by exhausting the server resources such as CPU, memory, disk/database bandwidth, and I/O bandwidth.[8]

- Exploit tools

  Publicly available and sophisticated tools that intruders of various skill levels can use to determine vulnerabilities and gain entry into targeted systems. An exploit is a program, or piece of code, designed to find and take advantage of a security flaw or vulnerability in an application or computer system, typically for malicious purposes such

[6] Marek Sikora, Radek Fujdiak, Karel Kuchar (2021): Generator of Slow Denial-of-Service Cyber Attacks, Multidisciplinary Digital Publishing Institute, https://www.ncbi.nlm.nih.gov/pmc/articles/PMC8401215/.

[7] S. U. Rehman, M. Khaliq, S. I. Imtiaz, A. Rasool, M. Shafiq, A. R. Javed, Z. Jalil, and A. K. Bashir (2021): DIDDOS: An Approach for Detection and Identification of Distributed Denial of Service (DDoS) Cyberattacks using Gated Recurrent Units (GRU), pp. 1–32, Elsevier, https://e-space.mmu.ac.uk/627611/1/FGCS-%20D IDDOS-%20DeepDDosDetectionAnalysis.pdf.

[8] S. U. Rehman, M. Khaliq, S. I. Imtiaz, A. Rasool, M. Shafiq, A. R. Javed, Z. Jalil, and A. K. Bashir (2021): DIDDOS: An Approach for Detection and Identification of Distributed Denial of Service (DDoS) Cyberattacks using Gated Recurrent Units (GRU), pp. 1–32, Elsevier, https://e-space.mmu.ac.uk/627611/1/FGCS-%20D IDDOS-%20DeepDDosDetectionAnalysis.pdf.

as installing malware. An exploit is not malware itself, but rather it is a method used by cybercriminals to deliver malware.[9] There are two types of exploits: (i) known exploit and unknown exploit. After an exploit is made known to the authors of the affected software, the vulnerability is often fixed through a patch to make the exploit unusable. That is different for unknown exploit, which occurs when a software or system architecture contains a critical security vulnerability of which the vendor is unaware.[10]

- Logic bombs

  A logic bomb is a programming code purposely inserted into a system that sets off malicious function when some specified condition (trigger) is met.[11] In other terms, it is a form of sabotage in which a programmer inserts code that causes the program to perform a destructive action when some triggering event occurs, such as terminating the programmer's employment.[12] Logic bombs have been suspected in several cyberespionage attacks. The United States is very vulnerable to this type of attack because its infrastructure is much dependent on computer networks in comparison with other countries.[13]

- Phishing

  Phishing is an example of a highly effective form of cybercrime that enables criminals to deceive users and steal important data.[14] It is a social engineering attack wherein a phisher attempts to lure the users to obtain their sensitive information by illegally utilizing a public or trustworthy organization in an automated pattern so that

---

[9] https://www.paloaltonetworks.com/cyberpedia/malware-vs-exploits.

[10] Cisco (2022): What Is an Exploit? https://www.cisco.com/c/en/us/products/security/advanced-malware-protection/what-is-exploit.html.

[11] Cindy Casy (2018): Logic Bombs—Blown to Bits, Gwynedd Mercy University, https://www.bucks.edu/media/bcccmedialibrary/con-ed/itacademy/fos2018/Casey-Logic-Bombs.pdf.

[12] Dorothy E. Denning (2000): Cyberterrorism: The Logic Bomb versus the Truck Bomb, Global Dialogue, Nicosia Vol. 2, No. 4 (Autumn 2000), pp. 29–37.

[13] Palash Sandip Dusane, Yallamandhala Pavithra (2020): Logic Bomb: An Insider Attack, International Journal of Advanced Trends in Computer Science and Engineering, Vol. 9, No.3, https://www.warse.org/IJATCSE/static/pdf/file/ijatcse176932020.pdf.

[14] Zainab Alkhali, Chaminda Hewage, Liqaa Nawaf (2021): Phishing Attacks: A Recent Comprehensive Study and a New Anatomy, Frontiers in Computer Science, https://www.frontiersin.org/articles/10.3389/fcomp.2021.563060/full.

the Internet user trusts the message, and reveals the victim's sensitive information to the attacker.[15] The most common threat derived by an attacker is deceiving people via email communications and this remains the most popular phishing type to date. Phishers aim to deceive Internet users into disclosing their personal data, such as bank and financial account information and passwords. The phishers then use that information for criminal purposes, such as identity theft and fraud. The number of phishing attacks reached a record high in the first quarter of 2022, exceeding one million, and the financial sector accounted for the highest amount, with 23.6% of all attacks, according to a recent report by Anti-Phishing Working Group (APWG).

• Sniffer

Sniffing is the process of capturing-decoding-inspecting—interpreting the data from the packets transmitted over the transmission channel.[16] It is a program that intercepts routed data and examines each packet in search of specified information, such as passwords transmitted in clear text. Sniffing enables the attacker to collect information on the vulnerabilities of the devices, protocols, and applications that can be exploited within the targeted network.[17]

• Trojan horse

A Trojan horse is any malware that misleads users of its true intent. The term is derived from the Ancient Greek story of the deceptive Trojan horse that led to the fall of the city of Troy. Trojan horse is considered one of the most serious threats to computer security.[18] A Trojan horse usually masquerades as a useful program that

[15] M. Jakobsson and S. Myers (2006). Phishing and Countermeasures: Understanding the Increasing Problems of Electronic Identity Theft. New Jersey: John Wiley and Sons.

[16] B. Prabadevi and N. Jeyanthi (2018): A Review on Various Sniffing Attacks and its Mitigation Techniques, Indonesian Journal of Electrical Engineering and Computer Science Vol. 12, No. 3 (December 2018), pp. 1117–1125.

[17] Marcin Gregorczyk and Piotr Żórawski (2020): Sniffing Detection Based on Network Traffic Probing and Machine Learning, IEEE Access, Vol. 8, pp. 1–15, https://ieeexplore.ieee.org/ielx7/6287639/8948470/09165714.pdf.

[18] Marie Antonette Acha, Carl Bueno, and Engel Pamittan (2016): Digital Warzone: An Analysis on Behavior Patterns of Trojan Attacks, https://www.researchgate.net/publication/309740333_Digital_Warzone_An_Analysis_on_Behavior_Patterns_of_Trojan_Attacks.

a user would wish to execute. Trojan horse gets hidden as an attachment in an email or a free-to-download file and then transfers onto the user's device. Once downloaded, the malicious code will execute the task the attacker designed it for, such as gain backdoor access to corporate systems, spy on users' online activity, or steal sensitive data. For instance, in June 2022, China's National Computer Virus Emergency Response Center and a leading cybersecurity company disclosed a new vulnerability attack weapon platform deployed by the U.S. National Security Agency (NSA), which experts believe is the main equipment of the NSA's computer network hacking operation team, and it targets the world with a focus on China and Russia.[19]

- Virus

  A program that infects computer files, usually executable programs, by inserting a copy of itself into the file. These copies are usually executed when the infected file is loaded into memory, allowing the virus to infect other files. Unlike a computer worm, a virus requires human involvement (usually unwitting) to propagate.

- Vishing

  A method of phishing based on voice-over-Internet-Protocol technology and open-source call center software that have made it inexpensive for scammers to set up phony call centers and criminals to send email or text messages to potential victims. If a visher gets the bank account or credit card information of a victim, he can gain access to their funds. That is because the routing numbers for bank accounts can be easily found online. With the combination of a bank's routing info and the victim's personal account number, the attacker can potentially withdraw or transfer funds from their account into their own.

- War driving

  War driving is a hacking method and has its origins in the movie War Games, which starred actor Matthew Broderick. A war driving is a method of gaining entry into wireless computer networks using a laptop, antennas, and a wireless network adapter that involves

---

[19] Zhao Siwei (2022): Exclusive: US Plants Trojan Horse Programs in Hundreds of Important Chinese Information Systems; New Cyber Weapon targets China, Russia, Global Times, https://www.globaltimes.cn/page/202206/1269300.shtml.

patrolling locations to gain unauthorized access.[20] War driving is restricted to collecting information about the wireless access points (WAPs), without using network services. Though war driving might seem like a thing of the past, security specialists still use it to research Wi-Fi security. Data accumulated in such a manner are valuable and help detect common mistakes and drawbacks. It also helps understand how open Wi-Fi networks protect their users.

- Worm

    A worm is a self-propagating computer program, which is often designed to cause harm to a computer and/or a computer network. A computer worm self-propagates by sending copies of itself from one node to another over a network. Such transmissions can occur without any user intervention, thereby allowing them to be spread quickly and easily.[21] Unlike computer viruses, worms do not require human involvement to propagate.

- Zero-day exploit

A zero-day (0 day) exploit is a cyberattack targeting a software vulnerability, which is unknown to the software vendor or to antivirus vendors. The attacker spots the software vulnerability before any parties interested in mitigating it, quickly creates an exploit, and uses it for an attack.[22] Such attacks are highly likely to succeed because defenses are not in place. This makes zero-day attacks a severe security threat. Responding to a zero day has posed to be a significant task. Since no known patch or fix is available at the time of a zero-day exploit, it is pertinent to have an efficient security framework that can reduce its impact[23] (Fig. 2.2).

---

[20] Antriksh Shah and Varun Haran (2011): Demystifying Wardriving: An Overview, ComputerWeekly.com, https://www.computerweekly.com/tip/Demystifying-wardriving-An-overview.

[21] N. Valliammal (2017): Comprehensive Study on Computer Worm—Cyber Attack, Journal of Network Communications and Emerging Technologies (JNCET) www.jncet.org, Vol. 7, No. 9, pp. 1–8, https://www.jncet.org/Manuscripts/Volume-7/Issue-9/Vol-7-issue-9-M-12.pdf.

[22] Almantas Kakareka (2014): Network and System Security (Second Edition), Detecting System Intrusions, Chapter 1, pp. 1–27. https://www.sciencedirect.com/science/article/pii/B9780124166899000010.

[23] A. E. Ibor (2017): Zero Day Exploits and national Readiness for Cyber-Warfare, Nigerian Journal of Technology (NIJOTECH), Vol. 36, No. 4, pp. 1174–1183.

Name	Description
Denial of service	A method of attack from a single source that denies system access to legitimate users by overwhelming the target computer with messages and blocking legitimate traffic. It can prevent a system from being able to exchange data with other systems or use the Internet.
Distributed denial of service	A variant of the denial of service attack that uses a coordinated attack from a distributed system of computers rather than from a single source. It often makes use of worms to spread to multiple computers that can then attack the target.
Exploit tools	Publicly available and sophisticated tools that intruders of various skill levels can use to determine vulnerabilities and gain entry into targeted systems.
Logic bombs	A form of sabotage in which a programmer inserts code that causes the program to perform a destructive action when some triggering event occurs, such as terminating the programmer's employment.
Phishing	The creation and use of e-mails and Web sites—designed to look like those of well-known legitimate businesses, financial institutions, and government agencies—in order to deceive Internet users into disclosing their personal data, such as bank and financial account information and passwords. The phishers then use that information for criminal purposes, such as identity theft and fraud.
Sniffer	Synonymous with packet sniffer. A program that intercepts routed data and examines each packet in search of specified information, such as passwords transmitted in clear text.
Trojan horse	A computer program that conceals harmful code. A Trojan horse usually masquerades as a useful program that a user would wish to execute.
Virus	A program that infects computer files, usually executable programs, by inserting a copy of itself into the file. These copies are usually executed when the infected file is loaded into memory, allowing the virus to infect other files. Unlike a computer worm, a virus requires human involvement (usually unwitting) to propagate.

Fig. 2.2 Evolution of U.S. cyber power (*Source* US GAO [2022]: The Evolution of U.S. Cyber power)

2.4   Cybersecurity Risk vs. Traditional Risk

One distinguishing feature of cyberattacks is that they may be designed for maximum disruption.[24] Aldasoro et al. analyze cyber events across sectors and find that losses are higher when cyber events affect larger firms or multiple firms at the same time, patterns that are very concerning in terms of systemic risk.[25] The most common types of cybersecurity available are.

2.4.1   *Application Security*

Application security describes security used by applications with the goal of preventing data or code within the app from being stolen or hijacked. These security systems are implemented during application development but are designed to protect the application after deployment, according to VMWare.

2.4.2   *Cloud Security*

The basic definition of Cloud computing is "A solution for providing a less complicated and reliable access to resources of IT." Cloud computing is an emerging technology similar like artificial intelligence both have security challenges.[26]

Cloud security involves the technology and procedures that secure cloud computing environments against both internal and external threats. These security systems are designed to prevent unauthorized access and keep data and applications in the cloud secure from cybersecurity threats, according to McAfee. It combines a number of computing concepts and technologies such as Service Oriented Architecture (SOA), Web 2.0, virtualization, and other technologies with reliance on the Internet, providing common business applications online through web browsers to

---

[24] Thomas M. Eisenbach, Anna Kovner, and Michael Junho Lee (2021): Cyber Risk and the U.S. Financial System: A Pre-Mortem Analysis, Federal Reserve Bank of New York Staff Reports, no. 909.

[25] Aldasoro, I., L. Gambacorta, P. Giudici, and T. Leach (2020). The Drivers of Cyber Risk. Working Paper 865, BIS.

[26] Rao Narendra, Sr Tadapaneni, and Habeebullah Hussaini Syed (2020): Cloud Computing Security Challenges, Novateur Publications, International Journal of Innovations in Engineering Research and Technology, Vol. 7, No. 6, ISSN: 2394–3696.

satisfy the computing needs of users, while their software and data are stored on the servers.[27]

2.4.3   Infrastructure Security

Critical infrastructure security is the area of concern surrounding the protection of systems, networks, and assets whose continuous operation is deemed necessary to ensure the security of a given nation, its economy, and the public's health and/or safety critical infrastructure security describes the physical and cyber systems that are so vital to society that their incapacity would have a debilitating impact on our physical, economic, or public health and safety, according to CISA. Critical infrastructures work together to provide a continuous flow of goods and services, which range from food and water distribution, power supply, military defense, and transport, to healthcare and government services.[28] Critical infrastructures use industrial control systems that enable operators to monitor and control components such as valves, pressure gauges, switches, and nodes from remote locations.[29]

2.4.4   Internet of Things (IoT) Security

The growth of the Internet of Things (IoT) offers numerous opportunities for developing industrial applications such as smart grids, smart cities, and smart manufacturers.[30] IoT-connected devices are predicted

---

[27] Keiko Hashizume, David G. Rosado, and Eduardo Fernández-Medina (2013): An Analysis of Security Issues for Cloud Computing, Journal of Internet Services and Applications, https://jisajournal.springeropen.com/articles/10.1186/1869-0238-4-5.

[28] William Hurst, Madjid Merabti, and Paul Fergus (2014): A Survey of Critical Infrastructure Security, Chapter 9.

[29] D. Kang, J. Lee, S. Kim and J. Park (2009): Analysis of Cyber Threats to SCADA Systems, Proceedings of the IEEE Transmission and Distribution Conference and Exposition: Asia and Pacific.

[30] Nasr Abosata, Saba Al-Rubaye, Gokhan Inalhan, and Christos Emmanouilidis (2021): Internet of Things for System Integrity: A Comprehensive Survey on Security, Attacks and Countermeasures for Industrial Applications, (Basel)—Multidisciplinary Digital Publishing Institute, Vol 21, No. 11, p. 3654, https://www.ncbi.nlm.nih.gov/pmc/articles/PMC8197321/.

to expand to 75 billion by 2025.[31] IoT is the concept of connecting any device to the Internet and to other connected devices. The IoT is a network of connected things and people, all of which share data about the way they are used and their environments, according to IBM. These devices include appliances, sensors, televisions, routers, printers, and countless other home network devices. Securing these devices is important, and according to a study by Bloomberg, security is one of the biggest barriers for widespread IoT adaption.

2.4.5   *Network Security*

Network security protects network and data from breaches, intrusions, and other threats. Network security consists of the policies, processes, and practices adopted to prevent, detect, and monitor unauthorized access, misuse, modification, or denial of a computer network and network-accessible. That is, network security is the protection of network infrastructure from unauthorized access, abuse, or theft. These security systems involve creating a secure infrastructure for devices, applications, and users to work together, according to CISCO.

2.5   Cybersecurity and the Banking Industry

As bank and non-bank institutions are going through an unprecedented digital transformation, shifting to digital channels such as online banking and mobile banking, digital platform financing, they have become the target of attacks known as cybercrimes: phishing, cross site scripting, vishing, cybersquatting, malware, SMS spoofing, denial-of-service attacks, pharming. Malicious actors are taking advantage of this digital transformation and pose a growing threat to the global financial system, financial stability, and confidence in the integrity of the system. The threats are even more insidious as the actors behind these attacks include not only increasingly daring criminals—such as the Carbanak group, which targeted financial institutions to steal more than $1 billion during 2013–18—but also states and state-sponsored attackers. North Korea, for example, has stolen some $2 billion from at least 38 countries in

---

[31] Girard M. (2020): Standards for Cybersecure IoT Devices: A Way Forward. JSTOR, Vol. 160, pp. 1–13.

the past five years.[32] A bank runs multiple servers that store enormous amounts of information and details of various operations such as credit cards, ATMs, real-time gross settlements, ATMs, and SWIFT (the global financial messaging service banks use to move funds), among others.[33] In 2021, ransomware comprises the majority of cyberattacks on the banking industry. According to a report published by the U.S. Treasury's Financial Crimes Enforcement Network (FinCen), the 635 suspicious activity reports (SARs) filed in the first half of 2021 represent a 30% increase over the entirety of 2020.[34]

2.6   INTERNATIONAL COOPERATION

Strong international partnerships and cooperation, in addition to national strategies and initiatives, can help support countries to adequately equip themselves to respond to and manage digital security threats (Fig. 2.3).

---

[32] IMF (2021): The Global Cyber Threat, Finance & Development.

[33] Dr. M. Lokanadha Reddy, and V. Bhargavi (2018): Cyber Security Attacks in Banking Sector: Emerging Security Challenges and Threats, American International Journal of Research in Humanities, Arts and Social Sciences.

[34] RSI Security (2021): Cyber Attacks on Banking Industry Organizations in 2021, https://blog.rsisecurity.com/cyber-attacks-on-banking-industry-organizations-in-2021/.

Country	GCI Score	Legal	Technical	Organizational	Capacity Building	Cooperation
Singapore	0.92	0.95	0.96	0.88	0.97	0.87
United States	0.91	1	0.96	0.92	1	0.73
Malaysia	0.89	0.87	0.96	0.77	1	0.87
Oman	0.87	0.98	0.82	0.85	0.95	0.75
Estonia	0.84	0.99	0.82	0.85	0.94	0.64
Mauritius	0.82	0.85	0.96	0.74	0.91	0.70
Australia	0.82	0.94	0.96	0.86	0.94	0.44
Georgia	0.81	0.91	0.77	0.82	0.90	0.70
France	0.81	0.94	0.96	0.60	1	0.61
Canada	0.81	0.94	0.93	0.71	0.82	0.70

(Source:International Telecommunication Union 2017)

Fig. 2.3 Most cyber-secured countries (*Source* International Telecommunication Union 2017)

CHAPTER 3

AML/CFT, Cybersecurity and International Organization

3.1 General

Cybersecurity is attracting focused attention from international governing, policymaking, law enforcement, and security bodies, including the United Nations (UN), the Organization for Economic Co-operation and Development (OECD), the North Atlantic Treaty Organization (NATO), and INTERPOL. According to Statista, by 2026, the global cybersecurity market size is forecast to grow to 345.4 billion U.S. dollars.

3.2 AML/CFT International Organizations

3.2.1 The Financial Action Task Force on Money Laundering (FAFT)

Formed in 1989 by the G7 countries, the Financial Action Task Force on Money Laundering (FATF) is an intergovernmental body whose purpose is to develop and promote an international response to combat money laundering. The FATF Secretariat is housed at the headquarters of the OECD in Paris. In October 2001, FATF expanded its mission to include combating the financing of terrorism. FATF is a policy-making body that brings together legal, financial, and law enforcement experts to achieve national legislation and regulatory AML and CFT reforms. As of 2014,

© The Author(s), under exclusive license to Springer Nature Switzerland AG 2023
F. I. Lessambo, *Anti-Money Laundering, Counter Financing Terrorism and Cybersecurity in the Banking Industry*, Palgrave Macmillan Studies in Banking and Financial Institutions, https://doi.org/10.1007/978-3-031-23484-2_3

its membership consists of 36 countries and territories and two regional organizations. FATF works in collaboration with a number of international bodies and organizations.[48] These entities have observer status with FATF, which does not entitle them to vote, but permits them full participation in plenary sessions and working groups. FATF has developed 40 recommendations on money laundering and 9 special recommendations regarding terrorist financing. FATF assesses each member country against these recommendations in published reports. Countries seen as not being sufficiently compliant with such recommendations are subjected to financial sanctions.

The role of FATF is to understand the risks of money laundering and terrorist financing, to develop and promote global policies and standards to counteract these risks, and to evaluate countries vis-à-vis these standards and thus contribute to security.[1]

FATF's three primary functions with regard to money laundering are:

1. Monitoring members' progress in implementing anti-money laundering measures,
2. Reviewing and reporting on laundering trends, techniques, and countermeasures, and
3. Promoting the adoption and implementation of FATF anti-money laundering standards globally.

The FATF currently comprises 34 members' jurisdictions and 2 regional organizations, representing most major financial centers in all parts of the globe.

3.2.2   The International Money Laundering Information Network (IMoLIN)

The International Money Laundering Information Network (IMoLIN), an Internet-based network assisting governments, organizations, and individuals in the fight against money laundering. IMoLIN, has been developed with the cooperation of the world's leading anti-money laundering organizations. Included herein is a database on legislation and

---

[1] Santiago Otamend (2018): State of Cybersecurity in the Banking Sector in Latin America and the Caribbean-FATF: Implementing Effective Legislative Frameworks to Combat Money Laundering in the Global Digital Economy.

regulation throughout the world (AMLID), an electronic library, and a calendar of events in the anti-money laundering field. Please be advised that certain aspects of IMoLIN are secured and therefore not available for public use. This multifaceted website serves the global anti-money laundering community by providing information about national money laundering and financing of terrorism laws and regulations and contacts for inter-country assistance. Inter alia, it identifies areas for improvement in domestic laws, countermeasures, and international cooperation. Policy practitioners, lawyers, and law enforcement officers all regularly use IMoLIN as a key reference point in their daily work. The information on IMoLIN is freely available to all Internet users, with the exception of AMLID, which is a secure database. The key features of the IMoLIN system are: The Anti-Money Laundering International Database (AMLID), a compendium of analyses of anti-money laundering laws and regulations, including two general classes of money laundering control measures (domestic laws and international cooperation) as well as information about national contacts and authorities. AMLID is a secure, multilingual database and is an important reference tool for law enforcement officers involved in cross-jurisdictional work. The AMLID questionnaire was updated to reflect new money laundering trends and standards, and takes into account provisions related to terrorist financing and other current standards, such as the revised FATF 40 + 9 Recommendations. In addition, the revised AMLID questionnaire now includes a Conventions Framework section. This new section gives an overview of the status of a country or territory to the international conventions applicable to anti-money laundering/countering the financing of terrorism (AML/CFT) as well as the status of a country or territory to bilateral/multilateral treaties or agreements on mutual legal assistance in criminal matters and extradition; the reference section that contains details of the UN's latest research, abstracts of the best new research from governments and international organizations, and a bibliography; and a click-on map that takes users to regional lists of national legislation.Eventually, this section will contain the full text or links to the full text of all national anti-money laundering/countering the financing of terrorism (AML/CFT) legislation and regulations throughout the world. The database now contains legislation from some 163 jurisdictions and, since January 2005, more than 250 new/amended AML/CFT legislation and regulations were collected to be included in the database; International Norms and Standards: model laws for common law and civil law systems, standards, conventions, and legal instruments; a worldwide calendar of events that lists current training events and conferences at national, regional, and international level; and a links section that includes links to the websites of related regional organizations active in the field of AML/CFT and financial intelligence units (FIUs).

3.2.3   Financial Action Task Force on Money Laundering in Latin America (GAFILAT)

A FATF-style regional body for Latin America, established in 2000. The intergovernmental organization in charge of international prevention of money laundering and terrorist financing, the Financial Action Task Force (GAFI), is divided into regional groups, corresponding in the case of Latin America to the Latin American Financial Action Group (GAFILAT). The aim of GAFILAT is to promote the implementation of best practices to combat money laundering and terrorist financing, mainly by communicating the 40 GAFI recommendations in this area (the 40 Recommendations). GAFILAT brings together Argentina, Bolivia, Brazil, Chile, Colombia, Costa Rica, Cuba, Ecuador, Guatemala, Honduras, Mexico, Nicaragua, Panama, Paraguay, Peru, the Dominican Republic, and Uruguay.

3.3   CYBERSECURITY IN INTERNATIONAL ORGANIZATIONS

Cybersecurity is attracting focused attention from international governing, policymaking, law enforcement, and security bodies, including the United Nations (UN), the Organization for Economic Co-operation and Development (OECD), the North Atlantic Treaty Organization (NATO), and INTERPOL. According to Statista, by 2026, the global cybersecurity market size is forecast to grow to 345.4 billion U.S. dollars.

One of the most infamous examples of ransomware is the WannaCry attack in 2017, in which North Korean hackers used loopholes developed by the United States National Security Agency in the Windows operating system to attack more than 200,000 computers across 150 countries. The IGOs, NGOs, and U.S. government agencies described below are key players in the global struggle against cybercrime.

3.3.1   The Council of Europe: Action Against Cybercrime

The Council of Europe (CoE) is a leading human rights' intergovernmental organization with 47 members comprising all European States with the exception of Belarus but including Russia, Turkey, and Azerbaijan. It is the body guaranteeing the European Convention on Human Rights and its protection by the European Court of Human Rights, the only international human rights protection mechanism in the world capable of providing individuals with direct access to judicial remedy in respect of States and their human rights obligations.

The Budapest Convention, which opened for signature 20 years ago, remains one of the world's most important international agreements regarding cybercrime both for the 66 states parties to the Convention, including non-members of the Council of Europe, but also for non-party states. More than 80% of world states have based their domestic legislation on cybercrime on this Convention. On November 23, 2001, the Convention and its first Additional Protocol concerning the criminalization of acts of a racist and xenophobic nature committed through computer systems create a framework for international cooperation between signatory parties to tackle cybercrime, including the harmonization of cybercrime legislation concerning both criminal and procedural law. Some non-party states seek to replace the Budapest Convention by creating a new cybercrime treaty. Most notable among them is Russia, which at the end of 2019 managed to pass a resolution at the UN establishing an ad hoc intergovernmental committee to create a draft of a global comprehensive cybercrime treaty. On 8 June 2017, the Cybercrime Convention Committee, in its 17th plenary session, approved the Terms of Reference for the Preparation of a Draft 2nd Additional Protocol to the Budapest Convention on Cybercrime, which laid down the scope of the Protocol. Civil society and other stakeholders were also involved in the drafting to incorporate cross-sectoral reservations. The new Protocol addresses more efficient mutual legal assistance; direct cooperation with service providers in other jurisdictions regarding requests for subscriber information, preservation requests, and emergency requests; safeguards for preserving human rights; and trans-border access to data. It aims to develop a framework for obtaining electronic evidence more effectively.

3.3.1.1   Mutual Legal Assistance

To enhance the time-consuming and 'inefficient' mutual legal assistance framework established by the Convention, the Protocol establishes emergency mutual assistance. Article 10 seeks to provide a rapidly expedited procedure for mutual assistance requests made in emergencies. By 'emergency', the Protocol means a 'situation in which there is a significant and imminent risk to the life or safety of any natural person' (Article 3 section 2. C). Under this provision, the requested state is required to respond to the request quickly. All states are required to ensure the permanent availability of members of their authorities responsible for responding to the mutual assistance requests. As the explanatory report para 177 puts it, 'authority should implement procedures to ensure that staff may be contacted in order to review emergency requests outside normal business hours.'

3.3.1.2   Direct Cooperation with Service Providers

Articles 6 and 7 address the direct cooperation of a requesting party with a service provider in another state. Under Article 6, entities providing domain name registration services are required to provide, on receiving a valid request from the law enforcement agency of another state, information for identifying or contacting the registrant of a domain name. The entities providing domain name registration services include organizations that sell domain names to the public as well as regional or national registry operators which keep authoritative databases of all domain names registered for a top-level domain and which accept registration requests. (Explanatory report par. 75).

Article 7 of the Protocol establishes direct cooperation with service providers. A law enforcement agency of the requesting country can obtain subscriber information directly from a service provider in the territory of another state. The article gives the option for states to require notification regarding such a request to a provider on its territory. Under this article, a state can also choose to guarantee human rights by requiring the order to be issued by or under the supervision of a prosecutor or other judicial authority or otherwise be issued under independent supervision. However, the information to be disclosed by the service providers under this article is limited to domain name registration or subscriber information containing the subscriber's identity, payment information, the type of communication service used, and the physical address of the subscriber (Explanatory report para 93).

Under these articles, the state issuing an order or request does not have to use the mutual legal assistance process, which could be time-consuming.

3.3.1.3   *Trans-border Access to Data*

Articles 11 and 12 address enhanced cooperation between parties. Article 11 deals with using video conferencing to take testimony or statements from a witness or expert. This should provide a timely solution to any issues that may arise concerning the execution of an order or request issued by another state.

Article 12 gives the competent authorities of two or more states the option to establish joint investigation teams that would facilitate a criminal investigation. Such a measure seems crucial in combating transnational cybercrime as it speeds up investigation. The states' authorities must then agree on the exact terms and conditions under which the joint investigation teams will operate. They should include 'specific purpose, composition, functions, duration, location, organization, transmitting and using the information of evidence, terms of confidentiality and others' (Explanatory report para 206).

3.3.1.4   *Human Rights Safeguards*

Article 13 requires parties to ensure that their domestic law adequately protects human rights and liberties. It also refers to Article 15 of the Convention, which addresses the state's obligations to protect fundamental human rights and liberties under international treaties. Protection of personal data is under Article 14 which provides specific safeguards for personal data transferred based on the Protocol. Given the different frameworks for data protection between states, implementation of this Article will be subjected to review under Article 23. The data protection measures include limitations on the use of the data to purposes described in the Protocol, safeguards for sensitive data, data retention requirements, restrictions on automated decisions, requirements for data security measures, limitations on onwards transfers, and requirements to have in place judicial and non-judicial remedies to provide redress for violations of this provision. The Protocol lists two exceptions from the required data protection. Under the first, if the requesting party and the receiving party are 'mutually bound by an international agreement that establishes a comprehensive framework between those Parties for the protection of personal data', the protections under Article 14 do not have to be employed. An example of such an international agreement is Convention 108+ (Explanatory report para 222). The second states that even if no international agreement on data protection binds both parties, they may transfer the data under an informal agreement between themselves. These informal agreements are not required to be made public, although the explanatory report in para 223 encourages parties to communicate such agreements to the public to maintain legal certainty and transparency. If there is a systematic or material breach of data protection obligations, a suspension may be invoked under Article 14 para 15. However, the suspension of transfers should be used only as a final measure. Suspension should therefore be employed when there is evidence of a systematic or material breach of the terms of the Protocol or if a material breach is imminent (Explanatory report para 282).

3.3.2   International Criminal Police Organization (INTERPOL)

The International Criminal Police Organization, or INTERPOL, is an independent multilateral organization with a general assembly made up of 188 member countries and an executive committee made up of thirteen elected members. As the world's largest international police organization, INTERPOL facilitates police cooperation across borders, even where diplomatic relationships do not exist between countries. Established as an institution to focus on criminal, rather than political issues (as indicated in Article 3 of its constitution), INTERPOL has been active in working with its member countries to address criminal and police issues relating to terrorism. As part of these efforts, INTERPOL facilitates the exchange of best practices and operational information about the organization and methods of active terrorist networks through its Fusion Task Force (a forum for counterterrorism experts). INTERPOL's core mission is to enable law enforcement agencies in its 190 member countries to work together to combat transnational crime, including cybercrime, and crimes against children. In addition to serving as a hub for information exchange and intelligence sharing, it also provides technical expertise, training, and capacity building.

INTERPOL has led several operations across different regions targeting organized cybercrime activity. These 'cyber surges' brought together investigators to act on threat information developed with private sector partners. After detecting a global crypto-jacking campaign exploiting a vulnerability in MikroTik routers, INTERPOL coordinated

Operation Goldfish Alpha in Southeast Asia, where more than 20,000 hacked routers were initially identified. Cybercrime investigators and experts from police and national Computer Emergency Response Teams (CERTs) in the region worked together to locate the infected routers, alert the victims, and patch the devices so they were no longer under the control of the cybercriminals, reducing the number of infections by 78 percent.

3.3.3   *International Telecommunications Union (ITU)*

The International Telecommunication Union (ITU) is the United Nations' specialized agency for information and communication technologies–ICTs. Founded in 1865 to facilitate international connectivity in communications networks, it allocates global radio spectrum and satellite orbits, develops the technical standards that ensure networks and technologies seamlessly interconnect, and strives to improve access to ICTs to underserved communities worldwide. ITU is committed to connecting all the world's people–wherever they live and whatever their means. Through its work, it protects and supports everyone's right to communicate and witness the infinite potential of an increasingly digitalized world. With billions of mobile phone subscribers, close to five billion people with access to television, and tens of millions of new Internet users every year, hundreds of millions of people around the world use satellite services–whether getting directions from a satellite navigation system, checking the weather forecast or watching television from isolated areas. Confronting with an increasingly interconnected world, ITU, is at the very heart of the ICT sector, brokering agreement on technologies, services, allocation of resources like radio-frequency spectrum, and satellite orbital positions in order to create a seamless global communications system that's robust, reliable, and constantly evolving. A fundamental role of ITU, based on the guidance of the World Summit on the Information Society (WSIS) and the ITU Plenipotentiary Conference, is to build confidence and security in the use of Information and Communication Technologies (ICTs). The ITU has developed a Global Cybersecurity Index. The Global Cybersecurity Index (GCI) is a trusted reference that measures the commitment of countries to cybersecurity at a global level–to raise awareness of the importance and different dimensions of the issue. As cybersecurity has a broad field of application, cutting across many industries and various sectors, each country's level of development or engagement is assessed along five pillars–(i) Legal Measures, (ii) Technical Measures, (iii) Organizational Measures, (iv) Capacity Development, and (v) Cooperation–and then aggregated into an overall score.

3.3.4   *United Nations Office of Drugs and Crime (UNODC)*

According to General Assembly resolution 65/230 and Commission on Crime Prevention and Criminal Justice resolutions 22/7 and 22/8, the Global Programme on Cybercrime is mandated to assist Member States in their struggle against cyber-related crimes through capacity building and technical assistance.

Prior to the commencement of the Global Programme, UNODC's open-ended intergovernmental expert group was established to conduct a comprehensive study of the problem of cybercrime and responses to it by Member States, the international community, and the private sector. This work includes the exchange of information on national legislation, best practice, technical assistance, and international cooperation. You can read more about the study and follow-up meetings. The Global Programme on Cybercrime is funded entirely through the kind support of the Governments of Australia, Canada, Japan, Norway, UK, and United States.

The Global Programme is designed to respond flexibly to identify needs in developing countries by supporting Member States to prevent and combat cybercrime in a holistic manner. The main geographic nexus for the Cybercrime Programme in 2017 are Central America, Eastern Africa, MENA and South East Asia, and the Pacific with key aims of:

- Increased efficiency and effectiveness in the investigation, prosecution, and adjudication of cybercrime, especially online child sexual exploitation and abuse, within a strong human-rights framework;
- Efficient and effective long-term whole-of-government response to cybercrime, including national coordination, data collection, and effective legal frameworks, leading to a sustainable response and greater deterrence;
- Strengthened national and international communication between government, law enforcement, and the private sector with increased public knowledge of cybercrime risks.

3.3.5 The Organization of Economic Cooperation and Development (OECD)

The Global Forum on Digital Security for Prosperity is an international multilateral and multidisciplinary setting for all stakeholder communities. It brings together experts and policy makers to foster regular sharing of experiences and good practice on digital security risk and its management, as well as mutual learning and convergence of views on digital security for economic and social prosperity. The Global Forum holds thematic events involving policy makers and experts from all stakeholder groups. The inaugural event took place on 13–14 December 2018 at OECD in Paris. The meeting explored the roles and responsibilities of actors: governance of digital security in organizations and security of digital technologies. Regarding Cyberspace activities, the OECD deals with the internet economy, e-government, internet governance, cybersecurity, and privacy. It is specialized in critical information and infrastructure protection, promotion of cybersecurity strategies, defense from malware and botnets, protection of minors online, and management of digital identity and its electronic authentication.

3.3.6 G8 24/7 Cybercrime Network

The G8 24/7 High Tech Crime Network (HTCN) is an informal network that provides around-the-clock, high-tech expert contact points, which permits the sharing of information on ongoing investigations against cyber criminals. Created in 1997, the G8 24/7 HTCN, which includes 45 countries, has, among other achievements, been used on several occasions to avert hacking attacks, including attacks on banks in the United States, Germany, and Mexico.

Meeting of the G8 Justice and Interior Ministers–December 1997 called for creation of a network.

- "With regard to high-tech crime, we must start by recognizing that new computer and telecommunications technologies offer unprecedented opportunities for global communication. As nations become increasingly reliant upon these technologies, including wireless communications, their exploitation by high-tech criminals poses an ever-greater threat to public safety."

Primary purpose of the Network is to preserve data for subsequent transfer through mutual legal assistance channels. To use this Network, law enforcement agents seeking assistance from a foreign Participant may contact the 24-hour point of contact in their own state or autonomous law enforcement jurisdiction, and this individual or entity will, if appropriate, contact his or her counterpart in the foreign Participant. Participants in the Network have committed to make their best efforts to ensure that Internet Service Providers freeze the information sought by a requesting Participant as quickly as possible. Participants have further committed to make their best efforts to produce information expeditiously. This is subject to the understanding that a requested Participant's legal, technical, or resource considerations may affect the extent to which–and the time frame within which–the Participant may produce evidence, as well as the process of Mutual Legal Assistance, by which the requesting country seeks release of that information though the usual MLAT or Letters of Request procedure."

3.3.7   The Internet Society (ISOC)

The Internet Society (ISOC) is an international nonprofit organization that handles Internet standards, education, and policy development. Founded in 1992, ISOC's mission is to ensure open Internet development by enhancing and supporting Internet use for organizations and individuals worldwide. ISOC was created to support the development process for Internet standards, while focusing on promoting key Internet development activities. ISOC leaders address issues confronting the future of the Internet and provide organizational infrastructure for Internet standards groups, including the Internet Architecture Board (IAB) and the Internet Engineering Task Force (IETF). ISOC handles Internet policy planning and deals with terminologies like the Internet Code of Conduct, Internet Law, and the Internet Ecosystem. ISOC has regular member meetings, workshops, and conferences on Internet use awareness and other topics of interest.

3.3.8   The International Cyber Security Protection Alliance (ICSPA)

The International Cyber Security Protection Alliance (ICSPA) was established to channel funding, expertise, and assistance directly to assist law enforcement cybercrime units in both domestic and international markets.

The International Cyber Security Protection Alliance (ICSPA) is a not-for-profit org supporting law enforcement units globally in their fight against cybercrime. ICSPA was established to channel funding, expertise, and assistance directly to assist law enforcement cybercrime units in both domestic and international markets. We are a business-led organization comprising large national and multinational companies who recognize the need to provide additional resourcing and support to law enforcement officers around the world, in their fight against cybercrime.

3.3.9 *International Association of Insurance Supervisors (IAIS)*

Established in 1994, the IAIS is a voluntary membership organization of insurance supervisors and regulators from more than 200 jurisdictions, constituting 97% of the world's insurance premiums. It is the global standard-setting body responsible for developing and assisting in the implementation of principles, standards, and guidance as well as supporting material for the supervision of the insurance sector. The IAIS mission is to promote effective and globally consistent supervision of the insurance industry in order to develop and maintain fair, safe, and stable insurance markets for the benefit and protection of policyholders, and to contribute to global financial stability.[2]

In 2016 the International Association of Insurance Supervisors (IAIS) produced a fact-finding document on the evolution of cyber risks, mitigation practices and the approaches adopted by the authorities.

3.3.10 *International Organization of Securities Commissions (IOSCO)*

The Committee on Payments and Market Infrastructures (CPMI) and the International Organization of Securities Commissions (IOSCO) have published a Guidance on cybersecurity which highlights the following points[3]:

---

[2] https://www.iaisweb.org/

[3] World Bank (2017): Financial Sector's Cybersecurity: A Regulatory Digest, p. 28; https://thedocs.worldbank.org/en/doc/524901513362019919-0130022017/original/FinSACCybersecDigestOct2017Dec2017.pdf.

- Sound cyber governance is key. Board and senior management attention is critical to a successful cyber-resilience strategy;
- The ability to resume operations quickly and safely after a successful cyberattack
- is paramount;
- Financial Market Infrastructures (FMI) should make use of good-quality threat
- intelligence and rigorous testing;
- FMIs should aim to instill a culture of cyber-risk awareness and demonstrate
- ongoing re-evaluation and improvement of their cyber-resilience at every level
- within the organization;
- Cyber-resilience cannot be achieved by an FMI alone; it is a collective endeavor of the whole ecosystem.

3.4   AN INTERNATIONAL STRATEGY

To achieve more effective protection of the global financial system against cyber threats, the Carnegie Endowment for International Peace released a report in November 2020 titled "International Strategy to Better Protect the Global Financial System against Cyber threats." Developed in collaboration with the World Economic Forum, the report recommends specific actions to reduce fragmentation by fostering more collaboration, both internationally and among government agencies, financial arms, and tech companies.

3.5   CYBERCRIME CONVENTIONS

3.5.1   The International Cybercrime Treaty

The treaty aims to foster a common criminal policy aimed at the protection of society against cybercrime. Since its initial release in April 2000, the treaty has been revised several times in response to much criticism over its language and the potential problems with its procedural implementation.[4] The treaty is drafted so broadly that it will affect far more than a

---

[4] Ryan M. F. Baron (2002): A Critique of the International Cybersecurity Treaty, Commlaw Conspectus, Vol. 10, pp. 263–278.

few hackers. That is, when significant human rights concerns are coupled with blind spots that could endanger cybersecurity research, it is apparent that an international instrument that is not carefully crafted could have unintended consequences, including undermining the very purpose for its existence.[5]

3.5.2   The UNDOP International Treaty on Cybercrime

In December 2019, the UN General Assembly adopted a resolution on "countering the use of information and communications technologies for criminal purposes", and introducing an Ad Hoc Committee. The committee was announced to elaborate a comprehensive international convention. Multiple governments around the world participated at the meeting with the UN, where they discussed and tried to find common ground on the treaty in order to facilitate global cooperation on cybercrime.

3.5.3   African Union Convention on Cyberspace Security and Personal Data Protection

An African Union Convention on Cyber Security and Personal Data Protection was drafted in 2011 to establish a 'credible framework for cybersecurity in Africa through organization of electronic transactions, protection of personal data, and promotion of cybersecurity, e-governance, and combating cybercrime. The Convention was finally adopted in June 2014.[6] The Convention addresses three main areas: (1) electronic transactions, (2) personal data protection, and (3) cybersecurity and cybercrime. The treaty will enter into force 30 days after the 15th instrument of ratification or accession is deposited.[7]

---

[5] Christian Ohanian (2022): The UN Cybercrime Treaty Has a Cybersecurity Problem In It, Just Security, https://www.justsecurity.org/83582/the-un-cybercrime-treaty-has-a-cybersecurity-problem-in-it/.

[6] https://ccdcoe.org/organisations/au/.

[7] https://ccdcoe.org/organisations/au/.

CHAPTER 4

AML and Cybersecurity in Banking Industry: Challenges

4.1 Overview

The banking industry relies heavily on technology. The sheer amount of transactions in modern banking makes the functioning of the financial sector infeasible without automated networking, information processing, and telecommunication services.[1] In 2019, the global financial services market was valued at about $22 trillion. The industry has seen steady growth in non-cash payments. Non-cash payments are multiplying due to increasing penetration of internet and mobile usage in developing countries and a global shift toward immediate payment schemes, which offer instant payments in real time.[2]

---

[1] StefanVarga, Joe Brynielsson, Ulrik Franke (2021): Cyber-Threat Perception and Risk Management in the Swedish Financial Sector, *Computers & Security*, Volume 105, June 2021, 102239.

[2] Steven Bowcut (2021): Cybersecurity in the Financial Services Industry, https://cybersecurityguide.org/industries/financial/.

4.2   AML and the Banking Industry

Banks are among the largest institutions in the field of finance. Since banks worldwide mediate millions of transactions throughout the day, these institutions are at a higher risk of financial crimes. And in fact, criminal organizations often carry out their money laundering activities through banks and other financial institutions. Therefore, banks must identify the risks by fulfilling their AML obligations and taking necessary precautions. More, the technological shift in financial infrastructure and the rise of online payments has increased the demand for more rigorous customer identity protection. In response to new and more stringent directives, banks and financial institutions adopt emerging trends in AI-based AML solutions to handle AML compliance with greater efficiency.[3]

4.3   Cybersecurity in the Banking Industry

Money can be moved among corporate entities and financial institutions in many countries in the blink of an eye through wire fund transfers, making the untangling more and more difficult at every stage.[4] As banks deal with a huge volume of financial data, cyber criminals are increasingly targeting customer banking credentials when carrying out attacks. Statistics show that in 2021, cybercrime was a top three most reported economic crime.[5] The cost of cyberattacks in the banking industry reached $18.3 million annually per company, and according to FBI, the amount paid to ransomware scammers has reached nearly $1

---

[3] Jackie Wheeler (2022): Guidance on Anti-Money Laundering (AML) in Banking and Finance for 2022, https://www.jumio.com/aml-guidance-banking-finance-2021/.

[4] Mohammed Issa, Samuel Antwi, and Solomon Koffi Antwi (2022): Anti-Money Laundering Regulations and Banking Sector Stability in Africa, *Cogent Economics & Finance*, Volume 10, No. 1, 2022.

[5] Jessica Day (2022): Cybersecurity in Digital Banking: Everything You Need to Know, https://stefanini.com/en/trends/articles/cybersecurity-in-digital-banking-everything-you-need-to-know.

billion per year.[6] With the introduction of several mobile banking applications, cyber criminals have more space to intrude into the network.[7] Although cybersecurity is essential to banks, they also need to provide convenience to their customers. If a bank's security measures are too strict, many people may switch their accounts to a bank with less stringent regulations. Conversely, if the security provided by a bank is not convenient, then there will be huge costs because of the extra security measures. More money will need to be spent on additional personnel, software, and hardware for the bank's security system. Therefore, banks must come up with the right balance of convenience and security to survive in the long run.

4.4   Core Cybersecurity Risks in the Banking

Cyber events are conventionally classified into three categories based on the technical nature of the event, introduced in the Federal Information Security Management Act[8].

4.4.1   The Compromising of Confidential data

Data Compromise refers to any actual or reasonably suspected unauthorized access, disclosure, or use of transmitted data that compromises the security, confidentiality, or integrity of the transmitted data. In March of 2019, Capital One was the victim of a wide-scale data breach that compromised more than 100 million customer accounts, including social security numbers, names, addresses, and credit card scores.[9] Two months later, in May of 2019, an attacker hit First American Financial Corp. in

---

[6] Archon Secure (2022): Cyber Threats in the Banking Industry, https://www.archon secure.com/blog/banking-industry-cyber-threats.

[7] Julie Clements (Apr 28, 2021): Cyber Security in the Banking Industry—Top Trends to Know, https://www.managedoutsource.com/blog/cyber-security-in-banking-industry-top-trends-to-know

[8] Thomas M. Eisenbach, Anna Kovner, Michael Junho Lee (2021): Cyber Risk and the U.S. Financial System: A Pre-Mortem Analysis, Federal Reserve Bank of New York Staff Reports, no. 909, January 2020; revised May 2021, https://www.newyorkfed.org/med ialibrary/media/research/staff_reports/sr909.pdf.

[9] Emily Flitter and Karen Weise (2019): Capital One Data Breach Compromises Data of over 100 Million, *The New York Times*, https://www.nytimes.com/2019/07/29/bus iness/capital-one-data-breach-hacked.html.

a massive data breach, exposing over 855 million real estate and mortgage documents to the public.[10] Due to a data management error, users were able to quickly lookup personal information, including social security numbers, mortgage and tax records, driver's license numbers, and more. Attackers could see them by simply altering a nine-digit transaction record.

4.4.2   The Compromising of Data Availability or Systems

Hackers are always looking for some open services, so that they can get into the system and bring havoc. In order to maintain a sustainable state of availability, it is necessary for an information system to have a check on the various services being accessed by various calling programs.[11] Availability events can immobilize capital and liquidity, and affect the ability of the bank to perform its core activities. Such events can therefore have considerable spillovers to the banks customers and counterparties, within and outside the financial sector.

4.4.3   The Compromising of Data Integrity

Data integrity is a guarantee of the accuracy and consistency of data throughout its life and is an important aspect of the design, implementation, and use of any system that stores, processes, or retrieves data. Banks can maintain data integrity through integrity constraints, which define the rules and procedures around actions like deletion, insertion, and update of information. For instance, in January 2008, Russian hackers injected malware through a web form on Heartland's website, resulting in the comprised of 130 million credit and debit card numbers.[12] The banking industry is making major investments in cybersecurity, across institutions

---

[10] A.J. Dellinger (2019): Understanding the First American Financial Data Leak: How Did It Happen and What Does It Mean? *Forbes*, https://www.forbes.com/sites/ajdellinger/2019/05/26/understanding-the-first-american-financial-data-leak-how-did-it-happen-and-what-does-it-mean/?sh=1c2a21a3567f.

[11] Suhail Qadir, S.M.K. Quadri (2016): Information Availability: An Insight into the Most Important Attribute of Information Security, *Journal of Information Security*, Volume 7 No.3, April 2016.

[12] Edward Kost (2022): 10 Biggest Data Breaches in Finance, UpGuard, https://www.upguard.com/blog/biggest-data-breaches-financial-services.

of varying sizes and credit quality, according to a report by Moody's. There are really three major attack vectors that banking institutions and financial organizations:

4.4.3.1 Personal Security of Individual Members Accessing Their Accounts

Banks and other financial institutions need to impose strict security requirements and controls on their web portals. This includes things like requiring strong passwords and implementing 2-factor authentication.

4.4.3.2 Security of the Tools to Access Their Clients' Accounts

Banks use sophisticated technology and monitoring techniques, intricate firewalls and other methods of securing customer data. Banks use more than one methods for verifying a customer's identity before granting online account access, for instance. Forms of identification include password or PIN. Likewise, Banks secure their customers' transactions and personal information using encryption software that converts the information into code that only bankers can read.

4.4.3.3 Internal Team Control as They Access Your Back-End Servers and Internal Network

Financial institutions and particularly Banks are subject to various safety and soundness standards, such as the standard to have internal controls and information systems that are appropriate to the institution's size and complexity and the nature, scope, and risk of its activities.[13] For instance, a bank can set up policies for approval and documentation standards by defining users' authority to access financial institution information systems, or limiting users' access rights across multiple information systems.

4.5   Ensuring Cyber Security in Banks

To remain protected against emerging threat trends, it is important for banking institutions to collaborate with their IT teams to establish strong security protocols. Here discussed are four ways to strengthen cyber security protocols within the banking sector:

---

[13] FFIEC (2005): Authentication and Access to Financial Institution Services and Systems, https://www.ffiec.gov/guidance/Authentication-and-Access-to-Financial-Institution-Services-and-Systems.pdf.

- Cyber Risk Assessment—Conducting a detailed cyber-risk assessment helps banks identify and manage vulnerabilities within their network environment in advance. By evaluating the potential risk factors that pose the greatest threat to a bank's financial business, you can prioritize remediation efforts and reorganize threat mitigation. This allows banks to proactively protect against data breaches while reducing costs and labor hours in the long run.
- Multi-factor Authentication (MFA)–MFA is an absolute necessity for financial organizations as it adds an additional layer of security when attempting to access valuable information. In simple terms, MFA is an authentication method in which access is only granted once a user presents two or more login credentials like passwords, pins, or fingerprints. When setting up MFA, make sure that login credentials do not come from the same source (i.e., two passwords) as this will weaken the security aspect.
- Cyber Insurance—Regarded as an important component of a cyber-security strategy, cyber insurance helps financial businesses to remain protected in the event of a data breach. Some insurance and reinsurance market participants have started to develop deeper competencies in cyber-risk underwriting.[14] Apart from covering legal expenses, cyber insurance carriers also notify customers of breaches so that organizations are in compliance with data breach regulations. In addition, cyber insurance will also help pay to fix damaged systems and restore compromised data.
- Employee Training—To make security programs more effective, it is essential to train banking employees on cyber hygiene best practices. When employees are trained to use cybersecurity systems properly, they can actively identify available or possible vulnerabilities within their systems and make sure they are resolved.
- Constant Evolution of Threats and Vulnerabilities

Another cybersecurity challenge faced by banks is the constant evolution of threats and vulnerabilities. Hackers are constantly updating their techniques to get around new security measures. Therefore, banks may need to continuously update their cybersecurity protocols to stay ahead

---

[14] Rupert Nicolay (2018): Keeping Ahead of Cybersecurity Challenges in Financial Services, https://cloudblogs.microsoft.com/industry-blog/financial-services/2018/10/24/keeping-ahead-of-cybersecurity-challenges-in-financial-services/.

of hackers every step of the way. Also, it requires a lot of time and money because banks need to hire more personnel, spend vast amounts on software, and buy new hardware for their security systems.

CHAPTER 5

AML/CFT and Cyber Security Laws in the United States

5.1 General

The phrase "money laundering" was officially coined by the US Government in the Money Laundering Control Act of 1986, which established it as a federal crime. In 1988, the United States passed the Anti-Drug Abuse Act, introducing new restrictions and legislative support to prevent money laundering, including the obligation to maintain full information about and the identification of persons who acquire bearer documents or transfer amounts greater than three thousand dollars (3000 USD).[1]

5.2 AML/CFT Laws

Banks and most financial institutions, and many non-financial institutions, are required to identify and report transactions of a suspicious nature to the financial intelligence unit in the respective country. Money laundering is the process of making illegally gained proceeds (i.e., "dirty money") appear legal (i.e., "clean"). Typically, it involves three steps:

---

[1] Willy Zapata Sagastume, Juan Carlos Moreno-Brid, Stefanie Garry (2016): Money Laundering and Financial Risk Management in Latin America, with Special Reference to Mexico, https://www.scielo.org.mx/scielo.php?script=sci_arttext&pid=S0188-338020160 00100009.

© The Author(s), under exclusive license to Springer Nature   57
Switzerland AG 2023
F. I. Lessambo, *Anti-Money Laundering, Counter Financing Terrorism and Cybersecurity in the Banking Industry*, Palgrave Macmillan Studies in Banking and Financial Institutions,
https://doi.org/10.1007/978-3-031-23484-2_5

placement, layering, and integration. First, the illegitimate funds are furtively introduced into the legitimate financial system. Then, the money is moved around to create confusion, sometimes by wiring or transferring through numerous accounts. Finally, it is integrated into the financial system through additional transactions until the "dirty money" appears "clean." Money laundering can facilitate crimes such as drug trafficking and terrorism, and can adversely impact the global economy. Money laundering can take several forms, although most methods can be categorized into one of a few types. These include bank methods, smurfing [also known as structuring], currency exchanges, and double-invoicing. In its mission to "safeguard the financial system from the abuses of financial crime, including terrorist financing, money laundering, and other illicit activity," the Financial Crimes Enforcement Network acts as the designated administrator of the Bank Secrecy Act (BSA). The BSA was established in 1970 and has become one of the most important tools in the fight against money laundering. Since then, numerous other laws have enhanced and amended the BSA to provide law enforcement and regulatory agencies with the most effective tools to combat money laundering. An index of anti-money laundering laws since 1970 with their respective requirements and goals are listed below in chronological order.

5.3   AML/CFT Legislations

5.3.1   The Bank Secrecy Act (aka the Financial Recordkeeping of Currency and Foreign Transactions Act of 1970

Initially adopted in 1970, the Financial Recordkeeping and Reporting of Currency and Foreign Transactions Act of 1970 (Known as the Bank Secrecy Act) establishes the basic framework for AML obligations imposed on financial institutions. Among other things, it authorizes the Secretary of the Treasury (Treasury) to issue regulations requiring financial institutions (including broker-dealers) to keep records and file reports on financial transactions that may be useful in investigating and prosecuting money laundering and other financial crimes. The Financial Crimes Enforcement Network (FinCEN), a bureau within Treasury, has regulatory responsibilities for administering the BSA. The Bank Secrecy Act aims to prevent financial institutions from laundering money, either willfully or through force during a cyberattack. The BSA forces financial institutions to work alongside the U.S. Government in the fight against financial crime. The implementing regulations under the BSA were originally intended to aid investigations into an array of criminal activities, from income tax evasion to money laundering. In recent years, the reports and records prescribed by the BSA have also been utilized as tools for investigating individuals suspected of engaging in illegal drug and terrorist financing activities. BSA compliance is regulated by the Office of the Comptroller of the Currency (OCC) through regular audits. Banks are expected to verify the legitimacy of all currency transactions. Under the BSA, national banks are expected to institute controls that:

- Detect and deter money laundering activities
- Detect terrorist financing
- Facilitate the timely notification of money laundering activities to law enforcement

The U.S. Bank Secrecy Act (BSA), as amended by the USA PATRIOT Act of 2001 (PATRIOT Act), contains anti-money laundering and financial transparency laws and mandated the implementation of various regulations applicable to all financial institutions, including standards for verifying client identification at account opening, and obligations to monitor client transactions and report suspicious activities. Through these and other provisions, the BSA and the PATRIOT Act seek to promote the identification of parties that may be involved in terrorism, money laundering, or other suspicious activities. Anti- money laundering laws outside the United States contain some similar provisions.

5.3.2   *Money Laundering Control Act (1986)*

The Money Laundering Control Act of 1986,[2] passed in 1986, is the first federal law that criminalized money laundering. The Money Laundering Control Act of 1986 was enacted as Title I of the Anti-Drug Abuse Act. It also amended the Bank Secrecy Act, the Change in Bank Control Act, and the Right to Financial Privacy Act. Section 1956 prohibits individuals from engaging in a financial transaction with proceeds that were generated from certain specific crimes, known as "specified unlawful activities" (SUAs). Additionally, the law requires that an individual specifically intend

---

[2] Public Law, 99–570.

in making the transaction to conceal the source, ownership, or control of the funds. There is no minimum threshold of money, nor is there the requirement that the transaction succeed in actually disguising the money. Moreover, a "financial transaction" has been broadly defined, and need not involve a financial institution, or even a business. Merely passing money from one person to another, so long as it is done with the intent to disguise the source, ownership, location, or control of the money, has been deemed a financial transaction under the law. Section 1957 prohibits spending in excess of $10,000 derived from an SUA, regardless of whether the individual wishes to disguise it. This carries a lesser penalty than money laundering, and unlike the money laundering statute requires that the money pass through a financial institution.

5.3.3   Anti-Drug Abuse Act (1988)

Enacted as part of the federal government war on drugs, the Anti-Drug Abuse Act of 1988 sought to increase penalties for those who were involved in the sale and use of illegal narcotics. Indeed, the U.S. government built upon the Anti-Drug Abuse Act of 1986 with changes which then became the Anti-Drug Abuse Act of 1988. In passing this legislation, Congress expressly intended to punish and deter anyone who intentionally kills or counsels, commands, induces, procures, or causes an intentional killing of: (A) any person while (1) engaging in or (2) working in furtherance of any continuing criminal enterprise, or (3) while engaging in a major federal drug felony; or (B) any law enforcement officer during or in relation to a federal drug felony. The Anti-Drug Abuse Act of 1988 contained a myriad of changes, enhancements, penalties, and funding for the war on drugs. It focused on both the seller and the user of illegal narcotics. It was the government's answer to battling the drug epidemic by providing changes to the law, making for harsher sentences for those involved in the drug trade.

5.3.4   Annunzio-Wylie Anti-money Laundering Act (1992)

Outlined the procedure to subpoena bank records. The Act amended federal law relating to international monetary instrument transaction reporting requirements to prohibit: (1) failure to file the requisite reports; (2) filing material omissions or misstatements of facts in such reports; and

(3) participation in structuring any importation or exportation of monetary instruments. The Act makes the penalty for conspiracy to commit a money laundering offense the same as the penalty for the substantive offense itself. More, it amended the Right to Financial Privacy Act of 1978 to prohibit certain personnel connected with a financial institution from disclosing the existence of a grand jury subpoena to a person named in such subpoena for bank records related to money laundering and controlled substance investigations. Also, it requires the Attorney General, the Secretary of the Treasury, and the head of any other federal agency or instrumentality to disclose to the appropriate federal banking agency any information raising significant concerns regarding the safety and soundness of any depository institution doing business in the United States.

5.3.5 *Money Laundering Suppression Act (1994)*

Money Laundering Suppression Act of 1994 Amends Federal law to prescribe guidelines for both mandatory and discretionary exemptions from monetary transaction reporting requirements for depository institutions.

5.3.5.1 *Section 402*
Section 402 directs the Secretary of the Treasury (the Secretary) to:

- submit an annual status report to the Congress on the consequent reduction in the overall number of currency transaction reports;
- streamline currency transaction reports to eliminate information of little value for law enforcement purposes;
- assign a single designee to receive reports of suspicious transactions; and
- submit annual reports to the Congress on the number of suspicious transactions reported.

5.3.5.2 *Section 404*
Section 404 requires each appropriate Federal banking agency to review and enhance:

- training and examination procedures to improve the identification of money laundering schemes involving depository institutions; and
- Procedures for referring cases to appropriate law enforcement agencies.

Further, it requires the Secretary and each appropriate law enforcement agency to provide information regularly to each appropriate Federal banking agency regarding money laundering schemes and activities involving depository institutions in order to enhance agency ability to examine for and identify money laundering activity. Last but not least, it requires the Financial Institutions Examination Council to report to the Congress on the usefulness of the reporting of criminal schemes by law enforcement agencies.

5.3.5.3   Section 405
Section 405 includes negotiable instruments drawn on foreign banks within the purview of monetary transactions subject to Federal record-keeping and reporting requirements.

5.3.5.4   Section 406
Section 406 requires the Secretary to delegate to Federal banking agencies any authority to assess civil money penalties.

5.3.5.5   Section 407
Section 407 expresses the sense of the Congress that the States should:

- establish uniform laws for licensing and regulating non- depository institution businesses which engage in currency transactions;
- provide sufficient resources for regulatory enforcement; and
- develop a model statute to implement the regulatory scheme.

Moreover, it directs the Secretary to study and report to the Congress:

- on the States' progress toward such a model statute;
- on possible federal funding sources to cover costs incurred by the States in implementing a licensing and enforcement scheme.

5.3.5.6   Section 408

Section 408 sets forth federal registration requirements for money transmitting businesses. Directs the Secretary to prescribe regulations establishing a threshold point for treating an agent of a money transmitting business as a money transmitting business. Establishes civil and criminal penalties for violation of such requirements.

5.3.5.7   Section 409

Section 409 amends federal law regarding monetary instruments transactions to include within the definition of "financial institution" a casino, gambling casino, or gaming establishment with specified annual gaming revenues which is either State-licensed, or a certain class of Indian gaming operation (thus subjecting Indian casinos to the more comprehensive currency reporting and recordkeeping requirements of the Bank Secrecy Act).

5.3.5.8   Section 411

Section 411 sets forth criminal penalties for structuring domestic and international transactions to evade federal reporting requirements (currently such violations must be willful in order to be penalized).

5.3.5.9   Section 412

Section 412 requires the Comptroller General to study and report to the Congress on:

- the vulnerability of cashiers' checks to money laundering schemes;
- the need for additional recordkeeping requirements for such checks.

5.3.6   *Money Laundering and Financial Crimes Strategy Act (1998)*

Money Laundering and Financial Crimes Strategy Act of 1998—Amends Federal law governing monetary transactions to redefine money laundering and related financial crimes as either:

- the movement of illicit cash or cash equivalent proceeds into, out of, or through the United States or through certain U.S. financial institutions; or

– the meaning given under State and local criminal statutes pertaining to the movement of illicit cash or cash equivalent proceeds. Section 5 of this Act directs the President (acting through the Secretary of the Treasury and in consultation with the Attorney General) to develop and submit to the Congress a national strategy, with five annual updates, for combating money laundering and related financial crimes. Requires such strategy to include:

(1) research-based goals, objectives, and priorities;
(2) prevention measures coordinated with other agencies;
(3) detection and prosecution initiatives (including seizure and forfeiture of proceeds and instrumentalities derived from such crimes);
(4) an enhanced partnership between the private financial sector and law enforcement agencies to target crime detection and prevention;
(5) enhanced intergovernmental cooperation between federal, State, and local officials; and
(6) a description of geographical areas designated as high-risk money laundering and related financial crime areas.

Section 2 also instructs the Secretary to submit to the Congress contemporaneously with such strategy an evaluation of the effectiveness of policies to combat money laundering and related financial crimes. Moreover, it requires: (1) an element of the national strategy to be the designation of certain geographic areas, industries, sectors, or institutions as areas in which money laundering and related financial crimes are extensive or present a substantial risk; (2) the Secretary to take specified factors into consideration when identifying such areas. It also authorizes certain federal, State, and local officials and prosecutors to submit a written request for: (1) the designation of a high-risk money laundering and related financial crimes area; (2) funding for a specific prevention or enforcement initiative, or to determine the extent of financial criminal activity in an area. It directs the Secretary to: (1) establish a grant program to support local law enforcement efforts in a money laundering detection, prevention, and suppression program; (2) report to specified congressional committees on the effectiveness and need for the designation of high-risk money laundering and related financial crime areas. Finally, it sets forth grant eligibility criteria, and authorizes the Secretary, one year after the national strategy is submitted to the Congress, to review, select, and award grants for State or local law enforcement agencies and prosecutors to provide funding necessary to investigate and prosecute money laundering and related financial crimes in high-risk areas.

5.3.7   Uniting and Strengthening America by Providing Appropriate Tools Required to Intercept and Obstruct Terrorism Act of 2001 (USA PATRIOT Act)

The purpose of the USA PATRIOT Act is to deter and punish terrorist acts in the United States and around the world, to enhance law enforcement investigatory tools, and other purposes, some of which include:

- to strengthen U.S. measures to prevent, detect, and prosecute international money laundering and financing of terrorism;
- to subject to special scrutiny foreign jurisdictions, foreign financial institutions, and classes of international transactions or types of accounts that are susceptible to criminal abuse;
- to require all appropriate elements of the financial services industry to report potential money laundering;
- to strengthen measures to prevent use of the U.S. financial system for personal gain by corrupt foreign officials and facilitate repatriation of stolen assets to the citizens of countries to whom such assets belong.

5.3.8   The USA Patriot Improvement and Reauthorization Act of 2005

The USA PATRIOT Act was enacted by Congress in 2001 in response to the September 11, 2001 terrorist attacks. Among other things, the USA PATRIOT Act amended and strengthened the BSA. It imposed a number of AML obligations directly on broker-dealers, including:

- AML compliance programs;
- customer identification programs;
- monitoring, detecting, and filing reports of suspicious activity;
- due diligence on foreign correspondent accounts, including prohibitions on transactions with foreign shell banks;
- due diligence on private banking accounts;

- mandatory information-sharing (in response to requests by federal law enforcement); and
- compliance with "special measures" imposed by the Secretary of the Treasury to address particular AML concerns.

5.3.8.1   Section 352

Section 352 of the USA PATRIOT ACT amended the BSA to require financial institutions, including broker-dealers, to establish AML programs. Broker-dealers can satisfy this requirement by implementing and maintaining an AML program that complies with SRO rule requirements. In September 2009, the SEC approved FINRA's new AML compliance rule, FINRA Rule 3310. FINRA's new rule adopts NASD Rule 3011 and most of NASD IM-3011-1 and deletes NYSE Rule 445 as duplicative. As with NASD Rule 3011 and NYSE Rule 445, FINRA Rule 3310 requires member organizations to establish risk-based AML compliance programs. Please note, however, that FINRA Rule 3310 does not contain the exception in NASD IM-3011-1 to the independent testing requirement. FINRA Rule 3310 became effective on January 1, 2010.

An AML program must be in writing and include, at a minimum:

- policies, procedures, and internal controls reasonably designed to achieve compliance with the BSA and its implementing rules;
- policies and procedures that can be reasonably expected to detect and cause the reporting of transactions under 31 U.S.C. 5318(g) and the implementing regulations thereunder;
- the designation of an AML compliance officer (AML Officer), including notification to the SROs;
- ongoing AML employee training; and
- an independent test of the firm's AML program, annually for most firms.

5.3.8.2   Section 326

Section 326 of the USA PATRIOT Act amended the BSA to require financial institutions, including broker-dealers, to establish written customer identification programs (CIP). Treasury's implementing rule requires a broker-dealer's CIP to include, at a minimum, procedures for:

- obtaining customer identifying information from each customer prior to account opening;
- verifying the identity of each customer, to the extent reasonable and practicable, within a reasonable time before or after account opening;
- making and maintaining a record of information obtained relating to identity verification;
- determining within a reasonable time after account opening or earlier whether a customer appears on any list of known or suspected terrorist organizations designated by Treasury; and
- providing each customer with adequate notice, prior to opening an account, that information is being requested to verify the customer's identity.

The CIP rule provides that, under certain defined circumstances, broker-dealers may rely on the performance of another financial institution to fulfill some or all of the requirements of the broker-dealer's CIP. For example, in order for a broker-dealer to rely on the other financial institution the reliance must be reasonable. The other financial institution also must be subject to an AML compliance program rule and be regulated by a federal functional regulator. The broker-dealer and other financial institution must enter into a contract and the other financial institution must certify annually to the broker-dealer that it has implemented an AML program. The other financial institution must also certify to the broker-dealer that the financial institution will perform the specified requirements of the broker-dealer's CIP.

5.3.8.3   Section 312, 313, and 319

Sections 312, 313, and 319 of the USA PATRIOT Act, which amended the BSA, are inter-related provisions involving accounts called "correspondent accounts.[3]" These inter-related provisions include prohibitions on certain types of correspondent accounts (those maintained for foreign "shell" banks) as well as requirements for risk-based due diligence of foreign correspondent accounts more generally.

In addition, Treasury has clarified that, for a broker-dealer, a "correspondent account" includes:

---

[3] A "correspondent account" is defined as: "any formal relationship established for a foreign financial institution to provide regular services to effect transactions in securities.".

- accounts to purchase, sell, lend, or otherwise hold securities, including securities repurchase arrangements;
- prime brokerage accounts that clear and settle securities transactions for clients;
- accounts for trading foreign currency;
- custody accounts for holding securities or other assets in connection with securities transactions as collateral; and
- over-the-counter derivatives contracts.

5.3.9 The National Defense Authorization Act for Fiscal Year 2021 (NDAA)

Congress passed the expansive AML Act on January 1, 2021. The Act has been heralded as a groundbreaking piece of BSA/AML legislation—but its potential promise inevitably will be tempered by its real-world implementation by regulators and affected stakeholders. The Anti-Money Laundering Act of 2020 (AMLA), signed into law on 1 January 2021, is intended to clarify and streamline certain AML and Bank Secrecy Act (BSA) obligations and establish new regulatory requirements to strengthen, modernize, and improve compliance programs.

5.4   CYBERSECURITY LAWS

Unlike the European Union, the US has no single federal law regulating cybersecurity and privacy. Several states have their own cybersecurity and data breach notification laws. Regulators in the United States have taken steps to promote faster incident reporting and more proactive cyber resiliency measures among banks and other financial-related industries.[4] In December 2020, the Federal Deposit Insurance Corp. and the Office of the Comptroller of the Currency proposed a 36-hour window for banks to notify regulators of a cyber incident that could materially disrupt operations.[5]

Cybersecurity legal parameters arise from multiple layers and sources (federal and States).

---

[4] David Jones (2021): Banks Outpace Other Industries in Cyber Investments, Defense Strategies: Report, https://www.cybersecuritydive.com/news/banks-cyber-security-invest ments/610045/.

[5] David Jones (2021): Banks Outpace Other Industries in Cyber Investments, Defense Strategies: Report, https://www.cybersecuritydive.com/news/banks-cyber-security-invest ments/610045/.

5.4.1 Comprehensive Crime Control Act of 1984

The Act prohibits the unauthorized use or accessing of computers in three relatively narrow areas. First, the Act makes it a felony to access or use a computer without authorization to obtain classified U.S. military or foreign policy information with the intent or reason to believe that such information will be used to harm the United States or to benefit a foreign nation. Second, the Act makes it a misdemeanor to access or use a computer without authorization to obtain financial or credit information that is protected by federal financial privacy laws. Third, the Act makes it a misdemeanor to access a federal government computer without authorization and thereby use, modify, destroy, or disclose any information therein, or prevent others from using the computer, if operation of the computer is thereby affected.[6]

5.4.2 The Computer Fraud and Abuse Act of 1986

In the early 1980s, law enforcement agencies faced the dawn of the computer age with growing concern about the lack of criminal laws available to fight emerging computer crimes. Although the wire and mail fraud provisions of the federal criminal code were capable of addressing some types of computer-related criminal activity, neither of those statutes provided the full range of tools needed to combat these new crimes.

The Computer Fraud and Abuse Act of 1986 is a U.S. cybersecurity legislation enacted in 1986 as an amendment to existing computer fraud law, which had been included in the Comprehensive Crime Control Act of 1984. The Computer Fraud and Abuse Act prohibits unauthorized computer access, interference, and obtaining data. The current version of the CFAA includes seven types of criminal activity. Conspiracy to commit and attempts to commit these crimes are also crime (Fig. 5.1).

---

[6] Joseph B. Thompkins, Linda A. Mar (1986): THE 1984 Federal Computer Crime Statute: A Partial Answer to a Pervasive Problem, UIC John Marshall Journal of Information Technology & Privacy, UIC John Marshall Journal of Information Technology & Privacy Law, Volume 6 Issue 3 Computer/Law Journal - Winter 1986.

Offense	Section	Sentence*
Obtaining National Security Information	(a)(1)	10 (20) years
Accessing a Computer and Obtaining Information	(a)(2)	1 or 5 (10)
Trespassing in a Government Computer	(a)(3)	1 (10)
Accessing a Computer to Defraud & Obtain Value	(a)(4)	5 (10)
Intentionally Damaging by Knowing Transmission	(a)(5)(A)	1 or 10 (20)
Recklessly Damaging by Intentional Access	(a)(5)(B)	1 or 5 (20)
Negligently Causing Damage & Loss by Intentional Access	(a)(5)(C)	1 (10)
Trafficking in Passwords	(a)(6)	1 (10)
Extortion Involving Computers	(a)(7)	5 (10)

* The maximum prison sentences for second convictions are noted in parentheses.

Fig. 5.1   Computer fraud & abuse/sentences

5.4.3   The Electronic Communications Privacy Act of 1986

The Electronic Communications Privacy Act and the Stored Wire Electronic Communications Act are commonly referred together as the Electronic Communications Privacy Act (ECPA) of 1986. The ECPA updated the Federal Wiretap Act of 1968, which addressed interception of conversations using "hard" telephone lines, but did not apply to interception of computer and other digital and electronic communications. Several subsequent pieces of legislation, including The USA PATRIOT Act, clarify and update the ECPA to keep pace with the evolution of new communications technologies and methods, including easing restrictions on law enforcement access to stored communications in some cases. In short, the Electronic Communications Privacy Act governs interception, access to data.

5.4.4   The Health Insurance Portability and Accountability Act (HIPAA) of 1996

The Health Insurance Portability and Accountability Act of 1996 (HIPAA) is a federal law that required the creation of national standards to protect sensitive patient health information from being disclosed without the patient's consent or knowledge. It mandates industry-wide standards for health care information on electronic billing and other processes, and requires the protection and confidential handling of protected health information. It sets boundaries on the use and release of health records. It establishes appropriate safeguards that health care providers and others must achieve to protect the privacy of health information.

5.4.5   Intelligence Reform & Terrorism Prevention Act (2004)

Subtitle G–Improving International Standards and Cooperation to Fight Terrorist Financing–of this Act works to better combat terrorist financing by requiring better coordination and building on international coalitions. It states the Sense of Congress that the Secretary of the Treasury should continue to promote the dissemination of international anti-money laundering and combating the financing of terrorism standards. It expands reporting requirements for the Secretary of Treasury to include assessments of progress made in these areas. It also requires the Secretary of Treasury to convene an inter-agency council to develop policies to be pursued by the United States regarding the development of common international anti-money laundering and combating the financing of terrorism standards.

5.4.6   The Cybersecurity Act of 2012

The destruction or exploitation of critical infrastructure through a cyber-attack, whether a nuclear power plant, a region's water supply, or a major financial market, could devastate the American economy, our national security, and our way of life.

The Cybersecurity Act of 2012 directs the Secretary of Homeland Security (DHS), in consultation with owners and operators of critical infrastructure, the Critical Infrastructure Partnership Advisory Council, and other federal agencies and private sector entities:

- to conduct a top-level assessment of cybersecurity risks to determine which sectors face the greatest immediate risk, and beginning with the sectors identified as having the highest priority, conduct, on a sector-by-sector basis, cyber risk assessments of the critical infrastructure;
- establish a procedure for the designation of critical infrastructure;

- identify or develop risk-based cybersecurity performance requirements; and
- Implement cyber response and restoration plans.

It sets forth requirements for securing critical infrastructure, including notification of cyber risks and threats and reporting of significant cyber incidents affecting critical infrastructure. It amends the Homeland Security Act of 2002 to consolidate existing DHS resources for cybersecurity within a National Center for Cybersecurity and Communications.

5.4.7 Cybersecurity Enhancement Act of 2014

The Act amended the USA PATRIOT Act to further loosen restrictions on Internet service providers (ISPs) as to when, and to whom, they can voluntarily release information about subscribers. It was signed into law December 18, 2014. It provides an ongoing, voluntary public-private partnership to improve cybersecurity and strengthen cybersecurity research and development, workforce development, and education and public awareness and preparedness.

5.4.8 The Infrastructure Security Services Act of 2015

Critical infrastructure protection is vital to keep essential services running and often relies on public-private cooperation models. Critical infrastructure describes the physical and cyber systems and assets that are so vital to the United States that their incapacity or destruction would have a debilitating impact on our physical or economic security or public health or safety (Fig. 5.2).

The Cybersecurity Act of 2015 establishes a portal at the DHS and its National Cybersecurity & Communications Integration Center (NCCIC) to facilitate private-public cyber-threat information sharing and clarifies NCCIC's statutory role in evaluating and responding to cybersecurity risks and threat indicators. The Act authorizes the President to transfer authority and responsibility to collect and disseminate cybersecurity threat information to an entity other than NCCIC (including outside the DHS), except that this role may not be transferred to the Department of Defense. The Act also allows the DHS, at its discretion, to disclose cyber-threat information it has received through the portal to other agencies or to the private sector.

cisa.gov

Fig. 5.2 Essential critical infrastructure workers

5.5 Federal Cybersecurity Laws in the Banking Industry

5.5.1 Federal Cybersecurity Laws

Certain cybersecurity laws are more specific to the banking industry.

5.5.1.1 The Gramm–Leach–Bliley Act (GLBA)

The Gramm–Leach–Bliley Act (GLBA) requires financial institutions to protect customer data and honestly disclose all data-sharing practices with customers. Under this U.S law, financial entities must establish security controls to protect customer information from any events threatening data integrity and safety. This includes strict financial information access controls to mitigate the chances of unauthorized access and compromise. GLBA compliance is mandatory for all U.S organizations selling financial products or services. The financial entities that must comply with GLBA include those that:

- sell financial products
- sell or offer financial services
- offer financial loans
- offer any financial or investment advice
- sell insurance

There are separate penalties for non-compliance, applicable to the violating organization and its officers and directors. The penalties for violating organizations are up to $100,000 per violation.

5.5.1.2   The Sarbanes-Oxley (SOX) Act of 2002 (SOX)

The Sarbanes-Oxley (SOX) act of 2002 is a law passed by U.S Congress to protect investors from financial scams. The SOX framework outlines best security practices for avoiding fraudulent financial transactions through a system of internal checks. Recently, SOX has evolved into more than just a framework for ensuring financial record accuracy. It now includes cybersecurity components to ensure financial institutions address common cybersecurity risks that could impact financial activity. An example of such a cyber threat is phishing attacks. During these attacks, hackers commonly pose as CEOs and CFOs to convince staff to initiate fraudulent transactions. Ubiquiti suffered from such an event. SOX has evolved into more than just a framework for ensuring financial record accuracy. It now includes cybersecurity components to ensure financial institutions address common cybersecurity risks that could impact financial activity.

SOX compliance now also supports the implementation of security controls across resources and IT infrastructures housing financial data. SOX compliance is mandatory for all public companies, including those in the financial sector. To prove SOX compliance, two yearly audits are required—one by an external independent auditing body and another by the organization–to highlight internal controls and management's contributions to supporting continuous improvement in financial data protection.

5.5.1.3   Payment Card Industry (PCI) Data Security Standards (DSS) PCI DSS

Payment Card Industry (PCI) Data Security Standards (DSS)—PCI DSS for short–is a set of standards for reducing credit card fraud and protecting the personal details of credit cardholders. The security controls of this regulation are designed to secure the three primary stages of the cardholder data lifecycle:

- processing;
- storage; and
- transfer.

Every organization that processes customer credit card information must comply with PCI DSS, including merchants and payment solution providers. PCI DSS is an internationally recognized standard that applies to all entities globally that process credit card data. Merchants are expected to complete Self-Assessment Questionnaires (SAQs) to validate compliance. There are varying degrees of compliance processes. For example, enterprise merchants processing millions of transactions require annual onsite audits conducted by a Qualified Security Assessor. Failure to comply with PCI DSS could result in fines ranging from $5,000 to $100,000 per month until compliance is achieved.

5.5.1.4 Cyber Events and Cyber-Enabled Crime

On October 25, 2016, the US Treasury Financial Crimes Enforcement Network (Fin-CEN) issued an Advisory to assist financial institutions in understanding their Bank Secrecy Act (BSA) obligations regarding cyber events and cyber-enabled crime. This advisory also highlights how BSA reporting helps U.S. authorities combat cyber events and cyber-enabled crime. Through this advisory FinCEN advises financial institutions on:

- Reporting cyber-enabled crime and cyber events through Suspicious Activity Reports (SARs);
- Including relevant and available cyber-related information (e.g., Internet Protocol (IP) addresses with timestamps, virtual-wallet information, device identifiers) in SARs;
- Collaborating between BSA/Anti-Money Laundering (AML) units and in-house cybersecurity units to identify suspicious activity; and
- Sharing information, including cyber-related information, among financial institutions to guard against and report money laundering, terrorism financing, and cyber-enabled crime.

5.5.2 Cybersecurity State Laws

Cybersecurity state laws aim to fill gaps in federal law, but can set de facto national standards. For instance, Massachusetts requires companies handling sensitive personal data must have Written Information Security Policy; encryption of personal data transmitted externally; and specific minimum "administrative, technical, and physical" security controls in order to prevent data breach.

Example 1: The Capital One Cyberattack
- In July of 2019, a Seattle software engineer was responsible for the hacking of Capital One. The breach started between the 22–23 of March and was discovered almost four months later by Capital One.
- The hacker stolen information included credit card numbers, birth dates, addresses, names, phone numbers, transaction history, 140,000 Social Security numbers and 80,000 bank account numbers, and personal data of over 100 million people.
- After initial speculations that pointed to a zero-day exploit, the culprit, an employee of Amazon Web Services (AWS), who used an SSRF attack, was arrested.
- The suspect, Paige Thompson, 33, was apprehended in Seattle after carelessly leaving clues about the breach on the internet and social media sites.
- According to the U.S. Attorney's Office on July 29, "Thompson posted on the information sharing site GitHub about her theft of information from the servers storing Capital One data."
- The intrusion occurred through a misconfigured web application firewall that enabled access to the data. On July 17, 2019, a GitHub user who saw the post alerted Capital One to the possibility it had suffered a data theft.
- After determining on July 19, 2019, that there had been an intrusion into its data, Capital One contacted the FBI.
- After three years, a federal jury convicted the former Seattle tech worker of several charges related to a massive hack of Capital One bank and other companies in 2019.
- Following a seven-day trial, the Seattle jury found her guilty of wire fraud, unauthorized access to a protected computer, and damaging a protected computer. The jury acquitted her of other charges, including access device fraud and aggravated identity theft.

Example 2: Flagstar Bank
- Flagstar is a Michigan-based financial services provider and one of the largest banks in the United States, having total assets of over $30 billion, and 150 branches in the United States.
- In June 2022, Flagstar notified its 1.5 million customers of a data breach where hackers accessed personal data during a December

2021 cyberattack, when intruders breached the bank's corporate network.
- The bank discovered on June 2, 2022 that the threat actors accessed sensitive customer details, including full names and social security numbers.
- The data breach affected 1,547,169 people in the United States. Flagstar linked the ransomware attack to Accellion software as the threat actors are said to have exploited the software vulnerability of Accellion's accounting software.

5.6   FEDERAL GOVERNMENT AGENCIES

Several federal government agencies are involved in cybersecurity:

5.6.1   Department of Justice–Division of Computer Crime & Intellectual Property Section (CCIPS)

- The CCIPS works with other federal agencies, the private sector, and foreign law enforcement agencies to prevent, investigate, and prosecute computer and intellectual property crimes. The following agencies, which fall under the DHS umbrella, also play a key role in combating cybercrime. When cyber incidents occur, the Department of Homeland Security (DHS) provides assistance to potentially impacted entities, analyzes the potential impact across critical infrastructure, investigates those responsible in conjunction with law enforcement partners, and coordinates the national response to significant cyber incidents. The Department works in close coordination with other agencies with complementary cyber missions, as well as private sector and other non-federal owners and operators of critical infrastructure, to ensure greater unity of effort and a whole-of-nation response to cyber incidents.[7]

---

[7] DHS Role in Cyber Incident Response, https://www.cisa.gov/publication/dhs-role-cyber-incident-response.

5.6.2   U.S. Secret Service

The U.S. Secret Service has extensive experience in cyber IR and the subsequent criminal investigations.[8] The Secret Service maintains an Electronic Crimes Task Force (ECTF) to investigate identify theft, network intrusions, attacks on business email systems, ransomware, and related matters. In 2018, transnational cybercrime investigation cases led by the U.S. Secret Service accounted for $1.9 billion in actual financial losses and $6.8 billion in potential losses averted due to law enforcement action.

5.6.3   Immigration & Customs Enforcement (ICE)

ICE operates the Cyber Crimes Center (C3), which provides technical support to domestic and international law enforcement agencies investigating cross-border crime. The Center is comprised of the Cyber Crimes Unit, the Child Exploitation Investigations Unit, and the Computer Forensics Unit. The HSI Cyber Crimes Center (C3) supports HSI's mission through the programmatic oversight and coordination of investigations of cyber-related criminal activity, and provides a range of forensic, intelligence, and investigative support services across all HSI programmatic areas. HSI C3 brings together highly technical assets dedicated to conducting trans-border criminal investigations of cyber-related crimes within the HSI portfolio of customs and immigration authorities. HSI C3 is responsible for identifying and targeting any cybercrime activity in which HSI has jurisdiction.[9]

---

[8] United States Secret Service Cybercrime Investigations (2020): Preparing for a Cyber Incident, pp. 1–10; https://www.secretservice.gov/sites/default/files/reports/2020-12/Preparing%20for%20a%20Cyber%20Incident%20-%20An%20Introductory%20Guide%20v%201.1.pdf.

[9] ICE: HSI Cyber Crimes Center, https://www.ice.gov/partnerships-centers/cyber-crimes-center.

CHAPTER 6

AML/CFT and Cybersecurity Laws in the European Union

6.1 General

The European Banking Authority (EBA) is required to ensure the integrity, transparency, and orderly functioning of financial markets. To that end, the EBA works to prevent the use of the financial system for the purposes of money laundering and terrorist financing (ML/TF). The EBA discharges its functions in this field by[1]:

(i) leading the development of AML/CFT policy and supporting its effective implementation by competent authorities and financial institutions across the EU to foster an effective risk-based approach to AML/CFT with consistent outcomes;

(ii) coordinating across the EU and beyond by fostering effective cooperation and information exchange between all relevant authorities in a way that supports the development of a common understanding of ML/TF risks, strengthens risk-based AML/CFT supervision, ensures that emerging risks are dealt with promptly

---

[1] EBA-Anti-Money Laundering and Countering the Financing of Terrorism, https://www.eba.europa.eu/regulation-and-policy/anti-money-laundering-and-countering-financing-terrorism.

© The Author(s), under exclusive license to Springer Nature Switzerland AG 2023
F. I. Lessambo, *Anti-Money Laundering, Counter Financing Terrorism and Cybersecurity in the Banking Industry*, Palgrave Macmillan Studies in Banking and Financial Institutions,
https://doi.org/10.1007/978-3-031-23484-2_6

across the single market, and ensures effective oversight of cross-border financial institutions; and

(iii) Monitoring the implementation of EU AML/CFT policies and standards to identify vulnerabilities in competent authorities' approaches to AML/CFT supervision and to take steps to mitigate them before ML/TF risks materialize.

6.2   AML/CFT in the EU

The fight against money laundering and terrorist financing is vital for financial stability and security in Europe. European legislators have taken various steps in recent years to strengthen the link between anti-money laundering/countering the financing of terrorism (AML/CFT) and prudential issues. In the fast-paced compliance world, financial institutions aren't just trying to keep up with bad guys and their inventive ways to commit crime. They also have to keep up with regulations that are updated every few years. 2018 will see three important regulatory changes that financial institutions need to be ready for. In this article, we discuss those changes, explaining how it'll affect banks and what you, as a compliance manager, can do to get ready for the future.

6.2.1   Fifth Anti-Money Laundering Directive

In 2017, we saw the Fourth Anti-Money Laundering Directive coming into effect. Financial institutions were expected to have had the changes implemented by the 26th of June. This year, however, we're expecting a final agreement on the Fifth Anti-Money Laundering Directive (a provisionary agreement was already made in December 2017).

A few of the expected additions to the Fourth Anti-Money Laundering Directive are that it:

- Clarifies enhanced customer due diligence
- Includes virtual currencies to anti-money laundering monitoring
- Prevents the abuse of anonymous prepaid cards
- Allows for more sharing of information between Financial Intelligence Units
- Requires financial institutions to share information with Financial Intelligence Units
- Gives the public access to beneficial ownership information.

The goal of the Fifth Anti-Money Laundering Directive is to create more transparency in banking after the Panama Papers revealed tax evasion practices by some of the world's wealthiest people, including 12 national leaders. It's also a measure against terrorism as it's believed that anonymous prepaid cards were used during the 2015 Paris attacks.

The Fifth AMLD contains some stricter rules:

- For 5AMLD upfront screening of customers' needs to become even more thorough. Monitoring of transactions needs to be more sensitive.
- - For GDPR audit trails need to become even more extensive and easier to share with the authorities. Personal data need protection against those that have no business in viewing that data and making it more easily accessible for clients.
- - For PSD2 a safe way to share information with third parties needs to be found while containing the new risks involved.

But banks should not just get ready for the year ahead, even if there are not any new regulations rolled out every few years, there's a need for banks to be future proof. After all, the world is advancing technologically and so are criminals. In order to create true transparency in banking, monitoring needs to become more than the question: "To process, or not to process this transaction?" Regulators have made it the bank's responsibility to know their clients and to actively battle criminals who keep on trying to use the banking infrastructure to further fund their illicit activities.

6.2.2 General Data Protection Regulation (GDPR)

The EU General Data Protection regulation enters into force on May 25, 2018. The new EU Regulation repeals the Data Protection Directive of 1995 and replaces local laws for data protection, bringing a single standard among all EU Member States. It applies to the processing of personal data in EU Member States and marks the shift from a formal to a substantive concept of data protection. The new rules are based on the principle of data protection by default and by design: personal data processing must be designed primarily to safeguard the right to confidentiality of the interested parties. To this end, both technical measures—including those pertaining to cybersecurity—and organizational models must be adopted to minimize the likelihood of wrongful access to information.[2] The European General Data Protection Regulation (EU-GDPR) is a security framework by the European Union designed to protect its citizens from personal data compromise. GDPR is applicable to entities outside the EU if they are servicing EU Member States. All businesses processing data linked to EU citizens, either manually or through automated mechanisms, must comply with the GDPR. The GDPR outlines separate security guidelines for both data controllers and data processors to secure the entire lifecycle of user data. The EU mandates GDPR compliance for financial services collecting or processing personal data from EU residents, regardless of the physical location of the business. Any organization must comply with the GDPR if it processes the data from EU citizens, meaning residents of any of the 27 EU countries. The maximum fine is €20 million (about 23 million USD) or 4% of annual turnover (whichever is larger). The GDPR also makes it incumbent on the data controller and data processor to implement adequate technical and organizational measures that ensure a level of security appropriate to the corresponding risk, which includes, for example: pseudonymization and the encryption of personal data; the ability to ensure the confidentiality; the integrity and resilience of processing systems and services on a permanent basis; and a procedure for testing and evaluating the effectiveness of the measures.

6.2.3   The Second Payments Services Directive (PSD2)

The Directive (PSD2) revises the PSD, adopted in 2007, "provides legal foundation for further development of a better integrated internal market for electronic payments within the EU." PSD2 is part of the Payment Card Industry Data Security Standard (PCI DSS) for financial data security. To ensure banking activities in the EU proliferate security, the PSD2 also includes regulations for protecting online payments, enhancing customer data security, and strong customer authentication (e.g., multi-factor authentication). All banks and financial institutions in the European Union must comply with the PSD2 directives. The penalty

---

[2] Caterina Beccarini e Claudia Biancotti (2018): Cybersecurity: The Contribution of the Bank of Italy and IVASS, pp. 16; http://www.bancadiitalia.it.

for not complying with PSD2 is a fine of up to EUR 20.000.000 (approx. 23 million USD) or 4% of annual revenue (whichever is greater).

It takes into account new market entrants offering services, specifically "account information services" (which allow a payment service user to have an overview of their financial situation at any time) and "payment initiation services" (which allow consumers to pay via credit transfer from accounts without intermediaries). This is made possible as banks will be required to open up customer data via a standard set of Application Programming Interfaces (APIs). It enhances consumer rights, including removal of surcharges for use of credit or debit card, reduced liability for non-authorized payments, and unconditional refund right for euro direct debits. It enhances to role of the EBA to develop a public central register of authorized payment institutions undated by national authorities, to resolve disputes from national authorities, develop regulatory technical standards on strong customer authentication and secure communication channels for all payment service providers, and develop cooperation and information exchange between the supervisory authorities.

With their client's consent, banks are required to give access to client information to third parties under the Second Payment Services Directive (implemented as of January 13, 2018). This act will open up the financial services market to new players. Those new players can service clients by collecting all financial information in one place as well as to initiate transactions for them. Financial institutions worry about the risks that could come with opening up their systems to third parties. There are also the questions: How to give access to that information? Should they give direct access to their systems? Should they create a third-party interface? Or, send data files to third parties? Every method will involve different risks. Compliance managers will need to control those new foreseeable and unforeseeable risks.

Not only are the Fifth Anti-Money Laundering Directive, GDPR, and PSD2 coming into effect this year, experts are also expecting the European Union to take the lead in fighting against anti-money laundering, terrorist financing, and other financial crimes in 2018. The EU will do so by tightening up surveillance and by making their enforcement stricter. We've seen that the enforcement actions of the European Union against financial institutions have already set record fines in 2017, this will only become worse for financial institutions that fail to comply. A logical reaction banks have to stricter enforcement is to be even more rigorous in their monitoring. It's a known fact that the workload at compliance departments is extremely high and almost unmanageable. That workload will again increase if banks start generating even more alerts out of fear for stricter law enforcement and higher fines by regulators. Resulting in even more work in analysis, investigation, and follow-up.

6.2.4   Sixth Anti-Money Laundering Directive

The European Union's 6th Money Laundering Directive (6AMLD) came into effect for Member States on December 3, 2020 and must be implemented by financial institutions by June 3, 2021. The 6th AML directive harmonizes the definition of money laundering across the EU with the goal of removing loopholes in the domestic legislation of Member States. Prior to 6AMLD, EU money laundering regulations sought only to punish those who profited directly from the act of money laundering, but under the new rules, so-called enablers will also be legally culpable. The current criminal framework against money laundering within the EU can properly be described as a mosaic of regimes and regulations rather than as a complete body. This system has led to a lack of legal clarity in certain individual cases and the lack of recognition of some crimes and security breaches by companies. Under the current rules, only individuals can be punished for the act of money laundering; however, 6AMLD will extend criminal liability to allow for the punishment of legal persons, such as companies or partnerships. Practically, the new rules will place AML/CFT responsibility on management employees along with employees acting separately. More, 6AMLD addresses the issue of dual criminality by introducing specific information sharing requirements between jurisdictions so that a criminal prosecution for the connected offenses can take place in more than one EU member state.

6th AMLD seeks to address these problems by hardening the definitions of offenses and penalties so that cases do not remain unsolved and includes the evolution of corporate responsibility. A total of 22 crimes have been established within the EU 6th directive AML, from those related to digital crime to tax crimes.

On July 20, 2021, the EU Commission is working on an AMLA, which aims to[3]:

---

[3] https://ec.europa.eu/commission/presscorner/detail/en/IP_21_3690.

- establish a single integrated system of AML/CFT supervision across the EU, based on common supervisory methods and convergence of high supervisory standards;
- directly supervise some of the riskiest financial institutions that operate in a large number of Member States or require immediate action to address imminent risks;
- monitor and coordinate national supervisors responsible for other financial entities, as well as coordinate supervisors of non-financial entities;
- Support cooperation among national Financial Intelligence Units and facilitate coordination and joint analyses between them, to better detect illicit financial flows of a cross-border nature.

Under the current proposal, AMLA's JSTs would consist of staff from both AMLA and national authorities, just as is the case in ECB Banking Supervision. 6th AMLD establishes three points to consider aggression: a criminal activity, the acquisition of any property through criminal act, and the laundering of it. The new AML 6 Directive also establishes and classifies as crimes the different methods of illegal acquisition of goods and money.

Article 7 of the new Anti-Money Laundering Directive 6 focuses on what RegTech companies are working, corporate responsibility, and identification: It specifies and sets that a legal person should be considered responsible in conditions where the "lack of supervision or control" by an actor with a "leadership position" has made the criminal act possible.

Articles 5 and 8 of the EU 6th money laundering directive focus on sanctions; for both companies and individuals:

- Denial of the right to governmental benefits or support and provisional or permanent prohibitions to access public funds, including grants and concessions.
- Temporary or permanent disability for commercial activities.
- Imposition of judicial surveillance.
- Judicial closure orders and temporary or permanent closure of establishments.
- Criminal punishment that could result in the imprisonment of responsible professionals.

6.3   CYBERSECURITY IN THE EU

EU cybersecurity legislation was first drafted in the early 2000s and focused on combatting crime. At the inception, the provisions on network security only applied to the telecommunications sector. As time passed by, the need to ensure the overall security of information was highlighted as key to pursuing the objectives of promoting the values of freedom and democracy. In 2008, with Council Directive 2008/114/EC on critical infrastructure, basic protection measures were introduced, including in respect of technological threats for European critical infrastructure.[4] In 2016, the EU adopted the NIS Directive concerning measures for a frequent level of security of network and information systems across the European Union. The NIS Directive's provisions apply to all businesses which fall under the definition of Digital Service Providers ("DSPs") or Operators of Essential Services ("OESs"); this includes the banking sector and financial market infrastructures (Annex 2 to the NIS Directive). EU Regulation No. 2019/881 ("ENISA Act") enrolled ENISA, the European Union Agency for Cybersecurity, with the task of contributing to the development and implementation of European Union policy and law in the field of cybersecurity and on sector-specific policy and law initiatives where matters related to cybersecurity are involved and assisting Member States to implement the EU policy and law regarding cybersecurity.

6.3.1   Budapest Convention on Cybercrime (2001)

The Convention on Cybercrime, opened for signature in Budapest, Hungary, in November 2001, is considered the most relevant international agreement on cybercrime and electronic evidence. It provides for (Fig. 6.1)[5]:

- the criminalization of conduct ranging from illegal access, data, and systems interference to computer-related fraud and child pornography;

---

[4] Caterina Beccarini e Claudia Biancotti (2018): Cybersecurity: The Contribution of the Bank of Italy and IVASS, pp. 15–16; http://www.bancadiitalia.it.

[5] Council of Europe (2020): The Budapest Convention on Cybercrime-Benefits and Impact in Practice, T-CY (2020)16_BC_Benefits_rep_Prov_1.docx.

Substantive criminal law: offences	Procedural law to secure evidence and investigate	International cooperation
Art. 2 – Illegal access	Art. 14 – Scope of procedural	Art. 23 – General principles
Art. 3 – Illegal interception	provisions	Art. 24 – Extradition
Art. 4 – Data interference	Art. 15 – Conditions and	Art. 25 – General rules
Art. 5 – System interference	safeguards	Art. 26 – Spontaneous information
Art. 6 – Misuse of devices	Art. 16 – Expedited preservation	Art. 27 – MLA in absence of treaty
Art. 7 – Computer-related	Art. 17 – Expedited preservation	Art. 28 – Confidentiality
forgery	and partial disclosure of traffic	Art. 29 – Expedited preservation
Art. 8 – Computer-related	data	Art. 30 – Partial disclosure traffic
fraud	Art. 18 – Production order	data
Art. 9 – Child pornography	Art. 19 – Search and seizure	Art. 31 – MLA accessing data
Art. 10 – IPR offences	Art. 20 – Real-time collection	Art. 32 – Transborder access
Art. 11 – Attempt, aiding,	traffic data	Art. 33 – MLA collection traffic data
abetting	Art. 21 – Interception of content	Art. 34 – MLA interception content
Art. 12 – Corporate liability	data	Art. 35 – 24/7 point of contact

Fig. 6.1 Budapest convention on cybersecurity (*Source* CoE [2020])

- the procedural law tools to investigate cybercrime and secure electronic evidence in relation to any crime; and
- The efficient international cooperation.

Though negotiated by members of the Council of Europe as well as Canada, Japan, South Africa, and United States, the treaty is open for accession by any state. The Convention is supplemented by an Additional Protocol covering the criminalization of acts of a racist and xenophobic nature committed through computer systems. That is, the Convention is more than a legal document; it is a framework that permits hundreds of practitioners from parties to share experience and create relationships that facilitate cooperation in specific cases, including in emergency situations, beyond the specific provisions foreseen in this Convention. Overall, the Convention provides numerous advantages, including, inter alia[6]:

- it represents a legal framework for criminal justice cooperation on cybercrime and any other crime where evidence is on a computer.
- It is the largest network of practitioners participating in the Cybercrime Convention Committee (T-CY) and in capacity-building activities who can call and rely on each other when needed in the investigation and prosecution of cases that more often than not

---

[6] Council of Europe (2020): The Budapest Convention on Cybercrime-Benefits and Impact in Practice, T-CY (2020)16_BC_Benefits_rep_Prov_1.docx.

are transnational in nature. The benefit of these relationships is immeasurable;

- It strengthens the laws, procedures, and mechanisms for international cooperation by the T-CY and capacity-building activities.

6.3.2   EU Network and Information Security (NIS) Directive

The Directive on security of network and information systems (the NIS Directive) provides legal measures to boost the overall level of cybersecurity in the EU by ensuring: Member States' preparedness, by requiring them to be appropriately equipped. It is the first piece of EU-wide cybersecurity legislation, aiming to enhance cybersecurity across the EU.[7] The NIS Directive has three parts:

- National capabilities: EU Member States must have certain national cybersecurity capabilities of the individual EU countries; for example, they must have a national CSIRT, perform cyber exercises, etc.
- Cross-border collaboration: Cross-border collaboration between EU countries, e.g., the operational EU CSIRT network, the strategic NIS cooperation group, etc.
- National supervision of critical sectors: EU Member States have to supervise the cybersecurity of critical market operators in their country: ex-ante supervision in critical sectors (energy, transport, water, health, digital infrastructure, and finance sector) and ex-post supervision for critical digital service providers (online market places, cloud, and online search engines).

6.3.3   Proposed EU General Data Protection Regulation

Regulation (EU) 2016/679 on the protection of natural persons with regard to the processing of personal data and on the free movement of such data EU-GDPR. EU Regulation 2016/679 repeals the Data Protection Directive of 1995 and replaces local laws for data protection, bringing a single standard among all EU Member States. It is an essential step to strengthen individuals' fundamental rights in the digital age and facilitate business by clarifying rules for companies and public bodies in

---

[7] https://www.enisa.europa.eu/topics/nis-directive.

the digital single market. A single law will also do away with the current fragmentation in different national systems and unnecessary administrative burdens. The directive protects citizens' fundamental right to data protection whenever personal data is used by criminal law enforcement authorities for law enforcement purposes. It will in particular ensure that the personal data of victims, witnesses, and suspects of crime are duly protected and will facilitate cross-border cooperation in the fight against crime and terrorism.

- Article 32 of the EU-GDPR

Pursuant to article 32 of the GDPR, where personal data have been violated, the data controller is required to notify the competent supervisory authority (the Guarantor for the Protection of Personal Data [GPPD]) of the violation without undue delay and, if possible, within 72 hours of becoming aware of the event, except where it is unlikely that the data breach poses a risk to individuals' rights.

- Article 33 of the EU-GDPR

Article 33 of the EU-GDPR provides for an obligation for all data controllers to notify any incidents to the competent data controlling body unless the personal data breach is unlikely to result in a risk to the rights and freedoms of natural persons.

- Article 34 of the EU-GDPR

Furthermore, the GDPR provides in article 34 that, in the event the violation of personal data is likely to present a high risk for the rights and freedoms of individuals, the data controller shall notify the injured party without delay. This notification is not required where the data controller has put in place adequate technical measures to protect the data subject to violation.

The GDPR sets out the obligation to appoint a DPO when (i) the data processing is carried out by a public authority or public body, (ii) the data processing requires regular and systematic monitoring on a large scale, and (iii) in cases of large-scale processing of sensitive data.

- Article 83 of the EU-GDPR

Under Art. 83 of the GDPR, non-compliance with the aforementioned requirements is subject to fines of up to EUR 10 million or 2% of the worldwide annual turnover, whichever is higher. Depending on the type of data protection infringement, the fine may even be higher.

All businesses processing data linked to EU citizens, either manually or through automated mechanisms, must comply with the GDPR. The GDPR outlines separate security guidelines for both data controllers and data processors to secure the entire lifecycle of user data. The EU mandates GDPR compliance for financial services collecting or processing personal data from EU residents, regardless of the physical location of the business. Any organization must comply with the GDPR if it processes the data from EU citizens, meaning residents of any of the 27 EU countries. The maximum fine is €20 million (about 23 million USD) or 4% of annual turnover (whichever is larger).

CHAPTER 7

AML/CFT and Cybersecurity Laws in Germany

7.1 AML LAWS IN GERMANY

The German national competent authority, i.e., BaFin, is in charge of AML/CFT supervision for both significant and less significant institutions. Under Section 25l of the Banking Act, banks are required to apply group-wide AML/CFT controls. The money laundering requirements are entirely codified in the federal Anti-Money Laundering Act (GWG) and partially in the Banking Act (KWG). Criminal money laundering pursuant to Section 261 of the German Criminal Code (StGB) comprises the following elements:

(1) Money or other assets are the proceeds of an offense;
(2) The proceeds were intentionally concealed, disguised, procured (for himself or a third party), used (for himself or a third party) by the offender or their origin, or tracing or confiscation was thwarted or endangered by the offender; and
(3) The offender is aware that the assets are the proceeds of an offense and acts with intent in this respect. It is also a criminal offense if an offender acts merely with gross negligence by not recognizing the criminal origin.

F. I. Lessambo, *Anti-Money Laundering, Counter Financing Terrorism and Cybersecurity in the Banking Industry*, Palgrave Macmillan Studies in Banking and Financial Institutions, https://doi.org/10.1007/978-3-031-23484-2_7

Financial institutions must retain records regarding large and complex transactions as part of their customer due diligence obligation, which they must do regardless of the client's risk qualification. Payments exceeding EUR 12,500 must be reported (Secttion 67 AWV): all residents in Germany including companies must report to the Federal Bank if they receive or make payments exceeding EUR 12,500 (or the equivalent in foreign currency) from a non-German resident or from a German resident, except for the account of a non-German resident (incoming and outgoing payments). BaFin has adopted a risk-based approach to AML/CFT supervision that is consistent with its approach to prudential supervision generally. Nonetheless, the SSM-wide supervision does take into account AML/CFT as part of its governance and broader compliance assessment. SSM-wide framework provides for consolidated supervision of banks operating outside of Germany (whether in an EU member or non-member state) including on a sub-consolidated and solo institution basis, but this does not cover AML/CFT specifically. BaFin conducts AML/CFT supervision of all institutions under its jurisdiction through its Department for the Prevention of Money Laundering (DPML). In contrast to the prudential supervision, the Bundesbank has no ongoing role in AML/CFT supervision. BaFin can apply sanctions for non-compliance with the AML/CFT legislation as well as sector-specific laws. BaFin and the Bundesbank receive consolidated annual accounts and other group-wide reports of banking groups, which contain inter alia assessments of AML/CFT compliance. BaFin relies mainly on external auditors to assess banks' compliance with AML/CFT requirements. The Audit Report Regulation defines the scope of AML/CFT obligations of auditors when conducting the annual or targeted audits on behalf of BaFin, but BaFin can also set the scope of auditors' inspections when necessary. Annual audit reports cover both prudential and AML/CFT issues and with respect to the latter focus mainly on banks' AML/CFT policies and systems, including domestic and overseas banking operations. The audit reports are sent to BaFin's DPML for analysis, which focuses on legal compliance and deficiencies in policies and systems. In addition, BaFin can conduct onsite inspections on its own or through auditors. As of January 1, 2020, crypto custody business has been incorporated into the KWG as a new financial service and is thus explicitly regulated by law. Anti-money laundering requirements apply to all financial services entities offering crypto custody business and to oblige persons in case of a transfer of crypto assets with an equivalent value of EUR 1,000 or more.

7.2   Cybersecurity Laws

Following a 1997 report by the U.S. government for the Protection of Critical Infrastructure, which exposed the vulnerability of networked IT systems, the German government set in place an ad hoc commission to examine potential cyber-threat scenarios.[1] The German government defined cybersecurity in 2011 as: "the desired objective of the IT security situation, in which the risks of the German cyberspace have been reduced to an acceptable minimum.[2] Since 2005, cybersecurity and the protection of critical infrastructure had become a national security issue.

7.3   Cybersecurity Laws and Regulations

Cybersecurity is governed by several acts. The main legal acts relating to cybersecurity are the GDPR, the Federal Data Protection Act, and the Act on the Federal Office for Information Security. The BSI is the main authority with respect to cybersecurity in Germany. This authority should be the main contact regarding questions about preventive security measures and is primarily responsible for receiving notifications about security breaches with respect to critical infrastructures. Financial services and telecommunications can now be considered critical infrastructure. Therefore, the main laws are:

7.3.1   Federal Data Protection Act (BDSG)

7.3.1.1   IT Security Act (ITSG) (2015)

The IT-Sicherheitsgesetz applied independently of the NIS Directive, since it was not based on the NIS Directive. However, once the NIS Directive entered into force, Member States must *transpose the NIS Directive into national law*. Critical infrastructure operators must:

- Establish and implement a minimum set of security measures;
- Verify implementation by conducting security audits;

[1] Klick, J., Lau, S. & Marzin, D. (2015). Cyber-Security aus Sicht der Sicherheitspolitik. Berlin, Germany: Freie Universität Berlin.

[2] BMI (2011). Cyber-Sicherheitsstrategie für Deutschland: 2011. Berlin, Germany: BMI.

 – Report incidents to Federal Office for Information Security (BSI).

7.3.1.2   IT Security Act 2.0

The Federal President of Germany passed the Information Technology Security Act 2.0 on May 27, 2021. The IT Security Act 2.0 has updated the First Act to increase the Security of Information Technology Systems increasing Cyber and information security against the cyberattacks and digitalization of everyday life. The IT Security Act 2.0 provides the following:

- Obligation for operators of critical infrastructure is introduced to register a critical infrastructure with the Federal Office for Information Security ("BSI");
- The IT Security Act 2.0 introduces, on the one hand, the obligation of operators of critical infrastructures to notify the Federal Ministry of the Interior, Building and Community ("BMI") of the planned first-time use of a critical component prior to its use, and on the other hand, the operator of critical infrastructure is obligated to obtain a declaration from the manufacturer of the critical components about its trustworthiness (so-called guarantee declaration). Only after obtaining such a guarantee declaration may the operator of a critical infrastructure use critical components. This declaration must be attached to the notification to the BMI.
- In accordance with the above-described obligation of the operators of critical infrastructures to use critical components only from those manufacturers who have issued a declaration of their trustworthiness to the operator of the critical infrastructure, the manufacturers will issue corresponding guarantee declarations vis-à-vis the operator of the critical infrastructure about the entire supply chain.
- The obligations applicable to operators of critical infrastructures are to be extended in a slightly modified form to further economic sectors, the companies in the special public interest. The obligations of companies in the special public interest differ depending on the category to which such a company belongs.
- The offenses subject to fines have been specified for better enforcement, especially of obligations to provide information and evidence, and have been considerably expanded in accordance with the newly introduced obligations described above. The fines themselves were

drastically increased to achieve a steering effect, as stated in the reasoning of the law. Instead of the fines of up to 100,000 EUR or up to 50,000 EUR possible under the previous BSI Act, administrative offenses can now—depending on the case—be punished with a fine of (i) up to 2,000,000 EUR, (ii) up to 1,000,000 EUR, (iii) up to 500,000 EUR, or (iv) up to 100,000 EUR.

- The IT Security Act 2.0 also expands the role of the BSI. The BSI is given several new tasks, including the following:

  - The performance of the tasks and powers of the BSI as the national cybersecurity certification authority within the meaning of Article 58 of Regulation (EU) 2019/881 of April 17, 2019, will be included in the catalogue of tasks of the BSI.
  - In order to take into account, the growing importance of cyber and information security for consumers, especially due to the increasing interconnectedness of private households and the dissemination of connected consumer products, consumer protection, and consumer information in the area of information technology security will be established as an additional task of the BSI.
  - Furthermore, the competence of the BSI for the development of specifications as well as the final evaluation of identification and authentication procedures from the point of view of information security will be clarified by law.

- The technical guidelines for the purpose of consumer protection, the competence of the BSI for the development of requirements, and recommendations together with conformity testing and confirmation for IT products are explicitly specified.
- The Act stipulates the authority of the BSI to be able to query inventory data from providers of telecommunications services to inform those affected about security vulnerabilities and attacks.
- To keep a check on the existence of security vulnerabilities and other security risks in the information technology of the Federation and in the information technology of critical infrastructures, digital services, and companies in the special public interest, the authority of the BSI to conduct so-called port scans is created. New Section 7b para. 4 of the new BSI Act also stipulates the authority of the BSI to use systems and procedures to fulfill its tasks, which simulate a successful

attack to collect and evaluate the use of malware or other attack methods (so-called honeypots).

- Finally, the BSI will have the power to issue orders vis-à-vis telecommunications and telemedia providers to avert specific threats to information security.

7.3.1.3   Telecommunications Act (2014)

Telecommunications Act of 2014 contains sector-specific data security provisions.

Section 109 requires the use of technical safeguards to prevent unauthorized access and imposes big fine on data controller for failure to adequately specify security controls to protect personal data in agreement with data processor. On May 27, 2020, the German Federal Constitutional Court invalidated Section 113 of the German Telecommunications Act (TKG) and several accompanying federal law provisions for non-compliance with the German Constitution.[3] Section 113 TKG enables German security authorities to request from providers of telecommunications services access to personal customer data linked to the conclusion or performance of a telecommunication services contract (Subscriber Data). In the view of the Federal Constitutional Court, Section 113 TKG violates the fundamental right to informational self-determination and the fundamental right to privacy of telecommunications of users of telecommunications services.[4]

7.4   Cybersecurity Laws in the Banking and Financial Sector

Under Section 25l of the Banking Act, banks are required to apply group-wide AML/CFT controls. In the case of branches and subsidiaries, the auditor must describe and assess to what extent the bank has implemented AML/CFT control measures in a uniform, group-wide basis. Auditors are also required to assess compliance with AML/CFT requirements in a foreign state where they are stricter than in Germany. If the AML/CFT

---

[3] Case nos. 1 BvR 1873/13 and 1 BvR 2618/13.

[4] Dr. Alexander Hardinghaus, Ramona Kimmich and Dr. Philipp Süss (2020): Highest German Court invalidates Section 113 of the German Telecommunications Act and abandons service providers' obligation to grant authorities access to subscriber data, Technology Law Dispatch.

control measures required in Germany are not permitted or cannot be applied in a third country, the auditor must also report and assess to what extent the institution has implemented appropriate measures.[5] Protecting the confidentiality, integrity, and availability of customer and bank details is a key priority at Deutsche Bank. To that end, the DB is engaged in the below activities or monitoring[6]:

7.4.1 Comprehensive Information and Security System

Deutsche Bank's security policies and standards are codified and updated on a regular basis, and vendors must comply with those policies and standards. IT vendors are also subject to Deutsche Bank's risk assessments and periodic vendor control assessments while they provide services.

7.4.2 Well-Established Information Network

This involves close and continuous collaboration between Deutsche Bank security experts and external security firms, research groups and other companies. Regular participation by Deutsche Bank security experts in security training and conferences is also part of the effort.

7.4.3 Regular Controls

Internal and external systems and electronic devices are regularly scanned to identify any vulnerabilities. In addition, "Red team" exercises are carried out to regularly check IT systems and compliance with security guidelines and standards. Moreover, constant monitoring of critical IT systems at Deutsche Bank.

---

[5] IMF Country Report No. 16/190 (2016): Germany- Anti-Money Laundering and Combating the Financing terrorism, pp. 1–31, https://www.imf.org/external/pubs/ft/scr/2016/cr16190.pdf.

[6] Security at DB, https://corporates.db.com/in-focus/Focus-topics/cyber-security/security-at-deutsche-bank.

7.4.4   *Employee Awareness*

This is achieving through:

- Regular security information training for employees worldwide.
- Increasing risk awareness through other channels, e.g., videos and an internal information security website providing new information every month.
- Cyber Security Hotline—available 24/7 and from anywhere. A global cybersecurity response process ensures that action can be taken at any time in response to potential security incidents.

DB also works closely with the European Central Bank. According to Art. 5 (1) (f) and Art. 32 of the GDPR, controllers are obliged to process personal data in a manner that ensures appropriate security of the personal data, including protection against unauthorized or unlawful processing and against accidental loss, destruction or damage, using appropriate technical or organizational measures. On May 31, 2022, the German financial regulator BaFin issued a fresh cybersecurity warning to the nation's financial sector due to the war in Ukraine following a recent increase in cyberattacks. The recent events had especially taken the form of 'distributed denial-of-service (DDoS)' attacks, in which hackers attempt to flood a network with unusually high volumes of data traffic in order to paralyze it.

CHAPTER 8

AML/CFT and Cybersecurity Laws in France

8.1 General

France has a robust and sophisticated framework to fight money laundering and terrorist financing that is effective in many respects, notably in law enforcement, confiscation areas, and international cooperation but needs to do more in areas such as the supervision of professionals involved in the activities of legal persons and the real estate sector.[1] Nonetheless, French anti-money laundering regulations present a formidable compliance challenge. The sheer amount of data that must be analyzed as part of the AML/CFT process means that employees completing the task manually risk committing errors and surfacing false positives, potentially frustrating customers or incurring compliance penalties.[2] The French Monetary and Financial Code (Book V, Title VI) and the French Criminal Code (Article 324-1, and Article 421-1-6) set out AML and CFT regulations in France. The Autorité des Marchés Financiers (AMF) is France's

---

[1] FATF (2022): France's measures to combat money laundering and terrorist financing, Mutual Evaluation France-2022, https://www.fatf-gafi.org/media/fatf/documents/reports/mer4/Mutual-Evaluation-France-2022.pdf.

[2] Comply Advantage (2022): AML France Regulations, https://complyadvantage.com/insights/aml-regulations-france/.

© The Author(s), under exclusive license to Springer Nature Switzerland AG 2023
F. I. Lessambo, *Anti-Money Laundering, Counter Financing Terrorism and Cybersecurity in the Banking Industry,* Palgrave Macmillan Studies in Banking and Financial Institutions,
https://doi.org/10.1007/978-3-031-23484-2_8

primary financial regulator with oversight of all financial institutions and a responsibility to prevent financial crime, money laundering, and the financing of terrorism. An independent body, the AMF has a range of powers to identify and prevent money laundering, including setting new rules, conducting investigations, and issuing penalties.

In a wider context, the AMF works with other French national and international authorities to contribute to the global fight against money laundering and to set AML policy.[3] France is a member of the intergovernmental Financial Action Task Force (FATF), so the AMF also works to implement FATF's 40 Recommendations as part of French AML/CFT policy. Nonetheless, France needs to improve its anti-money laundering and counter financing of terrorism (AML/CFT) performance around designated non-financial businesses and professions (DNFBPs).

8.2   AML/CFT Laws

Under AMF and FATF regulations, banks and financial institutions must facilitate transaction monitoring as part of their France AML policy. The monitoring process should automatically flag transactions that present a high risk of money laundering or terrorism financing and should factor in:

- The origin and destination of funds (to or from high risk countries).
- The nature or size of the transaction (unusual deposits or customer behavior).
- The legal structures or schemes connected to the transaction.

Individuals and institutions subject to AML requirements must report any suspicious transaction or activity or funds registered in their books, which they know, suspect, or have good reason to suspect is:

- The result of an offense punishable by a jail sentence of more than one year or is linked to the financing of terrorism; or

---

[3] Comply Advantage (2022): AML France Regulations, https://complyadvantage.com/insights/aml-regulations-france/.

- The result of tax fraud, when at least one criterion defined by law is met, such as the use of shell companies or anomalies in invoices or purchase orders.

The designated businesses subject to AML requirements are listed under article L.561-2 of the MFC. Targeted financial institutions refer to entities operating in the banking sector including credit and payment institutions, electronic money institutions, insurance companies, banking operations intermediaries, mutual societies and unions, retirement funds, intermediaries in banking, insurance and participative funding, the Banque de France, investment firms, and money changers, among others. In addition, other professionals subject to AML requirements include real estate agents, accountants, auditors, auction sellers, notaries, gambling and betting operators, sports agents, art and antiques dealers, and lawyers.

These financial institutions are all subject to specific requirements, including:

- The obligation to report to TRACFIN any sums entered in their books or transactions involving sums that they know, suspect, or have good reason to suspect derive from an offense punishable by a prison sentence of more than one year or are related to terrorism financing.
- A duty of care regarding their clients. In this vein, all the entities designated in article L.561-2 must identify their client and/or its beneficial owner. However, credit, payment, and electronic money institutions can be exempted from the obligation to identify their clients and/or their beneficial owners if there is no reason to suspect money laundering or terrorist financing, and subject to the respecting of strict conditions. Under this same duty of care, and unlike the other entities designated by article L.561-2, gambling and betting operators must in addition record the exchange operations of all payment methods, plates, tokens, and tickets whose amount exceeds a certain threshold.
- The implementation of internal processes and controls aiming at preventing money laundering and terrorism financing. If the entity is part of a group (i.e., a group of companies or a financial conglomerate), the processes and controls must be implemented at the group level.

Aside from these specific requirements, all companies and economic interest groups registered in France, all foreign commercial companies with a branch in France and all other legal entities registered in France are required to file at the Trade and Companies Registry a document identifying their beneficial owners, and the type of control over the legal entity such owners exercise. These general requirements are not applicable to companies whose securities are admitted to trading on a regulated market in France, in the EU, or in any country with similar legislation. Anti-money laundering ("AML") requirements are set out in the Monetary and Financial Code ("MFC"). As a European Union Member State, France is also under the obligation to implement the EU AML Directives.

The MFC imposes the following main obligations on financial institutions and other designated businesses concerning AML requirements:

Customer due diligence obligation, with a duty to clearly:

- Identify/verify the customer's identity;
- Identify/verify the beneficial owner's identity;
- Obtain information on the nature and purpose of the business relationship to establish the customer's risk profile; and
- Establish ongoing monitoring to report risky transactions and to maintain and update customer information.

The level of due diligence required depends on the level of AML risk to which the financial institution is exposed. It includes:

- Obligation to keep information records for five years from the account closure date or from the termination date of the business relationship.
- Obligation to report specific transactions or suspicious operations and activities, where applicable.
- Obligation to implement AML procedures and policies, as well as internal controls and compliance programs.

Enforcement is not centralized at the national level but handled by prosecutors with eight specialized interregional jurisdictions, based in Paris, Lyon, Marseille, Lille, Rennes, Bordeaux, Nancy, and Fort de France (the "JIRS"). Non-compliance with one or several of the AML requirements provided in Title VI of the MFC can lead to sanctions. A wide range of sanctions are available when the ACPR detects a breach of AML/CFT obligations. These include cease and desist orders, financial penalties, reprimand, and action letters. In the past four years, the ACPR has applied these sanctions. For instance, failure to carry out risk assessments or failure to report suspicious transactions, when required, could constitute a breach of AML obligations. In addition, specific supervisory authorities of self-regulatory organizations and professional associations supervise the compliance of their members with AML requirements. Most of them make guidelines publicly available or establish training.

In December 2021, the Paris Court of Appeal held that:

> The Swiss Bank UBS AG was guilty of unlawful solicitation and aggravated laundering of the proceeds of tax fraud relating to the bank's cross-border business activities in France between 2004 and 2012. The court imposed a fine of €3.75 million and also ordered the confiscation of €1 billion. In addition, the court awarded civil damages to the French State of €800 million.[4] Its subsidiary UBS (France) SA was found guilty of aiding and abetting unlawful solicitation. The court ordered a fine of €1.875 million. In December 2021, UBS filed an appeal with France's Supreme Court against the decision, which ordered the confiscation of 1 billion euros and awarded the French state 800 million in civil damages. Meanwhile, UBS has set aside some 1.1. billion euros in legal provisions to settle the case, which it noted remained subject to a "wide range of possible outcomes." UBS AG may launch an international arbitration against France by invoking the 1882 Switzerland-France Bilateral Convention of Establishment (Switzerland-France BCE) in conjunction with the 1993 France-Trinidad and Tobago Bilateral Investment Treaty (France-Trinidad and Tobago BIT) in an attempt to reduce the multi-billion euros penalty.[5]

---

[4] Lorenzo Migliorato (2022): French tax fraud verdict costs UBS $4.1bn of additional op RWAs, Risk Quantum, https://www.risk.net/risk-quantum/7947846/french-tax-fraud-verdict-costs-ubs-41bn-of-additional-op-rwas.

[5] Danilo Ruggero Di Bella (2022): Could UBS Dodge a $2 Billion Tax Penalty By Taking France to Arbitration?, https://blogs.law.ox.ac.uk/business-law-blog/blog/2022/07/could-ubs-dodge-2-billion-tax-penalty-taking-france-arbitration.

8.3   Cybersecurity

The France Cybersecurity Market is anticipated to grow with a CAGR of 6% during the forecast period (2022–2027). The market's expansion might be attributed to the sophistication of cyberattacks, which are rising. Hacking is a criminal offense pursuant to article 323-1 of the French Criminal Code ("FCC") relating to unauthorized access to an automated data processing system. The punishment for fraudulent access into an automated data processing system is imprisonment and a fine of up to €60,000. Article L.2321-4 of the Defense Code provides protection to any "ethical hacker" who informs the French National Cybersecurity Agency ("ANSSI") of the existence of a vulnerability concerning the security of an automated data processing security. Cybercrime covers a variety of offenses including hacking, fishing, identity theft, electronic theft, unsolicited penetration testing, and infection of IT systems with malware.

8.3.1   Cybersecurity Laws and Regulations

8.3.1.1   The Data Protection Act (1978)[6]

Under Article 1, Information technology must be at the service of every citizen. Its development shall take place in the context of international cooperation. It shall not violate human identity, human rights, privacy, or individual or public liberties. Article 2 goes on to state that the Act shall apply to automatic processing of personal data as well as non-automatic processing of personal data that are or may be contained in a personal data filing system, with the exception of processing carried out for the exercise of exclusively private activities, where the data controller meets the conditions provided for in Article 5. The Data Protection Act of January 6, 1978, was first amended by a law dated June 20, 2018, while its implementing Decree of October 20, 2005, was amended by a Decree of August 1, 2018. However, existing provisions adopted under the EU Data Protection Directive were still maintained in the amended French Data Protection Act.

---

[6] Act   n°78-17   of   6   January   1978   on   Data Processing, Data Files and Individual Liberties, https://fra.europa.eu/en/law-reference/act-ndeg78-17-6-january-1978-data-processing-data-files-and-individual-liberties.

8.3.1.2 *The Godfrain Law (n°88-19 of January 15, 1988)*

The 1988 Godfrain Act on IT fraud is a pioneering IT law that followed the Data Protection Act and was the first act on computer crime and hacking. It introduced the notion of an automated data processing system and sets out data controllers' security obligations. The Godfrain Act updated the French penal code by introducing a section regarding the intrusion in information systems (articles 323-1 to 323-7). The Godfrain Act has been updated several times since its introduction. The most recent modification occurred through the Act of June 21, 2004, Reinforcing Trust in the Digital Economy.[7]

8.3.1.3 *The Law for a Digital Republic n°2016-1321 of October 7, 2016, Amended by the Law Transposing the GDPR (Law n°2018-493 of June 20, 2018)*

On 28 September, the French Parliament adopted the Digital Republic Bill marking the end a year-long process which began in December 2015 to amend the laws regulating various aspects of the digital economy in France. The Act introduces new provisions that regulate the digital economy as a whole. The Digital Republic Act requires data controllers to inform their data subjects about the period during which the personal data will be stored, or if that is not possible, the criteria used to determine that period. Furthermore, all providers of online communication services to the public must inform their users specifically about the right to decide how their personal data will be processed following their death, including the right to provide their last instructions regarding the processing of their data.

8.3.1.4 *The Network and Information Systems Security Act ("NIS Act")*

The Network and Information Systems Security Act ("NIS Act") transposing the NIS Directive n°2018-133 of February 26, 2018, completed by Decree n°2018-384 of May 23, 2018, which details the application of the NIS Act and lists the sectors, types of operators and critical infrastructures concerned, and the Decree of September 14, 2018, defining the security rules (together, the "NIS Rules").

---

[7] Loi du 21 Juin 2004 pour la Confiance dans l'Economie Numérique.

8.3.2   Cybersecurity in Banking

The French Prudential Supervision and Resolution Authority (ACPR) is responsible for AML/CFT supervision of banks, including institutions that are part of the large financial groups subject to prudential supervision of the European Central Bank (ECB).[8] The financial services sector must comply with several requirements such as auditing IT systems, strengthening resistance to cyber risks, developing defenses adapted to the complexity of cyberattacks, and making several declarations to the ANSSI (ministerial orders of November 28, 2016). Pursuant to article L.225-100-1 of the French Commercial Code and article 222-3 of the General Regulations of the French Financial Markets Authority, listed and private companies must draw up an annual management report that contains a description of the main risks and uncertainties the company had to face or is facing (which implicitly includes cyber risks). Pursuant to article L.451-1-2 of the French Monetary and Financial Code, listed companies are required to submit this report to the French Financial Markets Authority and to publish it on their website. French banks are employing increasingly sophisticated tools, including machine learning, to carry out their due diligence obligations with respect to TF.

---

[8] Ke Chen, Kathleen Ka (2019): IMF- Financial Sector Assessment Program (FSAP)—Anti-Money Laundering and Combating the Financing of terrorism Regime in France, pp. 1–36, file:///C:/Users/LibKiosk/Downloads/1FRAEA2019009%20(1).pdf.

CHAPTER 9

AML/CFT and Cybersecurity Laws in Italy

9.1 AML/CFT Laws

Money laundering in Italy is a growing problem, despite the fact that the country is not a major regional or offshore financial center. Italy has a mature and sophisticated AML/CFT regime, with a correspondingly well-developed legal and institutional framework. Italy has a comprehensive institutional framework of LEAs responsible for ensuring that ML, TF, and predicate offenses are properly investigated. It is nonetheless confronted with a significant risk of money laundering (ML) stemming principally from tax crimes and activities most often associated with organized crime, such as corruption, drug trafficking, and loan sharking.[1] Money laundering is criminalized at the national level by article 648 bis of the Italian Criminal Code ("ICC").

---

[1] IMF (2016): Italy Report on the Observance of Standards and Codes (ROSC). P.4; https://www.imf.org/external/pubs/ft/scr/2016/cr1644.pdf.

© The Author(s), under exclusive license to Springer Nature Switzerland AG 2023
F. I. Lessambo, *Anti-Money Laundering, Counter Financing Terrorism and Cybersecurity in the Banking Industry*, Palgrave Macmillan Studies in Banking and Financial Institutions, https://doi.org/10.1007/978-3-031-23484-2_9

9.2   AML/ CFT Legislations

Italy was one of the first countries to introduce money laundering as a criminal offense. The first legislation to combat the phenomenon of money laundering dates back to Decree-Law No 143 of May 3, 1991, subsequently converted into Law No 197 of July 5, 1991.[2] Italian Legislative Decree no. 65/2018, adopted in the implementation of European Directive EU/2016/1148 (known as Network and Information Security (NIS) Directive), defines the object and scope of application, the obligations incumbent on operators of essential services (OESs) and digital service providers (DSPs) to guarantee the security of their networks and IT systems, as well as the rules regarding incidents and notification obligations. Italian Legislative Decree no. 82/2021, containing urgent provisions on cybersecurity, the definition of the national cybersecurity architecture and establishment of the National Cybersecurity Agency.

9.3   Cybersecurity Laws and Regulations

Italian cybersecurity regulation is currently based on two measures.

9.3.1   Prime Ministerial Decree of 17 February

Prime Ministerial Decree of February 17, 2017, confers on the Government's Security Intelligence Department (DIS) the responsibility for coordinating the prevention and management of cyber crises through the Cybersecurity Unit (Nucleo per la sicurezza cibernetica, NSC) composed, on a permanent basis, of representatives from the ministries sitting on the Interministerial Committee for the Security of the Republic (CISR), i.e., Defense, Interior, Foreign Affairs, Economy and Finance, Economic Development, and Justice.[3]

---

[2] Dimitri Barberini (2022): Anti-Money Laundering Regulations in Italy, Sanction Scanner, https://sanctionscanner.com/blog/anti-money-laundering-regulations-in-italy-411.

[3] Caterina Beccarini e Claudia Biancotti (2018): Cybersecurity: the contribution of the Bank of Italy and IVASS, pp. 8–9; http://www.bancadiitalia.it.

9.3.2   *Italian Legislative Decree No. 65/2018*

Italian Legislative Decree no. 65/2018, adopted in the implementation of European Directive EU/2016/1148 (known as Network and Information Security (**NIS**) Directive), defines the object and scope of application, the obligations incumbent on operators of essential services (**OESs**) and digital service providers (**DSPs**) to guarantee the security of their networks and IT systems, as well as the rules regarding incidents and notification obligations. In addition to these main legislations, the Italian cybercrime legal infrastructure includes.

9.3.3   *Italian Legislative Decree No. 105/2019*

On November 13, the Italian Parliament approved the Law Decree No. 105/2019, which significantly extends the scope of application of the Italian "golden powers" regulation, amending Law Decree No. 21/2012. The Decree Law extends the notification obligation to all the contracts relating to the development of 5G Technology.

9.3.4   *Italian Legislative Decree No. 82/2021*

Italian Legislative Decree no. 82/2021, containing urgent provisions on Cybersecurity, the definition of the national cybersecurity architecture and establishment of the National Cybersecurity Agency. The law creates the Interministerial Cybersecurity Committee under the Presidency of the Council of Ministers, granting it consultation powers and the functions of proposing and overseeing cybersecurity policies and activities concerning cyberspace national security. (Art. 4(1).) It also creates the Agency for National Cybersecurity to protect national interests in the field of cybersecurity. The agency is to be headquartered in Rome. (Art. 5(1).) For the performance of its functions, the agency may request the collaboration of other government bodies, according to their competence. (Art. 5(5).) The agency is also the national competent authority on the security of information networks and systems, and performs the necessary functions to support the Nucleus for Cybersecurity ("the Nucleus") (Art. 7(1)(c) & (d).) (Fig. 9.1).

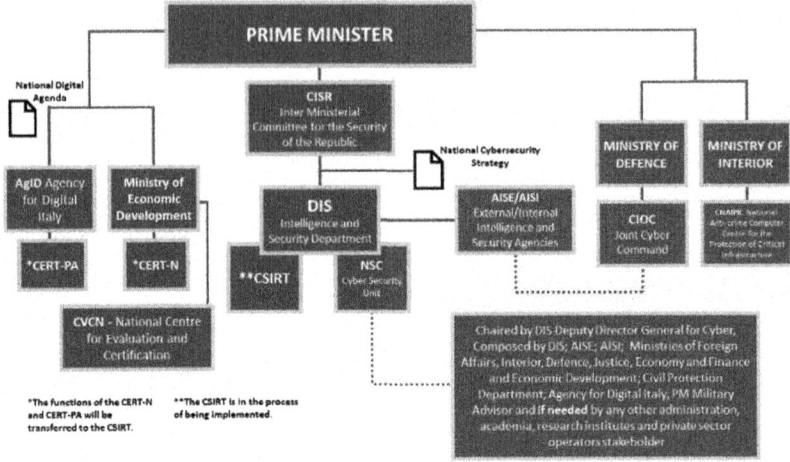

Fig. 9.1 Italian national cybersecurity architecture

9.4   Cybersecurity in the Banking Industry

Money launderers predominantly use non-bank financial institutions for the illicit export of currency—primarily U.S. dollars and Euros—to be laundered in offshore companies. Banks and other financial institutions are required to maintain records necessary to reconstruct significant transactions for ten years, including information about the point of origin of funds transfers and related messages sent to or from Italy.

Circular No. 285 of December 17, 2013, provides both specific security measures able to ensure security of information regarding banks activities and the compliance with privacy law and notification to Bank of Italy and European Central Bank in case of data breaches in the Italian banking sector. With the proliferation of attacks on banks and other financial institutions, the Bank of Italy is currently carrying out a number of activities to strengthen the security of its internal IT and that of the financial system. It also conducts research on the cybersecurity of the economy as a whole, as vulnerabilities in other sectors could also affect the security of the financial system.[4] Italy has strict

---

[4] Caterina Beccarini e Claudia Biancotti (2018): Cybersecurity: the contribution of the Bank of Italy and IVASS, p. 28; http://www.bancadiitalia.it.

laws on the control of currency deposits in banks. Banks must identify their customers and record and report to Italy's Financial Intelligence Unit (FIU), Italian Exchange Office (UIC), and any cash transaction that exceeds approximately $15,000.

CHAPTER 10

AML/CFT and Cybersecurity Laws in Spain

10.1 General

There is no legislation or policy in place in Spain that requires mandatory reporting of cybersecurity incidents. The legal framework for the protection of personal data in Spain is regulated by the Lisbon Treaty; Article 18(4) of the Spanish Constitution; the GDPR; and the Spanish Data Protection Law. The main obligations of data controllers and data processors are those set out in the GDPR and in the Spanish Data Protection Law, but sector-specific Spanish regulations may also provide specific rules on the processing of personal data in a specific sector or activity (e.g., data included in clinical records). Nonetheless, cybersecurity remains a challenge in Spain, where 43 percent of Spaniards lack basic digital skills. As such, training and education is a key component in the country's cybersecurity strategy. In 2021, Spain was one of the top three countries attacked by mobile banking malware.

© The Author(s), under exclusive license to Springer Nature Switzerland AG 2023
F. I. Lessambo, *Anti-Money Laundering, Counter Financing Terrorism and Cybersecurity in the Banking Industry*, Palgrave Macmillan Studies in Banking and Financial Institutions,
https://doi.org/10.1007/978-3-031-23484-2_10

10.2   AML/CFT Laws

Spanish AML/CTF legislation is the result of the transposition of EU legislation on the subject, in particular, of Directive 2005/60/EC of the European Parliament and Council, of October 26, 2005, and Commission Directive 2006/70/EC of August 1, 2006, laying down the implementing provisions of the former. Current Spanish AML/CTF legislation also includes the recommendations issued by the Financial Action Task Force ("FATF") on money laundering and terrorist financing. The money laundering law applies to most entities active in the financial system, including banks, mutual savings associations, credit companies, insurance companies, financial advisers, brokerage and securities firms, postal services, currency exchange outlets, casinos, and individuals and unofficial financial institutions exchanging or transmitting money (alternative remittance systems).

10.3   Cybersecurity Regulations

According to recent data, more than 13,000 legal proceedings for cybercrime took place in Spain, most of them corresponding with fraud or crimes against sexual freedom.[1] Some of the most relevant provisions under the Penal code are provided below.

10.3.1   Article 197

1. Any individual who, for the purpose of discovering the secrets or violating the privacy of another and without the consent of the latter, takes possession of that individual's papers, letters, electronic mail messages, or any other personal documents or belongings or intercepts his or her telecommunications or uses technical devices for listening, transmitting, recording, or reproducing sound or images or any other communications signal, will be punished by imprisonment from between one and four years and a fine of between twelve and twenty-four months [sic].
2. The same punishment will be applicable to any individual who, without authorization, seizes, uses, or modifies, to the detriment

---

[1] Statista Research Department (2022): Cybercrime in Spain - statistics & facts, https://www.statista.com/topics/7011/cyber-crime-in-spain/#topicHeader__wrapper.

of a third party, such private personal or family data of another individual as may be recorded on computer, electronic, or telematic files or media, or in any other type of file or record, whether public or private. The same punishment will be imposed on any individual who, without authority, accesses such data by any means or alters or uses such data to the detriment of the owner of the data or of a third party.

3. Punishment consisting of imprisonment from between two and five years will be imposed if the data or facts discovered or the images captured, as indicated in the proceeding paragraphs, are divulged, revealed, or transferred to third parties.

   Punishment consisting of imprisonment from between one and three years and a fine of between twelve and twenty-four months [sic] will be imposed on any individual who, with prior knowledge of the illicit origin of [such facts or data] [but] without having taken part in their discovery, commits the acts described in the preceding paragraph.

4. If the acts described in paragraphs 1 and 2 of this article are committed by the persons in charge of or responsible for the computer, electronic, or telematic files and media or files or records, punishment consisting of imprisonment from between three and five years will be imposed, and if such private data are disseminated, transferred or made public, the upper half [sic] of the punishment will be imposed.

5. In addition, when the acts described in the above sections involve personal data revealing the ideology, religion, beliefs, health, racial origin or sexual orientation, or if the victim is a minor or incapacitated, the upper half [sic] of the punishments Stipulated will be imposed.

6. If such acts are committed with intent to profit, the upper half [sic] of the punishments set forth respectively in paragraphs 1 through 4 of this article will be imposed. If in addition they involve the data mentioned in paragraph 5, the punishment will consist of imprisonment from between four and seven years.

10.3.2   Article 248

1. Any individual will be guilty of fraud who, with intent to profit, uses sufficient deceit to cause another individual to err, inducing him or her to commit an act of disposition to the detriment of him or herself or a third party.
2. Also guilty of fraud will be any individual who, with intent to profit and using computer manipulation or any similar contrivance, causes the unauthorized transfer of any personal asset to the detriment of a third party.

10.3.3   Article 264

1. Punishment consisting of imprisonment from between one and three years and a fine of between twelve and twenty-four months [sic] will be imposed on any individual who causes the injury identified in the preceding article in any of the following circumstances:

    1. The acts are committed for the purpose of preventing the free exercise of authority or in vengeance therefor, whether the crime is committed against public authorities or against private citizens who, whether acting as witnesses or in any other capacity, have contributed, or might in the future contribute, to the execution or application of the Law or General Provisions.
    2. Infection or contagion of cattle is caused by any means.
    3. Poisonous or corrosive substances are used.
    4. Assets in the public or community domain or assets designated for public or community use are involved.
    5. The acts lead to the bankruptcy of the individual affected or place him or her in a grave economic situation.

2. The same punishment will be imposed on any individual who, in any way, destroys, modifies, misuses, or otherwise damages such electronic data, programs, or documents of others as may be contained in computer networks, media, or systems.

10.3.4   Article 256

Any individual who makes use of any telecommunications terminal equipment without the consent of the owner thereof, causing damage to the latter in excess of fifty thousand pesetas, will be subject to punishment consisting of a fine of between three and twelve months [sic].

10.3.5   Article 270

Punishment consisting of imprisonment from between six months and two years or a fine of between six and twenty-four months [sic] will be imposed on any individual who, with intent to profit and to the detriment of a third party, reproduces, plagiarizes, distributes, or publicly communicates, either wholly or in part, a literary, artistic, or scientific work or the transformation, interpretation, or artistic execution thereof contained in any medium or communicated by any means, without the authorization of the holders of the corresponding intellectual property rights or successors thereof.

The same punishment will be imposed on any individual who intentionally imports, exports, or stores copies of such works or productions or executions without the authorization specified above. The same punishment will be imposed in the event of the manufacture, circulation, and possession of any medium specifically designed to facilitate the unauthorized suppression and neutralization of any technical device used to protect computer programs.

10.3.6   Article 273

1. Punishment consisting of imprisonment from between six months and two years and a fine of between six and twenty-four months [sic] will be imposed on any individual who, for industrial or commercial purposes, without the consent of the owner of a patent or utility model, and with prior knowledge of its registration, manufactures, imports, possesses, utilizes, offers, or introduces into the market items covered by such rights.

2. The same punishment will be imposed on any individual who, in the same fashion and for the above-indicated purposes, uses or offers the use of a procedure covered by a patent, or who possesses, offers,

introduces into the market, or uses the product directly obtained by the patented procedure.

3. The same punishment will be imposed on any individual who commits any of the acts characterized in the first paragraph of this article, under identical circumstances, with regard to objects covered in favor of a third party by an industrial or artistic model or drawing or topography of a semiconductor product.

The Spanish legal system is subject to the European Union (EU) legal acts: mainly Regulations and Directives. In the area of cybersecurity, the EU has worked to ensure greater security in networks and information systems. In this regard, the EU Cybersecurity strategy: An open, safe, and secure Cyberspace was published in February 2013. In Spain, Royal Decree-Law 12/2018 of 7 September on network and information system security transposes the Spanish legal system this Directive, with the aim of 'regulating the security of networks and information systems used for the provision of essential and digital services, while establishing an institutional framework for coordination between competent authorities and with the relevant cooperation bodies at Community level.' The CCN-CERT, according to the provisions of this Royal Decree Law, will exercise national coordination of the technical response of the three Reference CSIRTs established in the cases of special severity determined by regulation and which require a higher level of coordination than is necessary in ordinary situations.

10.4   Cybersecurity in the Banking Industry

The new European regulatory framework EBA/GL/2019/02 obliges European financial institutions to carry out security audits of all technology providers to whom they outsource critical tasks for the development of their operational and control functions.

CHAPTER 11

AML/CFT and Cybersecurity Laws in Switzerland

11.1 GENERAL

Swiss money laundering laws and regulations apply to both banks and Non-Bank Financial Institutions (NBFIs). Switzerland has significant AML legislation in place, making banks and other financial intermediaries subject to strict Know Your Customer (KYC) reporting requirements. Switzerland has also implemented legislation for identifying, tracing, freezing, seizing, and forfeiting narcotics-related assets. Switzerland has not yet adopted a general cybersecurity law to date, and there are also no plans to comprehensively address the issue in a bespoke legal instrument. Rather, cybersecurity remains regulated by a patchwork of various acts and regulatory guidance. Switzerland regulates cybersecurity with respect to specific objects (data, systems and products) and specific industries. Moreover, minimum cybersecurity measures are rarely defined by law, but are left to self-regulation.

© The Author(s), under exclusive license to Springer Nature
Switzerland AG 2023
F. I. Lessambo, *Anti-Money Laundering, Counter Financing Terrorism and Cybersecurity in the Banking Industry*, Palgrave Macmillan Studies in Banking and Financial Institutions,
https://doi.org/10.1007/978-3-031-23484-2_11

11.2   AML/CFT Laws

- Swiss Anti-Money Laundering Act (AMLA)

The Swiss Anti-Money Laundering Act (AMLA) has proved to be a highly successful law in practice. Since its introduction, it has become much more difficult to hide illicit money in a Swiss bank.[1] The Act is relatively simple in its concept, with five obligations to prevent and combat money laundering[2]:

- Identification of customers and any beneficial owners;
- Identification of the nature and purpose of the business relationship;
    - Informing the Money Laundering Reporting Office Switzerland (MROS) of suspected money laundering without informing customers or third parties.
- Designation of one or more qualified persons as an internal money laundering unit with responsibility for compliance functions;
- Documentation of the transactions carried out and of the financial intermediary's anti-money
- laundering measures.

As Switzerland is an international financial services center of the first order, the main source of criminal proceeds is from economic crime. On 19th March 2021, the Swiss Federal Council voted in favor of a reform of the anti-money laundering legislation. The primary goal of the revision is to allow Switzerland to pass its next FATF country audit in 2022. The new version of the Anti-Money Laundering Act (AMLA) applies to financial intermediaries and dealers that accept payments in cash. One important revision of the AMLA concerns: (i) the Verification of the identity of the person designated as a beneficial owner (UBO); (ii) Update of the clients' data (KYC profile). The Money Laundering Reporting Office Switzerland (MROS) similarly plays an important role in the prosecution of money laundering. Any violations of the reporting obligation (art.

---

[1] Stefan Mbiyavanga (2019): Applying the Swiss Anti-Money Laundering Act to gold refineries, Basel Institute on Governance, WP 31, pp. 1- 14, https://baselgovernance. org/sites/default/files/2019-12/working_paper_31_gold_en.pdf.

[2] Idem.

37 of the Federal Act on Combating Money Laundering and Terrorist Financing [AMLA]) are prosecuted by the Federal Department of Finance (art. 50 para. 1 of the Federal Act on the Swiss Financial Market Supervisory Authority [FINMASA]). Under Swiss law, the crime of money laundering pursuant to art. 305bis SCC protects the criminal authorities' right to forfeiture. Thus, in order to establish money laundering, the criminal authority has to prove:

- that a predicate offence (felony or qualified tax offence) has been committed;
- that assets originating from such predicate offence could be forfeited;
- that the offender intentionally committed an act aimed at frustrating the forfeiture of such assets; and
- that the offender knew or should have known that the assets originate from a predicate offence.

11.3   CYBERSECURITY LAWS

There is no overarching cybersecurity legislation in Switzerland to date. Nonetheless, personal data must be protected against unauthorized processing through adequate technical and organizational measures under the general Federal Act on Data Protection (FADP) and the Federal Council issued detailed provisions on the minimum standards for data security in the Ordinance to the Federal Act on Data Protection. The draft of Federal Act on Data Protection (FADP) and its relating Federal Council Dispatch were published on September 15, 2017.

Article 143bis of the Penal Code states[3]:

Anyone, who without authorization, and without the intent of procuring an unlawful gain, accesses a data processing system which are specially protected against unauthorized access, by electronic devices, shall be sentenced to imprisonment or fines.

Article 144bis of the same code, which sanctions damage to data states:

---

[3] https://www.cybercrimelaw.net/Switzerland.html.

1. Anyone, who without authorization alters, erases, or renders useless data which is stored or transferred by electronic or similar means, shall be punished by imprisonment for a term of up to three years or a fine of up to forty thousand Swiss francs if a complaint is made.

   If the offender has caused serious damage, a sentence of five years penal servitude can be imposed. The offence shall be prosecuted ex officio.

2. Any person who produces, imports, circulates, promotes, offers, or otherwise makes available programs, which he/she knows, or ought to assume, are to be used for purposes of committing an offence mentioned in paragraph 1 above, or gives instructions for the production of such programs, shall be punished by imprisonment for a term of up to three years or a fine of up to forty thousand Swiss francs.

   If the offender commits the offence on a habitual basis for profit, a sentence of up to five years' penal servitude can be imposed.

Switzerland has also been recognized by the EU as providing adequate protection of data, and has a data transfer agreement with the US in the form of the Swiss-US Privacy Shield. However, the FDPIC recently noted that the Swiss-US Privacy Shield does not guarantee adequate protection for transfers of data to the US. Furthermore, following the adoption of new Standard Contractual Clauses ('SCCs') for international data transfers by the European Commission in June 2021, the FDPIC announced, on 27 August, 2021, that the EU's SCCs could be used for transfers under Swiss law, subject to certain necessary adaptations and amendments.

11.4   CYBERSECURITY LAWS IN THE BANKING INDUSTRY

The Code of Criminal Procedure[4] provides for the possibility of monitoring the relations between a bank or bank-type institution and an accused person (Fig. 11.1).

in order to elucidate crimes or offences, subject to authorization by the court deciding on measures of constraint. The National Cyber Security Centre ('NCSC') announced, on April 5, 2022, that the Swiss Financial

[4] SR 312.0, in force as of 01.01.2011; Art. 284 and 285.

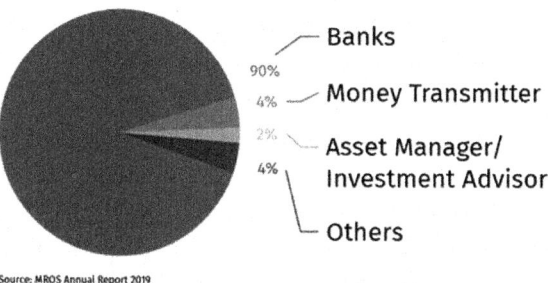

Source: MROS Annual Report 2019

Fig. 11.1 Cybersecurity in banking and other financial industry

Sector Cybersecurity Centre ('FS-CSC') association had been founded in Zurich. In particular, the NCSC highlighted that the FS-CSC association aims to strengthen cooperation between financial institutions and authorities in the fight against cyber threats, and to increase the resilience of the financial sector. Furthermore, the NCSC outlined that the FS-CSC association will also aim to facilitate the exchange of information between financial market players and improve cooperation with regard to sector-wide preventive measures and the management of systemic crises. The membership to the FS-CSC association is open to all banks, insurance companies, financial market infrastructures, and financial associations that have their registered office in Switzerland and have been authorized by the Swiss Financial Market Supervisory Authority ('FINMA'), further outlining that Swiss subsidiaries and branches of foreign banks and insurance companies with FINMA authorization can also join the association as members.

CHAPTER 12

AML/CFT and Cybersecurity Laws in China

12.1 General

China enacted the CSL on November 7, 2016. The CSL came into force on June 1, 2017, with the goal of establishing a uniform regulatory regime for cybersecurity and data protection in China. The Cyberspace Administration of China (CAC) has issued a series of regulations implementing the law.

Other sectoral regulators include Ministry of Science and Technology (MOST). On January 4, 2022, The Cyberspace Administration of China (the "CAC"), in conjunction with 12 other government departments (collectively, the "Working Mechanism"), issued the New Measures for Cybersecurity Review. The New Measures amends the Measures for Cybersecurity Review (Draft Revision for Comments) (the "Draft Measures") released on July 10, 2021 and will come into effect on February 15, 2022. The New Measures list the following main factors for assessing national security risk during cybersecurity review.

- The risk of any critical information infrastructure being illegally controlled, tampered with, or sabotaged after any product or service is used;

F. I. Lessambo, *Anti-Money Laundering, Counter Financing Terrorism and Cybersecurity in the Banking Industry*, Palgrave Macmillan Studies in Banking and Financial Institutions, https://doi.org/10.1007/978-3-031-23484-2_12

- The risk of an interruption in the supply of any product or service endangering the continuity of any critical information infrastructure;
- The security, openness, transparency, diversity of sources and reliability of any supply channel of any product or service, and the risk of its supply being interrupted due to political, diplomatic, trade, or other factors;
- The compliance of the provider of any product or service with the laws, administrative regulations, and departmental rules of China;
- The risk of any core data, important data, or a large amount of personal information being stolen, leaked, destroyed, illegally used, or illegally transferred abroad;
- The risk of any critical information infrastructure, core data, important data, or a large amount of personal information being affected, controlled, or maliciously used by foreign governments, as well as any network information security risk; and
- Any other factor that may endanger the security of any critical information infrastructure, network security, or data security.

12.2   AML/CFT Laws

The Anti-Money Laundering Law of the People's Republic of China was adopted at the 24th Meeting of the Standing Committee of the Tenth National People's Congress of the People's Republic of China on October 31, 2006. In June of 2021, the People's Bank of China (PBOC, China's central bank and major financial regulator) published the draft version of amended Anti-Money Laundering Law (Amended AML Law) seeking for public opinion. Amended AML Law contains major changes to improve the effectiveness of its legal framework to combat money laundering and terrorist financing and has expanded AML obligations to all individuals and organizations. In accordance with the Anti-Money Laundering Law, the People's Bank of China is responsible for supervising and reviewing financial institutions' performance in their fulfillment of the anti-money laundering obligations, and for coordinating and promoting the anti-money laundering supervision and administration over non-financial institutions.

12.3 CYBERSECURITY LAWS IN CHINA

The Chinese data protection model is built on two pillars: personal information protection and data security. The laws recognize the need to ensure that data flows and operations within government are properly regulated to prevent abuse and corruption.[1]

12.3.1 The Chinese Cybersecurity Law

On November 7, 2016, China enacted its comprehensive cybersecurity law, which entered into force on June 1, 2017. The CSL aims to establishing a uniform regulatory regime for cybersecurity and data protection in China. However, multiple government agencies are involved in implementing the CSL, including: (i) Cyberspace Administration of China (CAC) and its local offices, (ii) the Ministry of Public Security (MPS) and local Public Security Bureaus, (iii) the Ministry of Industry and Information Technologies (MIIT) and local Telecommunication Bureaus, and (iv) other sectoral regulators (such as the Ministry of Science and Technology (MOST), the National Energy Administration (NEA), and China Banking and Insurance Regulatory Commission (CBIRC).

In summary, the CSL is currently being enforced in the following ways:

- It imposes baseline data protection and cybersecurity obligations on network operators, including compliance obligations with Multi-Level Protection Scheme (MLPS) rules
- It provides a regulatory framework for critical information infrastructure (CII) operators
- It establishes a cybersecurity review mechanism for network products and services that may put China's national security at risk
- It establishes pre-sale certification requirements for critical network equipment and network security products
- It imposes requirements to protect data collected in the operations of networks
- It stipulates a wide array of sanctions and penalties for non-compliant companies

---

[1] Rogier Creemers (2022): China's emerging data protection framework, Journal of Cybersecurity, Volume 8, Issue 1, pp. 1–12, https://doi.org/10.1093/cybsec/tyac011.

12.3.2   The "Cybersecurity Multi-Level Protection System 2.0" or "MLPS 2.0

On December 1, 2019, China introduced the "cybersecurity multi-level protection system 2.0" or "MLPS 2.0," which includes three Chinese national standards (issued by the Chinese State Administration for Market Regulation and the Standardization Administration of China). The Chinese national standards require companies to fulfill cybersecurity protection obligations, which vary depending on the companies' nature of business or operation, to ensure their networks are free from interference, damage, or unauthorized access, and prevent network data from being divulged, stolen, or falsified. Under these standards, networks are classified into five levels, depending on their potential risk of harm in case of security breaches, with systems that would suffer the least harm classified as level 1 and those that would suffer the most harm classified as level 5. The national standards require companies' procurement and use of encryption products and services to be preapproved by the Chinese government for networks classified as level 2 or above. The standards further require companies (including Chinese affiliates of foreign companies) to set up their cloud infrastructure, including servers, virtualized networks, software, and information systems, in China. Such cloud infrastructures are subject to testing and evaluation by the Chinese government. Overseas operation and maintenance of Chinese cloud computing platforms must also follow Chinese laws and regulations. The national standards also state that customers' data and users' personal information processed by cloud service providers should be stored inside China, which is an additional requirement. It is currently uncertain how these national standards would be enforced and there has not yet been reports of enforcement.

On April 27, 2020, the Cyberspace Administration of China, the National Development and Reform Commission, and 10 other governmental departments jointly promulgated the Measures for Cybersecurity Review (effective June 1, 2020) to ensure the security of the supply chain of critical information infrastructure and to safeguard national security. The Measures apply to operators of critical information infrastructure, requiring national security and other reviews when purchasing network products and services.

12.3.3   Cybersecurity Protection of Critical Information Infrastructure (GB/T 39204-2020)

The Information Security Technology—Basic Requirements for Cybersecurity Protection of Critical Information Infrastructure (GB/T 39204-2020) was introduced in 2018 and is currently under final approval. The standard stipulates the overall cybersecurity framework of critical information infrastructure and the corresponding requirements for identification, safety protection, detection and evaluation, monitoring and early warning, and emergency response. In December 2019, the Chinese Information Security Standardization Technical Committee rolled out a pilot test on the practicality of the standard in order to accumulate experience and provide technical support for actual implementation. In August 2020, implementation plans for critical information infrastructure and classified protection of information systems were discussed in the 2020 Beijing Cyber Security Conference hosted by the investigation team of the Ministry of Public Security.

12.4   Cybersecurity in the Banking Industry

On November 11, 2020, the Peoples' Bank of China released a Guideline for the Implementation of Cybersecurity Level Protection in the Financial Industry (JR/T 0071-2020). In particular, the Implementation Guideline regulates, among other things, the basic framework and term definitions for the financial industry cyber security level protection work, as well as financial institutions cybersecurity job setting requirements including requirements for job competence and evaluation of cybersecurity personnel. Moreover, the Implementation Guideline is applicable to supervisors who guide financial institutions, evaluation institutions, and financial industry cybersecurity level protection.

CHAPTER 13

AML/CFT and Cybersecurity Laws in Japan

13.1 GENERAL

There is no special government entity that enforces the AML laws. Like criminal laws, the police departments of each prefecture and public prosecutor's offices enforce the AML laws. To prevent money laundering, Japan has established a domestic regulatory and oversight regime that imposes CDD (customer due diligence) and other necessary obligations on financial institutions and designated non-financial businesses and professions by the Act on Prevention of Transfer of Criminal Proceeds.

In Japan, the Act on the Protection of Personal Information (APPI) primarily handles the protection of data privacy issues. The APPI was drastically amended in 2016 and has been in full force since 30 May 2017.

13.2 AML/CFT

The Japanese Financial Services Agency (JFSA) is the AML/CFT supervisor of all banks and a number of non-bank FIs. Japanese AML laws can apply to non-citizens and non-residents who are involved in money

F. I. Lessambo, *Anti-Money Laundering, Counter Financing Terrorism and Cybersecurity in the Banking Industry*, Palgrave Macmillan Studies in Banking and Financial Institutions, https://doi.org/10.1007/978-3-031-23484-2_13

131

laundering activities within the jurisdiction.[1] There is no special government entity that enforces the AML laws. Like criminal laws, the police departments of each prefecture and public prosecutor's offices enforce the AML laws. The AML laws also applied to money laundering activities committed by Japanese nationals outside the jurisdiction's borders.

The AML/CFT legal framework in Japan is organized by the following Acts:

- The Act on the Prevention of Transfer of Criminal Proceeds (APTCP). The APTC was adopted in 2007. Major improvements to the APTCP were adopted in 2011 and 2014 and entered into force in 2013 and 2016, respectively. In 2016, the Act on Prevention of Transfer of Criminal Proceeds was amended to add virtual currency exchangers to covered institutions and persons in order to respond to the FATF's request. The APTCP requires the application of preventive measures, including STR reporting, by obliged entities and the conduct of AML/CFT supervision by relevant authorities.
- The Act on Punishment of Organized Crimes and Control of Proceeds (APOC). The APOC was enacted (enforced in February 2000) in Japan based on the FATF recommendations revised in June 1996. The APOC was last amended in 2017. It criminalizes money laundering and predicate offences (including tax crimes) and includes provisions on preservation of assets and confiscation. It designates the Financial Services Agency as the FIU of Japan, where money laundering information shall be collected, arranged, and analyzed to be disseminated to investigative authorities.
- The Act on Punishment of Financing to Offences of Public Intimidation (TF Act), which was adopted in 2002 and amended in 2015, criminalizes TF. In February 2018, the Financial Services Agency published the Guidelines for Anti-Money Laundering and Combating the Financing of Terrorism to clarify the basic stance on risk-management practices against money laundering and terrorism

[1] Yoshihiro Kai (2019): First-step Analysis: Anti-money Laundering Provisions in Japan, https://www.lexology.com/library/detail.aspx?g=59b1f93e-a48f-4f61-b828-d91dafcd707c.

financing to encourage financial institutions to improve their regimes to effectively prevent money laundering and terrorism financing.[2]

- The Foreign Exchange and Foreign Trade Act of 1949 (FEFTA) requires asset freezing on foreign transactions, and the Terrorist Asset Freezing Act (TAFA), adopted in 2014 to supplement the FEFTA for the implementation of targeted financial sanctions, requires asset freezing on domestic and foreign transactions.

13.3 CYBERSECURITY LAWS

13.3.1 *The Basic Cybersecurity Act*

The Basic Cybersecurity Act is the first cybersecurity-specific law that has been enacted among the G7 nations. It aims to move cybersecurity-related policies forward in a comprehensive and effective manner, and contribute to the creation of a more energetic and continuously developing economic society, consequently contributing to the national security of Japan.[3] On December 5, 2018, the Basic Cybersecurity Act was amended on 5 December, 2018 with a view to further ensure cybersecurity and to fully prepare Japan to host the Tokyo 2020 Olympic and Paralympic Games.

13.3.2 *The Unauthorized Computer Access Prohibition Act*

This Act prohibits computer fraud, malware, spyware, obstructing business by interfering, false data, and unauthorized computer access. Under this Act, any unauthorized access and usage or disclosure of the data obtained through unauthorized access can trigger civil liability based upon general tort laws and the Unfair Competition Prevention Act.

[2] Yoshihiro Kai (2019): First-Step Analysis: Anti-money Laundering Provisions in Japan, https://www.lexology.com/library/detail.aspx?g=59b1f93e-a48f-4f61-b828-d91dafcd707c.

[3] Kazuyasu Shiraishi, Masaya Hirano (2020): Cybersecurity in Japan, https://www.lexology.com/library/detail.aspx?g=5a1b0e44-9f84-432e-9bed-88523b2ebb6a.

13.3.3   The Specially Designated Secret Protection Act (Act no. 108 of 2013)

Act No. 108 of 2013 is a law in Japan allowing the government to designate defense and other sensitive information as "special secrets" that are protected from public disclosure. The Act requires the government to formulate standards to ensure uniform implementation in connection with the designation and termination of SDSs and the security clearance process. Access to SDS is limited to government personnel, employees of Government of Japan contractors, and prefectural police officers who, following the security clearance process, are identified as not risking unauthorized disclosure of SDS.

13.3.4   The Basic Act on the Formation of an Advanced Information and Telecommunications Network Society

The Basic Act on the Formation of an Advanced Information and Telecommunications Network Society was established in 2000. The purpose of this Act was to swiftly and thoroughly pursue strategies for the formation of a digital society by way of providing basic principles and basic policies for the development of strategies, determining the responsibilities of the government of Japan, local public entities, and business operators, establishing the Digital Agency, and providing for the development of a priority policy program on the formation of a digital society thereby contributing to the realization of the sustainable and sound development of the Japanese economy and happy lives for its citizens.

13.3.5   The Act on Electronic Signatures and Certification Business

The Act on Electronic Signatures and Certification Business, which came into effect on April 1, 2001 (the "E-signature Act") provides statutory support for the use of e-signatures.[4] Given the threat poses by cybersecurity, it is important for a company to conduct the proper KYC procedures before it executes e-contracts with a new counterparty.

---

[4] Kenji Miyagawa (2020): e-Signature Update (Japan), https://www.iltanet.org/blogs/kenji-miyagawa1/2020/12/22/e-signature-update-japan.

13.3.6   *The Act on the Protection of Personal Information (APPI)*

The Act on the Protection of Personal Information (APPI), adopted in 2003, was one of the first data protection regulations in Asia. It prescribes duty of companies to secure personal data they handle. It received a major overhaul in September 2015 after a series of high-profile data breaches shook Japan. The update brought with it the establishment of the Personal Information Protection Commission (PPC), an independent agency that, among others, protects the rights and interests of individuals and promotes the proper and effective use of personal information.[5] APPI distinguishes between two categories of protected data: personal information and "special care-required" personal information.[6] In 2020, and 2021, APPI received two major amendments. Key points for the amendment enacted in 2020 are the APPI's extraterritorial application, data transfers to third parties in a foreign country, and data breach reporting obligations. The other amendment enacted in 2021 having an impact on academic research institutions such as universities and public sectors in Japan.[7]

13.4   Cybersecurity in the Banking Industry

Recognizing that cybersecurity in the financial sector is of utmost importance for the stability of the entire financial system, the FSA formulated and published "The Policy Approaches to Strengthen Cybersecurity in the Financial Sector" (hereinafter referred to as "Policy Approaches") in July 2015 and updated it in October 2018, endeavoring to enhance cybersecurity in the financial sector.[8] The FSA conducted cybersecurity

---

[5] Andrada Coos (2022): Data Protection in Japan: All You Need to Know About APPI, https://www.endpointprotector.com/blog/data-protection-in-japan-appi/.

[6] Special care-required; personal information is a new category introduced under the 2017 amended APPI that refers to data that can be the basis for discrimination or prejudice. Medical history, marital status, race, religious beliefs, and criminal records, among others, fall under this category.

[7] Hiroto Imai, Mizue Kakiuchi, Sayuri Mori (2022): Data Privacy Laws and Regulations in Japan—Recent amendments to the APPI, Hogan Lovells, https://www.engage.hoganlovells.com/knowledgeservices/news/data-privacy-laws-and-regulations-in-japan-recent-amendments-to-the-act-on-the-protection-of-personal-information-appi.

[8] FSA (2020): Policies for Strengthening Cybersecurity in the Financial Sector, pp. 1–17, https://www.fsa.go.jp/en/news/2019/20190115/cyber-policy.pdf.

assessments for regional banks and credit associations/unions selected based on risks, such as those feared to delay the development of basic cybersecurity management systems, reaffirming their efforts to develop the basic systems and verifying the effectiveness of their cybersecurity countermeasures. Overall, the assessments found that while senior executives at some of these banks were proactively engaging in management and monitoring based on plans to enhance cybersecurity, others struggled to develop basic cybersecurity management systems. The FSA is also cooperating with local finance bureaus to follow up and promote their development of systems for resolving challenges under the leadership of their senior executive.[9]

---

[9] FSA (2020): Financial Sector Cybersecurity Report, pp. 1–18, https://www.fsa.go.jp/en/news/2020/20201127/cybersecurity.pdf.

CHAPTER 14

AML/CFT and Cybersecurity Laws in India

14.1 GENERAL

India has one of the robust AML/CFT legislation in Asia. The Finance Act of 2019 introduced amendments to the Prevention of Money Laundering Act, 2002 (PMLA) to tighten gaps and addressing ambiguities in the anti-money laundering law.[1] It widens the scope of "proceeds of crime" to include properties and assets created, derived, or obtained through any criminal activity related to the scheduled PMLA offence, and clarifies the continuing nature of the money laundering offence. Being among the top three countries in Asia to experience most server access and ransomware attacks, India has strengthened it cybersecurity laws to include its vital infrastructures.

14.2 AML/CFT LAWS

India has prohibited money laundering under the Prevention of Money Laundering Act, 2002 (PMLA) and also in the Narcotic Drugs and

---

[1] Faraz Alam Sagar, Pragati Sharma (2019): PMLA Amendment 2019—Plugging the Loopholes, India Corporate Laws, https://corporate.cyrilamarchandblogs.com/2019/09/finance-act-2019-prevention-money-laundering-act-amendment/.

© The Author(s), under exclusive license to Springer Nature Switzerland AG 2023
F. I. Lessambo, *Anti-Money Laundering, Counter Financing Terrorism and Cybersecurity in the Banking Industry*, Palgrave Macmillan Studies in Banking and Financial Institutions, https://doi.org/10.1007/978-3-031-23484-2_14

Psychotropic Substances Act, 1985 (NDPS Act) (amended in 2001). The Prevention of Money Laundering Act 2002 coupled with the rules issued under it and the rules and regulations formed by regulators such as the Reserve Bank of India (RBI) and the Securities and Exchange Board of India (SEBI) displays a broad framework for the anti-money laundering laws in India.

14.2.1   The Prevention of Money Laundering Act, 2002

In 1998, The Prevention of Money Laundering Bill was introduced in the Lok Sabha, passed in 2003, and came into force in 2005. It has gone through several amendments, with the last one being in 2019. Administration and enforcement authorities are chosen under PMLA to execute its provisions and rules. Certain powers are vested, which are very similar to those granted to the civil courts of the nation, to exercise the provisional attachment of properties that are involved in the offence under PMLA.

The PMLA attempts to combat acts related to money laundering in India and because of this, it has three main objectives:

- to prevent and control money laundering
- to confiscate and seize the property acquired from the laundered money
- to deal with any other issue in relation to money laundering in India.

Under the provisions of the PMLA, the Financial Intelligence Unit of India (FIU-IND) was formed in 2004 as the primary body for coordinating India's AML efforts. The primary function of FIU-IND is to receive, analyze, process, and disseminate information relating to suspect financial transactions. FIU-IND also coordinates and strengthens efforts of national investigation, international intelligence, and enforcement agencies in pursuing the global efforts against money laundering and financing of terrorism. In 2005, the Enforcement Directorate (ED) was introduced by the Government of India to utilize exclusive powers related to the investigation and prosecution under PMLA.

The primary legislation other than the Prevention of Money Laundering Act, 2002, which directly or indirectly focuses to curb and fight money laundering activities, is as follows:

14.2.2 The Conservation of Foreign Exchange and Prevention of Smuggling Activities Act, 1974

The act was passed in 1974 in furtherance to the government attempt to retain foreign exchange within the nation. The Act is established on the concept of Preventive Detention which, apart from being a colonial legacy, is also given explicitly in our constitution as 'the necessary evil' and laws exist under Article 22 of the Indian Constitution for the same reasons related to the security of the state and maintenance of public order. According to the provisions of Section 10, the stipulated period of detention is 1–2 years.

All decisions in furtherance of the Act may be taken by the state or central government. The relevant provisions in this regard which must be taken into consideration are Section 3 (power to make orders detaining certain persons), Section 4 (execution of detention orders), Section 5 (power to regulate place and conditions of detention), and Section 11 (revocation of detention orders).

14.2.3 The Benami Transactions (Prohibition) Act, 1988

A Benami transaction is a transaction in which property is transferred to one person for a value paid or provided by another person, and often, the identity of the persons involved is concealed. This Act was passed in 1988. It is to constrain Benami transactions and the right to recover property held by the Benami. Section 3 of the Act specifically debars anyone from getting into a Benami transaction. The Act further specifies those properties obtained under the Benami transaction which are liable to be acquired by the competent authorities without any need of compensation to be payable by such authority.

14.2.4 The Indian Penal Code, 1860 and Code of Criminal Procedure, 1973

The Indian Penal Code, 1860 is the primary substantive law that regulates a number of criminal activities and also prescribes penalties for them. The Code of Criminal Procedure, 1973 on the other hand is a part of procedural law that specifies procedures to be followed in criminal cases. A number of offences under the Indian Penal Code have been recognized as being scheduled offences within the meaning explained in the PMLA.

Further, Section 65 of the PMLA also specifies that the provisions of the Code of Criminal Procedure are to be followed in respect of the several proceedings prescribed under the PMLA.

14.2.5   The Narcotic Drugs and Psychotropic Substances Act, 1985

This Act was passed in 1985 with the aim of consolidation and amendment of laws relating to narcotic drugs. Keeping in line with its objectives identifies, lists, and explains several forms and types of narcotic drugs and psychotropic substances.

The Act in its essence attempts to stop and restrict the transport and vending of narcotic and psychotropic substances and does not mention money laundering activities. It may, however, be taken into consideration that the trade of narcotic substances does generate a lot of cash for people involved in it. So much so that a noticeable portion of the money involved in drug trafficking is then mobilized to give it legitimacy or in simple words, the same money gets laundered. The NDPS Act, by working against practices involving drug trading and trafficking, puts a direct restriction on the flow of money into illegitimate activities.

14.3   CYBERSECURITY LAWS

Since cybersecurity is a cross-cutting issue, India has a complex inter-ministerial and inter-departmental institutional framework for cybersecurity, with several ministries, departments, and agencies performing key functions.[2]

In India, cybercrimes are covered by the Information Technology Act, 2000 and the Indian Penal Code, 1860. It is the Information Technology Act, 2000, which deals with issues related to cybercrimes and electronic commerce.

14.3.1   The Information Technology Act of 2000 (IT Act)

The Information Technology Act addresses the protection of electronic data and computer-related offenses (e.g., hacking and tampering with computer source documents). The main objective of this act is to carry

---

[2] Vijayant Singh (2022): A Comparison of Cybersecurity Regulations: India, Asia Business Law Journal, https://law.asia/india-cybersecurity-regulations-2022/.

lawful and trustworthy electronic, digital and online transactions, and alleviate or reduce cybercrimes. It prescribes penalties for various cybercrimes and fraud through digital/electronic format.

- Section 43 of IT Act, 2000 states that any act of destroying, altering, or stealing computer system/network or deleting data with malicious intentions without authorization from owner of the computer is liable for the payment to be made to owner as compensation for damages.
- Section 43A of IT Act, 2000 states that any corporate body dealing with sensitive information that fails to implement reasonable security practices causing loss of other person will also liable as convict for compensation to the affected party.

The IT Act, 2000 was amended in 2008. This amendment introduced the controversial Section 66A into the Act, which gives authorities the power to arrest anyone accused of posting content on social media that could be deemed 'offensive'. However, the 2008 amendments (IT Act) does not criminalize hacking, but prohibits computer-related fraud and tampering with computer source documents.

14.3.2   *The Information Technology (Reasonable Security Practices and Procedures and Sensitive Personal Data or Information) Rules—"Privacy Rules"*

While organizations in India already adhere to international data privacy laws, including GDPR when serving overseas customers, India still struggles to pass a data privacy law. A proposed law ("the Personal Data Protection Bill") tailored under the EU GDPR is meeting fierce resistance in the Parliament. As of 3 August 2022, the Personal Data Protection Bill has been withdrawn and is no longer being considered in Parliament.

14.4   CYBERSECURITY IN THE BANKING INDUSTRY

In 2016, the Reserve Bank, had, provided guidelines on Information Security, Electronic Banking, Technology Risk Management, and Cyber Frauds. Banks are required to put in place a cybersecurity policy elucidating the strategy containing an appropriate approach to combat cyber threats given the level of complexity of business and acceptable levels of risk, duly approved by their Board.[3] The Cyber Security Policy required to banks must be distinct and separate from the broader IT policy/IS Security policy so that it can highlight the risks from cyber threats and the measures to address/mitigate these risks.

Cosmos Bank Pune India cyberattack
- Cyber criminals hacked the systems of India's Cosmos Bank and siphoned off nearly 944 million rupees ($13.5 million) through simultaneous withdrawals across 28 countries over the weekend.
- The unidentified hackers stole customer information through a malware attack on its automated teller machine (ATM) server, withdrawing 805 million rupees in 14,849 transactions in just over two hours on Aug. 11, mainly overseas.
- Several cloned debit cards of the Cosmos Cooperative Bank were used for thousands of ATM transactions from India and 28 other countries in a period of seven hours on August 11, 2018.
- Moreover, the hackers transferred 139 million rupees to a Hong Kong-based company's account by issuing three unauthorized transactions over the SWIFT global payments network.
- Interpol has issued a red corner notice against a prime suspect. Four persons are wanted in the case, of whom three, identified as Kunal Shukla, Abdul Bhai, and Sumer Shaikh, are suspected to be in Dubai.

---

[3] RBI (2016): Cyber Security Framework in Banks, https://www.rbi.org.in/Scripts/NotificationUser.aspx?Id=10435&Mode=0.

CHAPTER 15

AML/CFT and Cybersecurity Laws in South Korea

15.1 General

The Republic of Korea (South Korea) has a developed anti-money laundering system. South Korea has enacted anti-money laundering and combating the financing of terrorism laws and established a Financial Intelligence Unit. Money laundering is strictly regulated by the global standards. To this end, the Korea Financial Intelligence Unit was established in November 2001. FIU has been the primary executive agency responsible for implementing an effective Anti-Money Laundering and Combating the Financing of Terrorism regime in Korea.

15.2 AML/CFT Laws

Recently, South Korea has approved new anti-money laundering measures for the digital currency sector. The new rules came into force on April 25, 2021. The Korea Financial Intelligence Unit (KoFIU) is Korea's financial intelligence unit (FIU) and the lead agency in Korea for AML/CFT

© The Author(s), under exclusive license to Springer Nature Switzerland AG 2023
F. I. Lessambo, *Anti-Money Laundering, Counter Financing Terrorism and Cybersecurity in the Banking Industry*, Palgrave Macmillan Studies in Banking and Financial Institutions,
https://doi.org/10.1007/978-3-031-23484-2_15

matters.[1] On June 21, 2010, South Korea issued AML/CFT Regulation, which contains specific provisions concerning customer due diligence and other related preventive measures to be undertaken by financial institutions and casinos. The Regulation was issued based on Article 5 Paragraph 3 of the Enforcement Decree of the Financial Transaction Reports Act and contains legally binding obligations of financial institutions and casinos. Two statutes criminalize money laundering, besides the Prohibition of Financing for Offences of Public Intimidation Act (PFOPIA), which combats against terrorism financing.

15.2.1   The 1995 Act on Special Cases Concerning the Prevention of Illegal Trafficking in Narcotics, Psychotropic Substances and Hemp (ASPIT)

It aims to seek the repression and prevention of narcotics-related crimes through the prevention of activities that encourage narcotics-related illegal acts. Article 7(1) of ASPIT states:

> Any person who harbors or disguises the nature, location, origin, or restoration of illegal profits, etc. for the purpose of hindering the investigation or the detection of narcotics and other analogous substances related crimes or the source of illegal profits, etc. or avoiding the confiscation of illegal profits, etc. shall be either punished by imprisonment not exceeding seven years or a fine not exceeding 30 million won, or both penalties shall be imposed cumulatively.

15.2.2   The 2001 Proceeds of Crime Act (POCA)

This Act aims to contribute to the maintenance of a sound social order by regulating activities that disguise the acquisition of criminal proceeds related to specific crimes, conceal criminal proceeds for the purpose of encouraging specific crimes, or disguise such assets as legitimately acquired, and by fundamentally eliminating economic factors that encourage specific crimes through prescribing special cases regarding confiscation and collection of equivalent value with regard to proceeds of

---

[1] FATF (2009): South Korea- Anti-Money Laundering and Combating the Financing of Terrorism, https://www.fatf-gafi.org/media/fatf/documents/reports/mer/MER%20K orea.pdf.

crime related with specific crimes. Enacted in November 2001, it criminalizes money laundering and provides for the confiscation of criminal proceeds. Under Article 3 of POCA, any person who disguises the acquisition or disposition of criminal proceeds, disguises the origin of criminal proceeds, or conceals criminal proceeds is subject to imprisonment not exceeding five years or a fine not exceeding KRW 30 million. Article 8 of the POCA provides for the confiscation of criminal proceeds, and Article 10 of the same Act provides for the confiscation of property of equivalent value to criminal proceeds.[2]

15.2.3   *The Prohibition of Financing for Offences of Public Intimidation Act (PFOPIA)*

Enacted in December 2007 and came into force in December 2008, and the Act on Prohibition against the Financing of Terrorism and Proliferation of Weapons of Mass Destruction (PFOPIA) is Korea's anti-terrorist financing legislation.

15.3   CYBERSECURITY LAWS

Korea's cybersecurity effort began in earnest in the 1980s when the government first began to actively promote informatization of the economy, government, and society.[3]

15.3.1   *Act on the Protection of Information and Communications Infrastructure Information and Communications Network Act*

Enacted in 2001, South Korea's Communications Network Utilization and Information Protection Act is a personal privacy law. It has been amended several times since most recently in 2015. In conjunction with South Korea's Personal Information Protection Act of 2011 or PIPA, the Communications Network Utilization and Information Protection Act serves to protect the personal data and privacy of citizens within

---

[2] https://www.kofiu.go.kr/eng/regime/framework.do.

[3] So Jeong Kim, Sunha Bae (2021): Korean Policies of Cybersecurity and Data Resilience, Carnegie Endowment for International Peace, https://carnegieendowment.org/2021/08/17/korean-policies-of-cybersecurity-and-data-resilience-pub-85164.

South Korea. More specifically, the Communications Network Utilization and Information Protection Act protects the personal information of South Korean citizens as it pertains to the safe use of information and communications' technology networks within the country. It establishes various provisions that business entities within the country must follow as it pertains to the collection and processing of the personal information of South Korean citizens in regard to the use of information and communications services.

15.3.2   Personal Information Protection Act (PIPA)

South Korea's wide-ranging Personal Information Protection Act (PIPA) was passed on September 30, 2011, making the country one the world's strictest privacy regimes. The PIPA provides very prescriptive and specific requirements throughout the lifecycle of the handling of personal data. This includes requirements like prior notification, opt-in consent, and heavy sanctions prescribed by law, which makes it one of the strictest data protection laws in the world. The PIPA specifies that when obtaining consent from the data subjects, the personal information processor needs to notify the data subjects of the fact by separating the matters requiring consent from the ones who does not require consent. Additionally, you are expected to help the data subject with recognizing it explicitly. On March 30, 2021, adequacy talks were concluded between South Korea and the EU, with the effect being that personal data could potentially flow from the EU (And Norway, Liechtenstein and Iceland) to South Korea without any further safeguard being necessary. In other words, transfers to South Korea will be assimilated to intra-EU transmissions of data if passed.

15.4   CYBERSECURITY IN THE BANKING INDUSTRY

The Financial Supervisory Service (FSS), a quasi-governmental entity supervises, investigates financial institutions, and conducts AML supervision and inspection on behalf of KoFIU. The FSS has the power to demand sanctions against financial institutions violating AML laws and regulations as well as the officers and employees of those financial institutions.

CHAPTER 16

AML/CFT and Cybersecurity Laws in Indonesia

16.1 GENERAL

Indonesia has a well-developed anti-money laundering and counter-terrorism financing framework. A Financial Intelligence Unit and a system for reporting suspicious transactions have been established in the country. Bank Indonesia, Indonesia's central bank, and the Financial Services Authority of Indonesia, known as Otoritas Jasa Keuangan (OJK), are responsible for issuing AML regulations in Indonesia and have regulatory and supervisory authority over all banks and financial institutions. In 2021, a holistic national Risk Assessment on Money Laundering has been updated in with stakeholders' AML-CFT who are members of the Inter-Agency Working Group of the NRA Indonesia in 2021.[1]

16.2 AML/CFT LAWS

Indonesia has adopted several laws several laws to address money laundering and terrorist financing, including Law No. 3 of 2011, Law No.

---

[1] Mardiansyah (2021): Indonesia Risk Assessment on Money Laundering 2021, Indonesian Financial Transaction Reports and Analysis Center (INTRAC), Chapter 1, https://www.ppatk.go.id/backend/assets/uploads/20220412135927.pdf.

© The Author(s), under exclusive license to Springer Nature Switzerland AG 2023
F. I. Lessambo, *Anti-Money Laundering, Counter Financing Terrorism and Cybersecurity in the Banking Industry*, Palgrave Macmillan Studies in Banking and Financial Institutions,
https://doi.org/10.1007/978-3-031-23484-2_16

5 of 2018, Law No. 8 of 2010, and Law No. 9 of 2013. The principle anti-money laundering Indonesia legislation is OJK Regulation No. 12/POJK.01/2017 concerning the Implementation of the Anti-Money Laundering Program and Terrorism Funding Prevention in the Financial Service Sector.

AML regulators in Indonesia.

16.2.1   *Indonesia OJK Regulation No. 12/POJK.01/2017*

OJK Regulation No. 12/POJK.01/2017 compels institutions to implement a variety of anti-money laundering and counter-terrorism financing procedures that meet OJK and FATF standards. It applies to fintech providers that receive fees from customers in return for their services as peer-to-peer lenders and equity crowdfunding providers.

On September 30, 2019, the Financial Services Authority issued OJK Regulation No. 23/POJK.01/2019 on September 30, 2019 to amend several provisions of the previous OJK Regulation No. 12/POJK.01/2017 on the Implementation of Anti-Money Laundering and Prevention of Terrorism Funding in Financial Sector Programs. One major change introduced by POJK 23/2019 is to allow banks to engage third-party service providers to conduct their face-to-face on-boarding verification, whereas, previously, banks could only use their own electronic facilities for face-to-face verification.[2]

16.3   Cybersecurity Laws

Cybersecurity in Indonesia is governed by EIT Law and GR 71/2019, but they provide no specific definitions or terms on cybersecurity itself. A bill on cybersecurity was once proposed, but it was eventually rejected and failed to be enacted in 2019. Indonesia has established a governmental institution that oversees cybersecurity and encryption ("BSSN"), which functions include but not limited to identification, detection, protection,

---

[2] Vik Tang, David Dawborn, Teguh Arwiko and Michelle Virgiany (2020): Taking Indonesian Finance Digital—Recent Moves and Trends to Watch, https://www.herber tsmithfreehills.com/my/business-services/lang-ru/insight/taking-indonesian-finance-dig ital-%E2%80%93-recent-moves-and-trends-to-watch.

monitoring of the implementation of technical policies regarding cyber-security in e-commerce protection, cyberattacks, and/or cyber incidents in Indonesia.

16.3.1 Electronic Information and Transactions Law

The EIT Law serves as the principal policy for electronic information in Indonesia. Enacted in 2008, it was originally intended to respond to rapid developments in information technology, and fill legal gaps around issues such as electronic transactions and the position of digital information and signatures under Indonesian law. The EIT Law applies to everyone (individuals or legal entities whether Indonesian or foreign) conducting legal actions regulated in the territory of the Republic of Indonesia or outside the territory of the Republic of Indonesia to the extent such legal actions have legal consequences in the territory of the Republic of Indonesia and/or outside the territory of the Republic Indonesia and cause a loss to Indonesia. The EIT Law No 11 of regulates, among other things:

- the use of electronic documents and/or information as evidence before Indonesian Courts;
- electronic signatures;
- electronic transactions;
- domain name, intellectual properties, and protection of personal rights; and
- the illegal actions and criminal penalties may be imposed by GOI.

16.3.2 MoCI Regulation 20/2016

MOCI Regulation 20/2016 stipulates that the consent for Processing Personal Data must be in writing and can be provided manually or electronically. The consent should be in the Indonesian language, although there is no prohibition in having it in a bilingual format. In any case, the PDP Regulations do not state that the consent must be in the form of a separate stand-alone document.[3]

---

[3] Denny Rahmansyah, Saprita Tahir (2018): Data Protection in Indonesia: Processing Requirements, https://www.ssek.com/blog/data-protection-in-indonesia-processing-requirements.

16.3.3   GR 71/2019

As of October 10, 2019, GR 71 amends Indonesia's previous Government Regulation No. 82 of 2012 to provide more clarity around data localization requirements, including additional flexibility for private-sector ESOs to store systems and data outside Indonesia, subject to certain restrictions. GR No. 71/2019 classifies electronic system operators into two categories: public domain and private domain.

- Public domain consists of government institution and other institutions appointed by the government to administer electronic systems for them and on their behalf, excluding financial sector authorities (e.g., BI and OJK).
- Private domain consists of an individual (WNI or WNA), entity, or institution that operates the electronic system that is being used and offered within Indonesian territory.

16.4   CYBERSECURITY IN THE BANKING INDUSTRY

Under the FSA Law, the FSA is responsible for regulating and supervising banks and banking institutions, and bank solvency and prudential aspects.

As a Supervisory and Regulatory Bodies (LPP), Bank Indonesia has issued Bank Indonesia Regulation (PBI) No. 19/10/PBI/2017 concerning the Implementation of Anti-Money Laundering and Countering Terrorism Financing for Non-Bank Payment System Service Providers and Non-Bank Money Changers (PBI AML CFT). The Bank of Indonesia issued Regulation No. 14/27/PBI/2012 on implementation of Anti-Money Laundering and Combating the Financing of Terrorism Programs for Commercial Banks as well as Regulation No 19/10/PBI/2017 regarding the adoption of an "Anti-Money Laundering and Prevention of Terrorism Financing for Non-Bank Payment System Service Provider and Non-Bank Currency Exchange Service" Procedure. Extensive regulations exist related to the application of know your customer (KYC) standards. Meanwhile in the field of banking, personal data is also governed under the Bank Indonesia Regulation No. 22/20/PBI/2020 regarding Protection of Bank Indonesia Consumer, which regulates the obligation for banking or non-banking entities which are under the supervision of Bank Indonesia to keep the confidentiality and security of its consumer's data (e.g., requirement of consumer's consent before transferring their personal data).

CHAPTER 17

AML/CFT and Cybersecurity Law in the UK

17.1   GENERAL

The Financial Conduct Authority is the UK's main financial services regulator with authority over banks, building societies, credit unions, and other firms engaging in financial activities. Established in 2012 under the Financial Services Act, the FCA replaced the Financial Services Authority (FSA) and has a mandate to maintain the safety of the UK's financial system and its financial institutions. The FCA oversees compliance with AML regulations in the UK and has the power to investigate money laundering and terrorism financing offenses in conjunction with other law enforcement agencies and authorities, such as the Crown Prosecution Service (CPS). All banks and financial institutions in the UK must register with the FCA. The Terrorism Act imposes counter financing of terrorism obligations on banks and financial institutions, which also include customer due diligence, transaction monitoring, and reporting obligations. The Terrorism Act was first introduced in 2000 but was amended by the Anti-Terrorism, Crime and Security Act 2001, the Terrorism Act 2006, the Terrorism Act 2000, and Proceeds of Crime Act 2002 (Amendment) Regulations 2007).

© The Author(s), under exclusive license to Springer Nature Switzerland AG 2023
F. I. Lessambo, *Anti-Money Laundering, Counter Financing Terrorism and Cybersecurity in the Banking Industry*, Palgrave Macmillan Studies in Banking and Financial Institutions,
https://doi.org/10.1007/978-3-031-23484-2_17

17.2   AML/CFT Laws

Introduced in 2002, POCA is the UK's primary AML regulation and defines the offenses that constitute money laundering. Those activities cover the perpetration and facilitation of money laundering and the acquisition or distributions of its criminal proceeds. Under POCA, banks and financial institutions must put appropriate AML controls in place to detect money laundering activities: these include customer due diligence and Beyond POCA and the Terrorism Act, the next most important AML/CFT legislation is the Money Laundering, Terrorist Financing and Transfer of Funds (Information on the Payer) Regulations 2017. The MLR 2017 transposes the obligations set out in the EU's 5th AMLD, tightening controls in the private sector and introducing the need for firms to implement a written AML/CFT risk-assessment transaction monitoring measures, as well as a range of reporting requirements.[1] The Money Laundering and Terrorist Financing Regulations 2019 implemented the EU Fifth Money Laundering Directive in the UK, and came into effect on 10 January 2020. This legislation extends the scope of regulated industries and changes the way customer due diligence and enhanced due diligence is conducted.

17.2.1   *The Economic Crime (Transparency and Enforcement) Act 2022 (ECA 2022)*

The passing of the Economic Crime (Transparency and Enforcement) Act 2022 (**ECA 2022**), while rushed through Parliament due to Moscow's invasion of Ukraine, brings in a number of changes related to the identification of the beneficial ownership of overseas entities and provides regulators with the tools to obtain unexplained wealth orders more easily. The Economic Crime (Transparency and Enforcement) Act 2022 (ECA), which came into force on March 15, 2022 (subject to certain provisions not being operative at commencement), has three main features:

- the creation of a register of overseas entities and their beneficial owners

The ECA requires overseas entities that own or acquire property in the UK to register with Companies House. The new ROE is a public register

---

[1] https://complyadvantage.com/insights/anti-money-laundering-uk/.

and will require the disclosure of details of the beneficial owners or managing officers of overseas entities. The information held on the ROE is required to be updated annually.

- amendments to unexplained wealth orders (UWOs)

Unexplained Wealth Order (UWO) regime to enable law enforcement to investigate the origin of property and recover the proceeds of crime. The measures in the Bill aim to strengthen the UK's fight against serious economic crime; to clarify the scope of UWO powers; and to increase and reinforce operational confidence in using UWO powers.

- amendments to strengthening of sanctions legislation

The UK government may now impose sanctions without having to determine whether there are "good reasons to pursue" their given purpose, or if sanctions are "a reasonable course of action for that purpose". The ECA also amends the Policing and Crime Act 2017 to introduce a "strict liability test" for civil monetary penalties arising from sanctions breaches, which came into effect on June 15, 2022.

17.3 Cybersecurity Laws

In the UK, there is no overarching comprehensive national cybersecurity law, although the European Union's General Data Protection Regulation (GDPR), in which the UK was a member party, came pretty close.[2] For government, businesses, and other private-sector organizations, the UK's General Data Protection Regulation (UK-GDPR), the Data Protection Act (2018), and the NIS Regulations make up the bulk of the law relating to cybersecurity law and risk mitigation in the UK. For individuals and malicious parties, the UK's Computer Misuse Act, which was implemented back in 1990, continues to be a primary law at the forefront of interpersonal digital privacy, even 30 years later.

Nonetheless, the below Acts exist(ed) in the overall UK screen board:

---

[2] https://ico.org.uk/for-organisations/dp-at-the-end-of-the-transition-period/data-protection-and-the-eu-in-detail/the-uk-gdpr/.

17.3.1   Computer Misuse Act of 1990 (Amended in 2006)

This Act prohibits hacking, unauthorized access to computer systems, and purposefully spreading malware. The Computer Misuse Act 1990 creates three distinct criminal offenses:

- Unauthorized access to computers, including the illicit copying of software held in any computer. This carries a penalty of up to six months' imprisonment or up to a £5000 fine and will be dealt with by a magistrate. This covers hobby hacking and, potentially, penetration testing.
- Unauthorized access with intent to commit or facilitate commission of further offenses (such as fraud or theft), which covers more serious cases of hacking with a criminal intent. The penalty is up to five years' imprisonment and an unlimited fine.
- Unauthorized modification of computer material, which includes the intentional and unauthorized destruction of software or data; the circulation of "infected" materials online ("viruses"); and the unauthorized addition of a password to a data file ("crypto viruses"). The penalty of up to five years' imprisonment and an unlimited fine.

17.3.2   The UK Data Protection Act of 1998 (as Amended in 2018)

The Data Protection Act 2018 (DPA ACT) is a domestic law governing the use of personal data and the flow of information in the UK. The Data Protection Act 2018 is the UK's third generation of data protection legislation.[3] It replaces the previous 1998 law by the same name and modernizes the country's legal framework in response to new technologies. It sets out the framework for data protection law in the UK. It updates and replaces the Data Protection Act 1998, and came into effect on 25 May 2018. Since the UK is no longer part of the EU, the European GDPR no longer has application domestically in the UK, and so the Data Protection Act of 2018 has been amended to accommodate the post-Brexit changes to UK data privacy law that have taken place. The Data Protection Act frames the role–jurisdiction, function, and powers–of the Information Commissioner (ICO) as the leading data protection

---

[3] Annie Greenley-Giudici (2022): UK Data Protection Act & GDPR: No More Confusion, https://trustarc.com/blog/2022/06/15/uk-data-protection-act-gdpr/.

authority (DPA) in the UK. Another difference is that the UK-GDPR is solely focused on the protection of the personal data of UK residents.

17.4   Cybersecurity in the Banking Industry

Cyberattacks are on the rise. With the increasing sophistication of cyber-criminals, banks and financial institutions need every advantage in the information security fight. In the UK, individual banks are responsible for protecting themselves and their customers against cyberattacks, and all cyberattacks must be reported. The UK's financial regulator has told banks to strengthen and test their defenses against the threat of Russian-sponsored cyberattacks as the stand-off over the future of Ukraine deepens.[4]

Furthermore, in the UK, the Senior Managers and Certification Regime (SM&CR) has applied to the banking sector since March 2016 and to dual regulated insurers since December 2018. Under the SM&CR, individuals who perform the 'Chief Operations' senior management function are required to have responsibility for managing the internal operations or technology of the firm or of a part of the firm. This includes responsibility for cybersecurity.[5] The UK government has increasingly demonstrated its commitment to investigating and prosecuting serious financial misconduct and has levied historic fines against financial services institutions that fall afoul of the country's AML regulations at all levels. Record fines against financial institutions such as NatWest and HSBC have all contributed to a climate of increasing AML enforcement actions. This festival of enforcement in the UK extends beyond Financial Conduct Authority (FCA)-led actions and include actions by other regulatory bodies such as the Solicitors Regulation Authority (SRA), which has fined one of the UK's most prestigious law firms the record amount of £232,500 (approximately $315,000) for failing to carry out the required level of due diligence or ongoing monitoring.

---

[4] Stephen Morris and Laura Noonan (2022): UK Regulator Warns Banks Over Threat of Russian-Sponsored Cyber-Attack, Financial Times, https://www.ft.com/content/4ea d59e6-260c-445d-850c-43f54c69bef9.

[5] Jonathan Herbst, Simon Lovegrove, Katie Stephen (2020): Cybersecurity: Not just an IT issue, But a Regulatory One Too, https://www.nortonrosefulbright.com/en/knowle dge/publications/b8178be8/cybersecurity-not-just-an-it-issue-but-a-regulatory-one-too.

17.4.1   The NatWest Case

In December 2021, NatWest was fined £264,772,619.95 (approximately $350 million) after the UK-based financial services provider was convicted of three offences of failing to comply with money laundering regulations. The charges against NatWest cover a range of failures including NatWest's failure to investigate and take action on money laundering "red flags" surrounding the activity of a commercial customer, who deposited approximately £365 million with the bank, of which around £264 million was in cash. This conviction and fine marks the first successful criminal prosecution under the MLR 20,071 by the FCA and the first prosecution under the MLR against a bank.

17.4.2   The HSBC Bank Plc Case

In December 2021, the FCA fined HSBC Bank plc (HSBC) a discounted amount of £63,946,800 (approximately $80 million) for several AML failures between 2010 and 2018, including a failure to improve its internal controls and risk assessment processes. Specifically, the FCA faulted HSBC, which uses automated processes to monitor transactions, for not: (1) considering whether scenarios used to identify indicators of money laundering of terrorist financing were adequate until 2014 and not conducting risk assessments for new scenarios until 2016; (2) appropriately testing and updating the system parameters used to flag suspicious activity; and (3) checking the accuracy and completeness of data in the monitoring systems. HSBC did not dispute the FCA's findings. HSBC received a 30% discount for agreeing "to settle at the earliest possible opportunity." HSBC also agreed to implement FCA-supervised remediation of its AML processes.

CHAPTER 18

AML/CFT and Cybersecurity Law in Canada

18.1 General

Canada's Anti-Money Laundering and Anti-Terrorist Financing (AML/ATF) Regime (the AML/ATF Regime), which was first established in 2000–2001, has been regularly upgraded to adapt and evolve to changes in its operating environment and changes to international standards. As Canada's financial intelligence unit and anti-money laundering and anti-terrorist financing regulator, the Financial Transactions and Reports Analysis Centre of Canada (FINTRAC) helps to combat money laundering, terrorist activity financing and threats to the security of Canada, while ensuring the protection of personal information under its control. FINTRAC is one of 13 federal departments and agencies that play a key role in Canada's Anti-Money Laundering and Anti-Terrorist Financing regime.[1] The AML regime is being bolstered by the introduction of a beneficial ownership registry in 2023.

---

[1] https://www.fintrac-canafe.gc.ca/fintrac-canafe/1-eng.

© The Author(s), under exclusive license to Springer Nature Switzerland AG 2023
F. I. Lessambo, *Anti-Money Laundering, Counter Financing Terrorism and Cybersecurity in the Banking Industry*, Palgrave Macmillan Studies in Banking and Financial Institutions,
https://doi.org/10.1007/978-3-031-23484-2_18

18.2   AML/CFT Laws

Canada's anti-money laundering and terrorist financing laws are primarily contained in two statutes: The Criminal Code and the Proceeds of Crime (Money Laundering) and Terrorist Financing Act (PCMLTA). The Criminal Code applies to all individuals and businesses. Under the Criminal Code, it is an offence to knowingly deal with any property or provide or facilitate any financial or related service for any terrorist activity or any terrorist group or "listed person" (i.e., a person or entity on a government or other agency list). The test for "knowledge" includes not being wilfully blind.

The PCMLTA applies to "reporting entities". These entities include financial institutions, credit unions, life insurance companies, loan companies, securities dealers, foreign exchange dealers, money services business, casinos, real estate brokers and developers. Under PCMLTA, reporting entities have four main obligations:

- establish a compliance program,
- identify and verify clients,
- maintain certain specified records, and
- Report certain specified transactions.

On April 27, 2022, FINTRAC imposed AML obligations on both crowd-funding platforms and entities that perform "payment functions" (i.e., PSPs). Therefore, both crowdfunding platforms and PSPs that perform MSB activities must[2]:

- register with FINTRAC;
- develop and maintain a compliance program;
- carry out KYC (know your customer) requirements, including verifying the identity of persons and entities for certain activities and transactions;
- keep certain records, including records related to transactions and client identification; and
- Report certain transactions to FINTRAC.

---

[2] Jack Frankli, Zain Rivzi, Gillian Stacey (2022): Filling the Gap: Scope of Canadian Anti-Money Laundering Laws Expanded, https://www.jdsupra.com/legalnews/fil ling-the-gap-scope-of-canadian-anti-1511836/.

Pursuant to subsection 9(2) of the Proceeds of Crime (Money Laundering) and Terrorist Financing Suspicious Transaction Reporting Regulations, "the person or entity shall send the report to the Centre as soon as practicable after they have taken measures that enable them to establish that there are reasonable grounds to suspect that the transaction or attempted transaction is related to the commission of a money laundering offence or a terrorist activity financing offence.[3]"

These measures include:

- screening for and identifying suspicious transactions;
- assessing the facts and context surrounding the suspicious transaction;
- linking ML/TF indicators to your assessment of the facts and context; and
- Explaining your grounds for suspicion in an STR, where you articulate how the facts, context and ML/TF indicators allowed you to reach your grounds for suspicion.

18.3   CYBERSECURITY IN CANADA

In Canada, data protection and cybersecurity are governed by a complex legal and regulatory framework. Canada's two departments responsible for securing and defending government information systems, and preventing and responding to cyber incidents on critical infrastructure are the Canadian Centre for Cyber Security (Cyber Centre) within the Communications Security Establishment and the National Cybercrime Coordination Unit (NC3) within the RCMP. The Canadian Criminal Code prohibits (i) any fraudulently and without color of right obtaining any computer service; or willful "mischief" to interfere with computer use or tamper with data; (ii) interception, access to electronic communications, but exceptions for consent ("express or implied") or to protect the network.

---

[3] Government of Canada (2021): Reporting Suspicious Transactions to FINTRAC, https://www.fintrac-canafe.gc.ca/guidance-directives/transaction-operation/Guide3/str-eng.

18.3.1   Personal Information Protection & Electronic Documents Act (PIPEDA) (2005)

PIPEDA aims to establish, in an era in which technology increasingly facilitates the circulation and exchange of information, rules to govern the collection, use and disclosure of personal information in a manner that recognizes the right of privacy of individuals with respect to their personal information and the need of organizations to collect, use or disclose personal information for purposes that a reasonable person would consider appropriate in the circumstances.[4]

PIPEDA applies to private-sector organizations across Canada that collect, use or disclose personal information in the course of a commercial activity. The law defines a commercial activity as any particular transaction, act, or conduct, or any regular course of conduct that is of a commercial character, including the selling, bartering or leasing of donor, membership or other fundraising lists. All businesses that operate in Canada and handle personal information that crosses provincial or national borders in the course of commercial activities are subject to PIPEDA, regardless of the province or territory in which they are based (including provinces with substantially similar legislation).

Under PIPEDA, personal information includes any factual or subjective information, recorded or not, about an identifiable individual. This includes information in any form, such as:

- age, name, ID numbers, income, ethnic origin, or blood type;
- opinions, evaluations, comments, social status, or disciplinary actions; and
- employee files, credit records, loan records, medical records, existence of a dispute between a consumer and a merchant, intentions

In June 2015, PIPEDA was amended to require that organizations notify the Office of the Privacy Commissioner of Canada (the "OPC"), affected individuals, and organizations or government institutions that may be able to reduce or mitigate the risk of harm, if it is reasonable to believe that a breach of the security safeguards protecting personal information poses a "real risk of significant harm" to the affected individuals. Moreover,

---

[4] Personal Information Protection and Electronic Documents Act, S.C. 2000, c. 5, Assented to 2000-04-13.

organizations are required to keep a record of all breaches. Knowingly failing to report or record a breach will be an offence punishable by fines of up to C$100,000. These new provisions have not yet come into force, but will become mandatory once the associated regulations have been enacted.

18.4   Cybersecurity Laws in the Banking Industry

Banks in Canada are at the forefront of the prevention and detection of cyber security threats and work closely with each other and with bank regulators, law enforcement and all levels of government to share best practices and other information to address the growing challenges posed by cybercrime.[5] Canadian Banks have sophisticated security systems in place to protect customers' personal and financial information. As part of a normal course of business, they actively monitor their networks and continuously conduct routine maintenance to help ensure that online threats do not harm their servers or disrupt service to customers. The banking industry provides active leadership to improve the resiliency of the financial sector against cyber threats, in partnership with key stakeholders within the government and law enforcement. The Bank of Canada has established critical foundational programs such as penetration testing and identity and access management, which have become core elements of the Bank's operations.[6]

[5] Canadian Banker Association (2022): Focus: Banks and Cyber Security, https://cba.ca/banks-and-cyber-security.

[6] Filipe Dinis (2022): Cyber Security Strategy 2022–24- Reducing Risk Promoting Resilience, https://www.bankofcanada.ca/wp-content/uploads/2022/02/2022%E2%80%932024-Cyber-Security-Strategy.pdf.

CHAPTER 19

AML/CFT and Cybersecurity Law in Australia

19.1 GENERAL

Australia has a strong institutional framework for combatting ML, TF, and proliferation financing. The Anti-Money Laundering and Counter-Terrorism Financing Act 2006 (AML/CTF Act) is the main piece of Australian government legislation that regulates AUSTRAC's functions. On December 17, 2020, the Australian Government passed the Anti-Money Laundering and Counter-Terrorism Financing and Other Legislation Amendment Bill 2020 (the Amendment), which introduces a raft of measures aimed at strengthening Australia's anti-money laundering and terrorism financing framework. The amendment introduces changes to customer identification procedures, correspondent banking relationships, tipping-off offences, access to information, and the cross-border movements of money. All private sector firms that provide designated financial services must register with AUSTRAC in order to obtain an operating license.

© The Author(s), under exclusive license to Springer Nature
Switzerland AG 2023
F. I. Lessambo, *Anti-Money Laundering, Counter Financing Terrorism and Cybersecurity in the Banking Industry*, Palgrave Macmillan Studies in Banking and Financial Institutions,
https://doi.org/10.1007/978-3-031-23484-2_19

19.2   AML/CFT Laws

Australia's anti-money laundering efforts are guided by international legal obligations and the International Standards on Combating Money Laundering and the Financing of Terrorism and Proliferation as defined by FATF. Money laundering and terrorism are criminalized under Division 400 of the Commonwealth Criminal.[1]

19.3   Code

19.3.1   *The Anti-Money Laundering and Counter-Terrorism Financing Act 2006*

The AML/CTF Act provides the means to help detect and deter money laundering and terrorism financing. It also provides financial intelligence to revenue and law enforcement agencies. The AML/CTF Act 2006 establishes a risk-based regulatory framework in which certain businesses that offer 'designated services' are required to identify their customers and their customers' financial activities that might pose a high risk of involvement in money laundering or financing of terrorism and report these to AUSTRAC.[2] It imposes 5 key obligations on regulated businesses:

- Enrollment: all regulated businesses need to enroll with AUSTRAC and provide prescribed enrollment details
- establishing and maintaining an AML/CTF program to help identify, mitigate, and manage the money laundering and terrorism financing risks a business faces
- customer due diligence: identifying and verifying the customer's identity, and ongoing monitoring of transactions
- reporting: notifying authorities of suspicious matters, threshold transactions, and international funds transfer instructions

[1] Doron Goldbarsht (2021): The Adequacy and Efficacy of Australia's Anti-money Laundering and Counter-Terrorism Financing (AML/CTF) Regime. See also: Mathew Leighton-Daly, Money Laundering Offences: Out with Certainty, in with Discretion? Revenue Law Journal, Volume 24, Issue 1, 2015, p. 1.

[2] Julie Walters, Russell G Smith, Brent Davis (2012): The Anti-money Laundering and Counter-Terrorism Financing Regime in Australia: Perceptions of Regulated Businesses in Australia, AIC Reports Research and PUBLIC Policy Series 117, https://www.aic.gov.au/sites/default/files/2020-05/rpp117.pdf.

  – record keeping: businesses are required to keep records of transactions, customer identification, electronic funds transfer instructions, and details of AML/CTF programs.

On 3 April 2018, the AML/CTF Act was amended to include a new designated service applicable to cryptocurrency products. Persons who exchange digital currency for money or exchange money for digital currency, where the exchange is provided in the course of carrying on a digital currency exchange business, are REs and must comply with the AML/CTF Act. Providers of this designated service must also register on the Digital Currency Exchange Register maintained by AUSTRAC. The regulations thereof required digital currency exchanges (DCEs) to register with AUSTRAC, to collect and store information on customer identity, to report suspicious activity, and to report all transactions over AUD 10,000.[3]

19.4   Cybersecurity Laws

19.4.1   Telecommunications (Interception and Access) Act 1979

The TIA Act protects the privacy of Australians by prohibiting interception of communications and access to stored communications. The privacy of Australians is also protected by the Telecommunications Act 1997, which prohibits telecommunications service providers from disclosing information about their customers' use of telecommunications services. The TIA Act sets out certain exceptions to these prohibitions to permit eligible Australian law enforcement and security agencies (agencies) to:

  – obtain warrants to intercept communications;
  – obtain warrants to access stored communications; and
  – authorize the disclosure of data.

---

[3] Alicia Schmidt (2022): Virtual Assets: Compelling a New Anti-money Laundering and Counter-Terrorism Financing Regulatory Model, International Journal of Law and Information Technology, Volume 29, Issue 4, Winter 2021, pp. 332–363, https://doi.org/10.1093/ijlit/eaac001.

19.4.2   *Privacy Act 1998 (Amended 2017)*

The Privacy Act 1988 regulates information privacy in the Commonwealth public sector and the national private sector. It covers personal information and sensitive in formation (i.e., health information, ethnicity, sexual preference, trade union membership).[4] It was amended in 2017. The Privacy Amendment (Notifiable Data Breaches) Act 2017 imposes mandatory data breach notification on Australian Privacy Principle (APP) entities, when there has been an eligible data breach. Data breaches occur where there is either (i) an unauthorized access to, or unauthorized disclosure of, personal information about one or more individuals (affected individuals), or (ii) where personal information of affected individuals is lost in circumstances that may give rise to unauthorized access or unauthorized disclosure. Failure to comply exposes entities to penalties, including fines of $360,000 for individuals and $1.8 million for organizations.

19.4.3   *Assistance and Access Act (AA Act, as Amended in 2018)*

The Assistance and Access Act allows law enforcement and security agencies to seek assistance from the full scope of companies that supply communications services and devices in Australia. The 2018 amendment to the Act empowers law enforcement and national security agencies to request, or compel, assistance from telecommunications providers. It also established powers which enable law enforcement and intelligence agencies to obtain warrants to access data and devices, and amended the search warrant framework under the Crimes Act and the Customs Act to expand the ability of criminal law enforcement agencies to collect evidence from electronic devices.

19.4.4   *Consumer Data Right*

On November 26, 2017, the Australian Government introduced Consumer Data Right (CDR), which gives consumers greater access to and control over their data and improves consumers' ability to compare

---

[4] David Watts, Pompeu Casanovas (2018): Privacy and Data Protection in Australia: A Critical Overview (extended abstract), pp. 1–5, https://www.w3.org/2018/vocabws/papers/watts-casanovas.pdf.

and switch between products and services. The Consumer Data Right (CDR) is a secure online system that enables consumers to get value from data that is collected about them through the provision of specific goods and services by consenting to that data being shared with trusted accredited third parties. CDC is available to consumers who are 18 or older. Small, medium, and large businesses can use the Consumer Data Right (i.e., to manage their bills or for bookkeeping and accounting).

19.4.5   *The Security of Critical Infrastructure Act 2018 (SOCI) (Amended in 2021)*

The Security of Critical Infrastructure Act 2018 (the Act) aims to manage the complex and evolving national security risks of sabotage, espionage, and coercion posed by foreign involvement in Australia's critical infrastructure. The SOCI Act was amended to strengthen the security and resilience of critical infrastructure by expanding the sectors and asset classes the SOCI Act applies to, and to introduce new obligations. The Act applies to 22 asset classes across eleven sectors including: communications, data storage or processing, defense, energy, financial services and markets, food and grocery, health care and medical, higher education and research, space technology, transport, water, and sewerage. In March 2022, additional amendments to the SOCI Act introduced the following key measures:

- a new obligation for responsible entities to create and maintain a critical infrastructure risk management program (the Minister for Home Affairs will consult with industry before the rules are made setting out the requirements for a risk management program) and
- a new framework for enhanced cybersecurity obligations required for operators of systems of national significance (SoNS), Australia's most important critical infrastructure assets (the Minister for Home Affairs will consult with impacted entities before any declarations are made).

19.4.6   *The Consumer Privacy Protection Bill (CPPA) (2022)*

Introduced on June 16, 2022, the CPPA aims to modernize Canada's now 22-year-old Personal Information Protection and Electronic Documents Act (PIPEDA) with the Consumer Privacy Protection Act (CPPA).

If passed, CPPA would strengthen the rights of data subjects and significantly alter the obligations of organizations who collect, use, or disclose personal information. It would also create a new tribunal to handle privacy matters.

19.5   Cybersecurity Laws in the Banking Industry

The Consumer Data Right was introduced in the banking sector in July 2020 and will be rolled out across other sectors of the economy. Banks with a significant customer base but relative lower revenue numbers, such as several regional banks, have a high risk of a data breach.[5]

---

[5] Simone Fox Koob (2022): Cyberattack on Australian Bank Could Threaten Financial System, but Risk Is Low, The Sydney Morning Herald, https://www.smh.com.au/business/banking-and-finance/cyberattack-on-australian-bank-could-threaten-financial-system-but-risk-is-low-20221005-p5bng1.html.

CHAPTER 20

AML/CFT and Cybersecurity Laws in Russia

20.1 General

Russia is generally perceived as a source country for proceeds of crime, and is not a major center for laundering the proceeds of crime committed in other countries. The Russian Federation (Russia) has an in-depth understanding of its money laundering and terrorist financing risks and has established policies and laws to address these risks. The Federal Financial Monitoring Service (FFMS) is the main AML/CTF supervisory authority that conducts financial intelligence investigations, collects data, and monitors transactions of controlled entities in accordance with the AML Law.

Other authorities monitor compliance with the AML Law as part of their competences, including the Central Bank of Russia (the CBR), the Federal Tax Service, the Federal Bailiff Service, and the Federal Customs Service. Under the Central Bank of Russia Law and the Banking Law, the CBR is responsible for regulating banking activities and is authorized to adopt mandatory regulations concerning banking and currency operations.

© The Author(s), under exclusive license to Springer Nature   169
Switzerland AG 2023
F. I. Lessambo, *Anti-Money Laundering, Counter Financing Terrorism and Cybersecurity in the Banking Industry*, Palgrave Macmillan Studies in Banking and Financial Institutions,
https://doi.org/10.1007/978-3-031-23484-2_20

20.2   AML/CFT Laws

The Federal Financial Monitoring Service ("the FFMS") is the main AML/CTF Supervisory authority in Russia. The other authorities that monitor compliance in Russia with the AML law as part of their competences include the following: (i) the Central Bank of Russia ("the CBR"); (ii) the Federal Tax Service; (iii) the Federal Bailiff Service; and the Federal Customs Service. Federal Law No. 115-FZ is the primary legislative act in the Russian Federation. Federal Law No. 115-FZ "On Combating Money Laundering and the Financing of Terrorism" (the "AML Law") came into force on February 1, 2002, and has been revised a number of times to reflect the global developments in this area. It aims to prevent money laundering activities and the financing of terrorism, and is supported by numerous recommendations, binding instructions, and regulations of the CBR and other authorities.[1] The Bank of Russia regulates the activities of credit institutions and non-credit financial institutions in the field of AML/CFT/CFPWMD and monitors and oversees the compliance with statutory requirements by these entities. To that end, credit institutions and non-credit financial institutions are required to implement a wide range of measures aimed at preventing the use of the Russian financial system for illegal purposes.[2]

20.3   Cybersecurity Laws

The two main legislations are: The Federal Law No. 152-FZ dated 27 July 2006 "On Personal Data" (the "Data Protection Law"), and The Labor Code of the Russian Federation (for personal data of employees).

20.3.1   The Federal Law No. 152-FZ Dated 27 July 2006 "On Personal Data" (the "Data Protection Law")

The Personal Data Law covers almost all aspects of data protection: what is considered personal data, what types of data can be collected and

---

[1] Konstantin Baranov, Elena Tchoubykina (2020): Anti-Money Laundering Laws in Russia, https://seamless.legal/en/rus/publication/doing-business-in-russia-2020/banking-sector/the-anti-money-laundering-law.

[2] Bank of Russia (2022): Countering Money Laundering and Currency Control, https://www.cbr.ru/eng/counteraction_m_ter/.

processed, how and in what cases can data be collected and processed, and what technical and organizational measures must be applied by companies or individuals that collect data. Any individual or entity working with personal data is considered a personal data operator and is thus governed by the Personal Data Law. In 2014, the Russian parliament adopted amendments to the Personal Data Law (that then became known as the Data Localization Law) that require data operators that collect Russian citizens' personal data to store and process such personal data using databases located in Russia. Subsequent amendments require companies that provide video, audio, or text communication services (usually 'messengers') to register with the authorities, to store users' messages or audio or video calls for up to six months, and to provide the security authorities with decryption keys if the messages are encrypted.

20.3.2   The Labor Code of the Russian Federation (for Personal Data of Employees)

The main objectives of the labor law shall be creating the necessary legal conditions for achieving an optimal harmonization of the parties to labor relations' interests, the state's interests as well as legal regulation of labor relations and other relations directly linked to them as for[3]:

- organization of labor and management of labor;
- job placement with a specific employer;
- professional training, re-training, and skill improvement of employees directly at a certain employer's facilities;
- social partnership, collective bargaining, concluding collective contracts and agreements;
- participation of employees and of labor unions in determining working conditions and in applying the labor law in the cases stipulated by the law;
- material liability of employers and employees in the sphere of labor;
- surveillance and control (including control by labor unions) of compliance with the labor law (including the law on occupational safety); and

---

[3] Russian Federation—LABOR CODE OF THE RUSSIAN FEDERATION OF 31 DECEMBER 2001 (Federal Law No. 197-FZ of 2001).

– settlement of labor disputes.

20.4   CYBERSECURITY IN THE BANKING INDUSTRY

On April 16, 2019, Russia adopted the Runet Isolation Law, which came into force on November 1, 2019.[4] Under this law, the DPA received broad powers to control the internet. In 2019, Russia signed the Protocol to the Council of Europe Convention No. 108. It is expected new amendments to the Personal Data Law that would harmonize the law with Convention No. 108.

---

[4] Vyacheslav Khayryuzov (2021): The Privacy, Data Protection and Cybersecurity Law Review: Russia, Law Review, https://thelawreviews.co.uk/title/the-privacy-data-protection-and-cybersecurity-law-review/russia.

CHAPTER 21

AML/CFT and Cybersecurity Laws in Turkey

21.1 GENERAL

The main legislation against money laundering activities in Turkey is the Law on Prevention of Money Laundering No. 4208 dated November 11, 1996 ('Money Laundering Law'). The Financial Crimes Investigation Board (MASAK) is an intelligence agency that helps create an efficient economy and a crime-free society by combating laundering illicit proceeds and corruption effectively. MASAK imposes administrative fines on organizations that do not fulfill their anti-money laundering obligations in accordance with Article 13 of Law No. 5549. The Law on the Prevention of the Funding of Terrorism (No. 6415), passed by the Turkish government in February 2013, expanded the definition of terrorist financing offenses and gave authorities an additional legal authority to prosecute cases of alleged terrorist financing.

21.2 AML/CFT LAWS

21.2.1 Law No. 5549 on the Prevention of the Laundering of the Proceeds of Crime

The main legislation in Turkey regarding the prevention of money laundering is the Law on Prevention of Laundering Proceeds of Crime No.

© The Author(s), under exclusive license to Springer Nature Switzerland AG 2023
F. I. Lessambo, *Anti-Money Laundering, Counter Financing Terrorism and Cybersecurity in the Banking Industry*, Palgrave Macmillan Studies in Banking and Financial Institutions, https://doi.org/10.1007/978-3-031-23484-2_21

173

5549 developed upon the recommendations of The Financial Action Task Force. Article 5 of Law No. 5549 addresses the regulations that determine the procedures and principles of taking necessary measures including training, internal auditing, and control and risk management systems on a risk-based approach.[1]

- The Law on the Prevention of the Financing of the Proliferation of Weapons of Mass Destruction No. 7262.
- Law No. 6415 on the Prevention of the Financing of terrorism.
- Banking Law No. 5411.

21.3   CYBERSECURITY LAWS

The National Cybersecurity Strategy and Action Plan 2013–2014 was the first comprehensive strategic planning document in the field of cybersecurity in Turkey and was published in the Official Gazette in June 2013.[2] Nonetheless, the Constitution and subsequent laws lay the foundation of Cybersecurity in Turkey.

21.3.1   The Constitution of the Turkish Republic

The Turkish Constitution does not directly set out any provision on cybersecurity. However, as cybersecurity is an umbrella term for both personal and non-personal data protection, it can be considered that cybersecurity is partly and indirectly set out under (i) Article 20(3), which provides the right to protection of personal data and (ii) Article 22, which provides the freedom of communication, as an individual right to any person.

Article 20(3) states: "Unless there exists a decision duly passed by a judge in cases explicitly defined by law, and unless there exists an order of an agency authorized by law in cases where delay is deemed prejudicial, neither the person himself nor any private papers, nor any belongings of an individual may be searched, nor may they be seized."

[1] Altug Ozgun, Burcu Seven (2021): Six Legal Requirements for Organizations in Turkey to Prevent Money Laundering, https://www.lexology.com/library/detail.aspx?g=e25a7bde-9d0d-4df1-95ba-440d33e84cbd.

[2] Emre Halisdemir (2021): National Cybersecurity Organization: TURKEY, pp. 1–22, https://ccdcoe.org/uploads/2021/08/TUR_country_report_final_clean_ver_2408.pdf.

In the same vein, Article 22 expands to state:

> Everyone has the right to freedom of communication. Secrecy of communication is fundamental. Communication shall not be impeded nor its secrecy be violated, unless there exists a decision duly passed by a judge in cases explicitly defined by law, and unless there exists an order of an agency authorized by law in cases where delay is deemed prejudicial. Public establishments or institutions where exceptions to the above may be applied will be defined by law.

21.3.2   The Data Protection Laws

The Data Protection Law provides the guidelines, in line with the constitutional principles protecting privacy and confidentiality of personal life, applicable to the processing of personal data. The Data Protection Law which is modeled after European Union practices is applicable to any entity that processes, for any reason, any kind of personal data of real persons. Personal data must be maintained only for the time required by the relevant legislation or for the purpose for which it is processed. The Law set up a special "Board," the Data Protection Board (KVKK) as the ultimate authority responsible for enforcing the Data Protection Law and resolving complaints against data controllers arising out of alleged breaches of the Data Protection Law, has clarified that an explicit consent request must be sufficiently informative in nature. Certain data as classified as "sensitive," which must be processed based on the data subject's explicit consent or if allowed by law. This category includes data relating to race, ethnic origin, political opinion, philosophical belief, religion, sect and other beliefs, clothing, membership in associations, foundations or trade unions, health, sexual life, criminal record and biometric, and genetic features.

21.3.3   Internet Law No. 5651 of 2007

The Turkish government passed its first internet-specific legislation in 2007: Law No. 5651, Regulation of Publications on the Internet and Suppression of Crimes Committed by Means of Such Publications. This law, briefly known as the Internet Law, defined important concepts related to internet governance, provided a list of "internet" crimes and established the legal framework for banning websites. Law No. 5651 established the Telecommunications Communication Presidency (TIB) as the organization responsible for monitoring internet content and executing blocking orders issued by judges and public prosecutors.[3] The law also provided a catalogue of crimes with reference to the provisions of the Turkish Penal Code (TCK) and other related laws. In July 2020, Law No. 5651 was amended by the new Internet Law (No. 7253), which imposes new obligations for content and hosting providers, add port numbers to the monitoring scope of traffic information, and introduce a version of the right to be forgotten.

21.3.4   Law on Electronic Communication No. 5809 ("Law No. 5809")

The Electronic Communications Law has been published in the Official Gazette in Turkey on November 10, 2008. It aims to create effective competition, to ensure the protection of consumer rights, to promote the deployment of services throughout the country, to ensure efficient and effective use of the resources, to promote the new investments and technological developments in communications infrastructure, network and services through regulations and inspections in electronic communications sector and to determine relevant principles and procedures thereto. Article 12(5) of the Electronic Communication Law regulates rights and obligations of the operators by stating "the operators are obliged to build the technical infrastructure to provide electronic communications services by meeting the relevant obligations related to national security and the regulations of Laws No. 5397, No. 5651 and other relevant Laws. Operators, which have already been providing electronic communications services, are obliged to build the technical infrastructure with the same conditions within a period of time prescribed by the Authority, undertaking all necessary expenses."

---

[3] Gülcin Balamir Coskun (2021): Turkey's New Internet Law and Its Effects on Freedom of Media, https://www.resetdoc.org/story/turkey-internet-law-freedom-media/.

21.3.5   *Turkish Criminal Code No. 5237*

Article 282 of Turkish Criminal Law No. 5237 states:

- A person who transfers abroad the proceeds obtained from an offence requiring a minimum penalty of six months or more imprisonment, or processes such proceeds in various ways in order to conceal the illicit source of such proceeds or to give the impression that they have been legitimately acquired shall be sentenced to imprisonment from three years up to seven years and a judicial fine up to twenty thousand days.
- A person who, without participating in the commitment of the offence mentioned in paragraph (1), purchases, acquires, possesses or uses the proceeds which is the subject of that offence knowing the nature of the proceeds shall be sentenced to imprisonment from two years up to five years.
- Where this offence is committed by a public officer or professional person in the course of his duty then the penalty to be imposed shall be increased one half.
- Where this offence is conducted in the course of the activities of an organization established for the purpose of committing an offence, the penalty to be imposed shall be doubled.
- Where a legal entity is involved in the commission of this offence it shall be subject to security measures.
- In relation to the offences defined in this article, no penalty shall be imposed upon a person who directly enables the securing of financial assets, or who facilitates the securing of such assets, by informing the relevant authorities of the location of such before the commencement of a prosecution.

21.4   Cybersecurity Laws in the Banking Industry

21.4.1   *Banking Law No. 5411*

Law No. 5411 aims to regulate the principles and procedures of ensuring confidence and stability in financial markets, the efficient functioning of the credit system and the protection of the rights and interests of depositors. Article 2 of the Law states:

"The depos it banks, participation banks, development and investment banks, the branches in Turkey of such institutions established abroad, financial holding companies, Banks Association of Turkey, Participation Banks Association of Turkey, Banking Regulation and Supervision Agency, Savings Deposit Insurance Fund and their activities shall be subject to provisions of this law.

The provisions of this law shall also apply to banks that have been established as per their special laws, on the condition to preserve the provisions of their special laws."

In 2020, Banking Law No. 5411 was amended. The Amendment covers various topics such as the scope of the risk group of banks, new regulations regarding loans and administrative fines. Article 73 of the Banking Law No. 5411 ("Law") authorizes the Banking Regulatory and Supervisory Authority ("BRSA") to determine the scope, form, procedures, and principles regarding the sharing and transferring of client information.

CHAPTER 22

AML/CFT and Cybersecurity Laws in Brazil

22.1 General

Brazil (GOB) has a comprehensive Anti-Money Laundering (AML) regulatory regime in place. In 1998, the GOB enacted Law 9.613 criminalizing money laundering related to drug trafficking.[1] Brazil's Law 9.613 provides information for crimes related to money laundering or the concealment of assets, rights, and valuables. This and other laws require financial institutions to train their employees on how to recognize suspicious activity that may be tied to money laundering or terrorist financing activities.

22.2 AML/CFT Laws

AML requirements under Brazilian law are set forth in Law No 9.613, of March 3, 1998 ('Law 9.613/98'). In 2012, Law 9.613/98 was amended and updated by Law No 12,683, of July 9, 2012 ('Law 12,683/12'), making the rules broader and more stringent. Such laws establish that

---

[1] Anti-Money Laundering (AML) in Brazil, http://bankersacademy.com/resources/free-tutorials/57-ba-free-tutorials/626-aml-brazil.

© The Author(s), under exclusive license to Springer Nature Switzerland AG 2023
F. I. Lessambo, *Anti-Money Laundering, Counter Financing Terrorism and Cybersecurity in the Banking Industry*, Palgrave Macmillan Studies in Banking and Financial Institutions,
https://doi.org/10.1007/978-3-031-23484-2_22

AML rules are applicable to financial institutions and to a comprehensive list of entities engaging in financial and payment-related activities including, among others, companies rendering consulting, accounting, auditing, advisory, as well as assistance or accessory services, of any nature, in financial transactions.[2]

22.2.1   Law No. 12,683, of July 9, 2012 ('Law 12,683/12')

Law No. 12,683 amends the law that provides, inter alia, for the punishment of crimes involving money laundering as well as concealment of the utilization of assets, legal rights, and valuables resulting from criminal acts. It removes the list of previous offenses, allowing to configure the concealing or hiding of the origin of proceeds from any crime or misdemeanor, such as illegal lottery games and the exploitation of slot machines, as money laundering crimes.[3] It also broadens the list of persons required to send information about suspicious transactions to the Council for Financial Activities Control Council for Financial Activities Control (COAF) and reaches, for example, money changers, people who negotiate rights of athletes or sell luxury goods, among other activities. Moreover, it raises the limit of the fine to be imposed on those who disobey the obligations of transmission of information, from approximately USD$100,000 to USD$10 million.[4]

22.3   Cybersecurity Laws

Brazil does not have a cybersecurity-specific regulator. Different regulatory agencies deal with cybersecurity regulations. These regulatory

---

[2] José Luiz Homem de Mello, Ricardo Binnie, Ana Cristina do Val Fausto (..): The New Regulatory Framework for AML in Brazil, International Bar Association, https://www.ibanet.org/article/D7273F5F-ABAF-4B44-90AB-16CF5095FBB6.

[3] UNODC (2012): Brazil Moves Forward in the Fight Against Money Laundering, https://www.unodc.org/lpo-brazil/en/frontpage/2012/07/10-brasil-avanca-no-combate-a-lavagem-de-dinheiro.html.

[4] UNODC (2012): Brazil Moves Forward in the Fight Against Money Laundering, https://www.unodc.org/lpo-brazil/en/frontpage/2012/07/10-brasil-avanca-no-combate-a-lavagem-de-dinheiro.html.

agencies include the Central Bank, the Securities and Exchange Commission, the National Telecommunications Agency, and the Brazilian Private Insurance Authority.

The regulatory authority for cybercrime is the Ministry of Justice and Public Security. There are no dedicated laws related specifically to cybersecurity in Brazil.[5] However:

- The Consumer Code and the Internet Act provide for certain principles and rules;
- The Criminal Code (Decree Law 2,848/1940) establishes the crime of "invasion" of a computing device;
- LGPD extends to any category of personal data (both offline and online).

Despite the lack of cybersecurity-specific law or regulator, an "E-Ciber" strategy was introduced in 2020:

- It aims to make Brazil into a "country of excellence" in the sector;
- It has set out ten strategic ways to strengthen the cybersecurity arena, including: centralization of the national cybersecurity system; an increase in international cooperation; an improvement in cyber governance in both the public and private sectors; and enhanced protection of critical infrastructure;
- It also envisages the creation of a new cybersecurity law (yet to materialize).

22.4   CYBERSECURITY IN THE BANKING INDUSTRY

Under Law 9,613/98, as amended, the Central Bank enacted certain regulations specifically related to compliance and adoption of AML controls. Currently, the main banking AML regulation is Circular No 3,461, dated July 24, 2009 ('Circular 3,461/09'), which concentrates

---

[5] Carolina Vaissman Uribe (2021): Data Protection and Cybersecurity Laws in Brazil, CMS, https://cms.law/en/int/expert-guides/cms-expert-guide-to-data-protection-and-cyber-security-laws/brazil.

the AML rules and procedures that must be adopted by financial institutions and other institutions authorized by the Central Bank. This rule was recently reviewed and will be replaced from October 1, 2020, by Circular No 3,978, of January 23, 2020 ('Circular 3,978/2020'). The first provides a more detailed AML procedure, while the last focuses on a risk-based approach.[6]

[6] José Luiz Homem de Mello, Ricardo Binnie, Ana Cristina do Val Fausto (..): The New Regulatory Framework for AML in Brazil, International Bar Association, https://www.ibanet.org/article/D7273F5F-ABAF-4B44-90AB-16CF5095FBB6.

CHAPTER 23

AML/CFT and Cybersecurity Laws in Mexico

23.1 General

In Mexico, money laundering and terrorism financing are federal crimes. Mexico is a risky area for money laundering and other crimes. The Mexican government has identified money laundering and other crimes and aimed to prevent their occurrences. Enforcement of money laundering crimes may occur at both the national or local levels. Most local (state-level) regulation regarding money laundering crimes overlaps with the regulation applicable at national level. Mexico has an institutional framework in place to investigate and prosecute terrorism financing, with an ad hoc unit, the Specialized Unit on Terrorism, Arms Stockpiling, and Trafficking (UEITA). However, this unit does not have protocols or manuals containing guidelines for the clear identification and prioritization of potential terrorism financing cases.[1] The SHCP[2] is the body responsible for the overall regulation of compliance with AML/CFT

---

[1] IMF (2017): IMF Country Report No. 17/405 Mexico Detailed Assessment Report—Anti-Money Laundering and Combating the Financing of Terrorism, http://www.imf.org/external/np/exr/facts/aml.htm.

[2] Ministry of Finance and Public Credit.

© The Author(s), under exclusive license to Springer Nature Switzerland AG 2023
F. I. Lessambo, *Anti-Money Laundering, Counter Financing Terrorism and Cybersecurity in the Banking Industry*, Palgrave Macmillan Studies in Banking and Financial Institutions, https://doi.org/10.1007/978-3-031-23484-2_23

183

obligations, but operational responsibility is delegated by statute to the CNBV,[3] CNSF, CONSAR, and SAT, respectively.

23.2   AML/CFT LAWS

Mexico's official AML law came into force in 2013. This law aims to prevent illegal income and protect the national economy. It also plays an effective role in preventing crimes such as drug trafficking, fraud, corruption, and tax evasion.

In May, 2018, Mexico's Federal Law for the Prevention and Identification of Transactions with Resources of Illicit Origin (commonly referred to as the Anti-Money Laundering Law) was amended in order to regulate transactions with "virtual assets"—that is, cryptocurrencies.[4] The new law defines virtual assets as representations of value electronically registered and utilized by the public as a means of payment for all types of legal transactions, which may be transferred only electronically. It also provides that Mexico's legal currency may not, under any circumstances, be considered a virtual asset. (Id.) Providing services involving virtual assets is an activity classified by this Law as vulnerable to money laundering. Thus, providers of such services must report to the Mexican government relevant transactions that reach or exceed a particular amount (equivalent to approximately US$2,638 as of May 2018) starting in September 2019. (Id.)

Furthermore, providers of such services will have a number of additional duties, including:

- identifying their clients and verifying their identity through official identification documents, a copy of which must be kept by the provider;
- asking the client for information on his or her occupation if a business relationship is established; and
- Keeping records pertaining to transactions and clients (Id. arts. 17, 18).

---

[3] National Banking and Securities Commission.

[4] Library of Congress (2018): Mexico: Amendment to Anti-Money Laundering Law Pertaining to Cryptocurrencies, https://www.loc.gov/item/global-legal-monitor/2018-05-22/mexico-amendment-to-anti-money-laundering-law-pertaining-to-cryptocurrencies/.

Regulations further detailing pertinent requirements for financial companies were published in August 2018.

23.3 CYBERSECURITY LAWS

The cost of cybercrime incidents in the world has gone from US$3 trillion in early 2015 to a projected US$6 trillion by 2021. Mexico's National Cybersecurity Strategy sets forth a guide toward 2030 and aims to prepare the country for future activities in an increasingly complex digital world. The Strategy aims to place Mexico as a resilient nation in Cyberspace. It is broad reaching and general to stand as a guide to new activity over time.[5] Several cover the cybersecurity laws in Mexico, including:

23.3.1 *The Mexican Constitution*

Article 16 paragraph 2 of the Mexican Constitution provides:

> All people have the right to enjoy protection on his personal data, and to access, correct, and cancel such data. All people have the right to oppose the disclosure of his data, according to the law. The law shall establish exceptions to the criteria that rule the handling of data, due to national security reasons, law and order, public security, public health, or protection of third party's rights.

Adding to the aforementioned, paragraph 12 goes on to state:

> Private communications shall not be breached. The law shall punish any action against the liberty and privacy of such communications, except when they are voluntarily given by one of the individuals involved in them. A judge shall assess the implications of such communications, provided they contain information related to the perpetration of a crime. Communications that violate confidentiality established by law shall not be admitted in any case.

---

[5] Luisa Parraguez (2017): The State of Cybersecurity in Mexico: An Overview, at: https://www.researchgate.net/publication/315728675.

23.3.2   The Data Protection Law

The Federal Law on the Protection of Personal Data held by Private Parties (the "Data Protection Law") entered into force on July 6, 2010. It requires data controllers to have in place appropriate administrative, technical, and physical safeguards to ensure the protection of personal data.

- The Federal Law on Transparency and Access to Public Information;
- The General Law on Transparency and Access to Public Information;
- The Federal Labor Law;
- The Federal Criminal Code;
- The Law of the National Security Guard;
- The National Strategy of Cybersecurity 2017; and
- The White Paper on National Defense of the Mexican State.

23.4   Cybersecurity Laws in the Banking Industry

Mexico's financial sector is dominated by banks and highly concentrated around conglomerate structures, which usually include a bank and entities in the insurance and securities sector.[6] Banks are most at threat, but other sectors are vulnerable to money laundering activities as well. Banks dominate the financial sector, handle a high volume of transactions, and are well interconnected to the international financial system. The banking sector, in particular, the seven largest banks (G-7) pose the highest money laundering risks followed by brokerage firms (which offer money/value transfer services and handle large amounts of cash in U.S. dollars) and various money service providers (e.g., exchange houses, exchange centers, and money transmitters), due to the types of activities and services performed. The G-7 banks account for about 80% of total bank assets. The G-7 banks all have product and service risk characteristics (e.g., cash transactions, exchange transactions, domestic and foreign transfers, transactions through commission agents may be executed, products or services that make it possible for at least one of the parties in the transaction not to be identified). Brokerage firms and DNFBPs,

---

[6] IMF (2017): IMF Country Report No. 17/405 Mexico Detailed Assessment Report—Anti-Money Laundering and Combating the Financing of Terrorism, http://www.imf.org/external/np/exr/facts/aml.htm.

notably notaries and real estate agents, are involved in a high volume of transactions and are exposed to ML threats.[7] On June 21, 2020, the CNBV enacted extraordinary KYC simplification measures for AML/CFT purposes applicable to banks and legal entities authorized to give loans as their main corporate purpose that have patrimonial ties to financial groups (Sociedades Financieras de Objeto Múltiple Reguladas).

[7] IMF (2017): IMF Country Report No. 17/405 Mexico Detailed Assessment Report—Anti-Money Laundering and Combating the Financing of Terrorism, http://www.imf.org/external/np/exr/facts/aml.htm.

CHAPTER 24

AML/CFT and Cybersecurity Laws in Argentina

24.1 GENERAL

Argentina has successfully made significant progress in strengthening the anti-money laundering and counter-terrorist financing framework. It was not until march 2005 that Argentina enacted the Law 26,026 thereby approving the United Nations International Convention on Combating the Financing of Terrorism. In June 2007, the Argentine Congress passed legislation (Law No. 26,268) criminalizing terrorism and terrorist financing, and establishing terrorist financing as a predicate offense for money laundering.

24.2 AML/CFT LAWS

In April of 2000, the Anti-Money Laundering Law No. 25,246 was implemented. The new Law established of a functionally independent Financial Information Unit (UIF) within the Ministry of Justice and Human Rights of the Nation and a more stringent regulatory framework for the financial industry and a list of individuals and companies responsible for reporting suspicious activities to the Financial Information Unit. Beside the Financial Information Unit, the Argentine Central

© The Author(s), under exclusive license to Springer Nature Switzerland AG 2023
F. I. Lessambo, *Anti-Money Laundering, Counter Financing Terrorism and Cybersecurity in the Banking Industry*, Palgrave Macmillan Studies in Banking and Financial Institutions, https://doi.org/10.1007/978-3-031-23484-2_24

Bank (BCRA) plays a prominent role in anti-money laundering and counter-terrorist financing issues.

24.2.1   Resolution 30-E/2017 on AML/CFT

On June 16, 2017, the Financial Information Unit passed Resolution 30-E/2017 revoking Resolution 121/2011 on anti-money laundering and the financing of terrorism (AML/FT). Resolution 30-E/2017, which replaces FIU resolution No. 121/2011, aims at financial entities and foreign currency exchange offices. Under Resolution No. 30-E/2017, these entities are required to categorize their clients by low, medium, and high risk; in accordance with the level of risk of their clients, products and services, distribution channels, and geographic area.[1] Moreover, the aforementioned entities must implement a system to prevent money laundering and financing of terrorism, which must include the policies, procedures and controls for identifying, assessing, mitigating, and monitoring the entities' risks of ML/FT. Furthermore, the Resolution establishes mitigation measures, which must be adopted in accordance with the classification of risks and the statement of risk tolerance related to ML/FT. It is worth mentioning that the Resolution authorizes the aforementioned entities to outsource the identification and verification of the identity of their client.

24.3   CYBERSECURITY LAWS

Though Cybersecurity is a relevant topic for executives within the financial sector; specifically banks,[2] it is not yet regulated in Argentina. However, there are some regulations enacted by the National Central

---

[1] Canosa Abogados (2017): Argentina: AML Rules in Argentina. New Scenario. Financial Information Unit: Resolution 30-E/2017, https://www.mondaq.com/arg entina/money-laundering/614916/aml-rules-in-argentina-new-scenario-financial-inform ation-unit-resolution-30-e2017.

[2] Idem.

Bank and the National Securities Commission regarding data security obligations for financial institutions and publicly listed companies.[3] Nonetheless, Decree 577/2017 has created the Cybersecurity Committee, which mainly focus on creating a regulatory framework, educating people on the importance of cybersecurity, creating a national cybersecurity plan, and creating general guidelines for security breaches. On April 26, 2018, Argentine entered into a memorandum of understanding on cooperation in cybersecurity, cybercrime, and cyberdefense between Argentina and Chile aimed at, inter alia, strengthening the coordination and cooperation, promoting joint initiatives, exchanging good practices, and developing and implementing new legislation and national strategies to response to incidents, information exchange, education, and training.[4]

24.3.1 Privacy and Data Protection

Privacy and data protection are expressly acknowledged by the Argentine Constitution several International Treaties executed by Argentina; the Argentine National Civil and Commercial Code and more specifically by Argentine Data Protection Act No 25,326 (PDPA). Executed in 2000, PDPA aims to protect the privacy of personal data, and to give individuals access to any information stored in public and private databases and registries. The PDPA aligns with the European legislative model for protecting data privacy, and Argentina was the first country in Latin America to achieve an 'adequacy' qualification for data transfers from the EU. Under PDPA, any personal database must be registered with the Agency. Registration requires the following information:

(i) the name and domicile of the person in charge of that database;
(ii) the characteristics and purpose of the database;
(iii) the nature of the personal data contained in each file;
(iv) the method of collecting and updating the data;
(v) the recipients to whom such data may be transmitted;

---

[3] Adrian Furma, Francisco Zappa (202): The Privacy, Data Protection and Cybersecurity Law Review: Argentina, The Law Reviews, https://thelawreviews.co.uk/title/the-privacy-data-protection-and-cybersecurity-law-review/argentina.

[4] Idem.

(vi) the manner in which the registered information can be interrelated;

(vii) security measures;

(viii) data retention period; and

(ix) Means for individuals to access, correct and update their data.

The security obligations in the DPA require data controllers and data processors to use measures to detect any unauthorized access or amendment to personal data. Furthermore, under the duty of confidentiality, any third party providing data processing services may: (i) only use the relevant personal data for the purposes specified on the corresponding service contract; and (ii) not disclose that personal data to any third party, even for storage purposes. Last but not least, the Data Protection Authority issued the Resolution 47/2018 establishes the recommendation to notify any data breach as a demonstration of good practices.

24.4   Cybersecurity in the Banking Industry

Argentina's banks are turning to new authentication strategies to step up their cybersecurity defenses against an evolving series of digital risks.[5] They are adopting biometrics and multi-factor authentication in a bid to keep their platforms secure. The UIF has also the power of requesting reports, background screening information, and documents from the banks and other businesses if they become flagged as being involved in money laundering or assisting criminals to use Argentina's legal financial systems to launder their illicit earnings.

---

[5] Katie Llanos-Small (2021): Old Infrastructure, New Services Create Fresh Bank Cybersecurity Risks, https://iupana.com/2019/05/06/cybersecurity-in-argentina-banks-financial-services/?lang=en.

CHAPTER 25

AML/CFT and Cybersecurity Laws in Saudi Arabia

25.1 General

Saudi Arabia is the foremost country to retaliate the illegal money laundering activities to combat as well as comply with the rules. The legal AML framework in KSA is composed of Shari'ah law and the Anti-Money Laundering Statute (AMLS). As per the Anti-Money Laundering Law issued by Royal Decree No. M/20 dated 5/2/1439H, A person shall be considered to have committed a money laundering offence if he/she conducts any of the following acts[1]:

- Converts or transfers or conducts any transaction on funds that the person knows are proceeds of crime for the purpose of disguising or concealing the illegitimate origin of the funds, or to help a person involved in the commission of the predicate offense that generated the funds to evade the legal consequences for his/her acts;
- Acquires, possesses, or uses funds that the person knows are proceeds of crime or from illegal source;

---

[1] Manual for Anti-Money Laundering and Combating the Financing of Terrorism, https://www.awqaf.gov.sa/sites/default/files/2020-08/Manual%20for%20Anti-Money%20Laundering%20and%20Combating.pdf.

© The Author(s), under exclusive license to Springer Nature   193
Switzerland AG 2023
F. I. Lessambo, *Anti-Money Laundering, Counter Financing Terrorism and Cybersecurity in the Banking Industry*, Palgrave Macmillan Studies in Banking and Financial Institutions, https://doi.org/10.1007/978-3-031-23484-2_25

– Conceals or disguises the true nature, source, movement, ownership, place, disposition, or manner of disposition, or rights with respect to funds that the person knows are proceeds of crime;
– Attempts to conduct any of acts stated in Paragraphs (1), (2), and (3) in this Article, or participates in such acts by means of agreement, providing assistance, abetting, providing counseling or advice, facilitation, collusion, cover-up, or conspiring.

Combating-Terrorism Crimes and its Financing Law issued by Royal Decree No. M/21 dated 12/2/1439H stipulates that a terrorism financing crime is:

Providing funds for committing a terrorist crime or for the benefit of a terrorist entity or a terrorist individual in any form stipulated in this Law, including financing the travel and training of a terrorist individual.

25.2   AML/CFT Laws

Saudi Arabian AML regime started in 2003 when the Saudi Government passed an Anti-Money Laundering Statute 2003 and its Implementing Regulations in 2005.[2]

The Anti-Money Laundering and Counter-Terrorist Financing Rules (the "AML/CTF") issued by the Saudi Capital Market Authority (the "CMA") amended by CMA Board Resolution No. 1-85-2017.

25.3   Cybersecurity Laws

25.3.1   *The Anti-Cybercrimes Law of 2017*

The Anti-Cybercrimes Law of 2017 (the "Cybersecurity Law") is a general law that applies across the board and addresses data protection in the context cybercrimes.

---

[2] Madhura Phadtare (..):Money Laundering Challenges in Saudi Arabia, https://regtec htimes.com/aml-certification-in-saudi-arabia/.

25.3.2 *The National Data Governance Interim Regulations of 2020*

The "National Data Regulations" issued by the National Data Management Office deal mainly with government-related data. Part 5 of the National Data Regulations, however, deals with personal data protection and is stated to apply to all entities in KSA that process personal data in whole or part, as well as all entities outside KSA that process personal data related to individuals residing in KSA. The legal status of the National Data Regulations remains slightly unclear at the time of writing and it is not clear if they are being actively enforced. No sanctions for breach are specified, which is unusual for a law which is intended to be enforced. Clearly, the potential scope of Part 5 is very extensive and, on the face of it, would catch numerous businesses with no local presence in the Kingdom, such as cloud service providers. Now that the PDPL has been published, we assume that the National Data Regulations are not intended to apply to private businesses in KSA.

25.4 Cybersecurity in the Banking Industry

The SAMA Anti-Money Laundering and Terrorist Financing Guidelines requires that all Banks within Saudi Arabia establish a dedicated Unit to combat money laundering and terrorist financing. The AML/CTF Division is responsible for and principally tasked with the monitoring, investigation, and reporting of suspicious or unusual transactions to the relevant Authorities. The AML/CTF Division is manned by specialized human resources committed to address any and all relevant questions and issues pertaining, among others, to AML/CTF Investigations, Sanctions, AML/CTF Efficiency, and AML/CTF Monitoring.

Saudi Arabian money laundering gang sentenced to twenty years in prison and fined £14.5million.

The Riyadh Court of Appeal has sentenced the 24 members of a criminal gang which laundered SR17b (£3.3b) to terms of up to 20 years each. The court also fined the gang SR75m (£14.5 m) and seized all funds discovered at the crime scene, an amount thought to be in the billions. Additionally, the Saudi citizens convicted received 20-year travel bans, while the expatriates are to be deported once they have served their sentences.

Authorities say the group laundered the funds as part of an organized criminal network, using commercial enterprises such as factories, companies, institutions, and medical facilities as a cover. The individual roles played by the gang members included money laundering, collecting and depositing illicit funds, and transferring money abroad.

CHAPTER 26

AML/CFT and Cybersecurity Laws in South Africa

26.1 General

Money laundering is considered a major crime in South Africa. The Financial Intelligence Centre (FIC) was established in 2001 to act as the primary authority over Anti-Money Laundering (AML) efforts in South Africa. The FIC is responsible for establishing an AML regime and maintaining the integrity of the South African financial system by enforcing recordkeeping and reporting procedures of financial institutions within the country.[1] In April 2012, the government of SA established the anti-money laundering and counter financing of terrorism (AML/CFT) Division within the Prudential Authority ((PA) previously the Bank Supervision Department) to supervise and enforce compliance with the FIC Act.[2] The South African Government (SAG) estimates that between $2 and $8 billion is laundered each year through South African financial institution.

---

[1] Anti-Money Laundering (AML) in South Africa, http://bankersacademy.com/resources/free-tutorials/57-ba-free-tutorials/610-aml-southafrica-sp-280.

[2] South African Reserve Bank—Prudential Authority (2022): Anti-Money Laundering and Countering the Financing of Terrorism (AML/CFT, https://www.resbank.co.za/en/home/what-we-do/Prudentialregulation/anti-money-laundering-and-countering-the-financing-of-terrorism.

F. I. Lessambo, *Anti-Money Laundering, Counter Financing Terrorism and Cybersecurity in the Banking Industry*, Palgrave Macmillan Studies in Banking and Financial Institutions, https://doi.org/10.1007/978-3-031-23484-2_26

26.2   AML/ CFT Laws

The Financial Intelligence Centre Act, No 38 of 2001 (the FIC Act) together with the Prevention of Organized Crime Act, 1998 (POCA), the Prevention and Combatting of Corrupt Activities Act, 2004 (PRECCA), and the Protection of Constitutional Democracy against Terrorist and Related Activities Act, 2004 (POCDATARA) were introduced to combat money laundering and terrorist financing.

26.2.1   *The Financial Intelligence Centre Act, No 38 of 2001 (The FIC Act)*

The Financial Intelligence Centre Act 38 of 2001 ('FICA') in aggregate with the Prevention of organized Crime Act 121 of 1998 ('POCA') form the backbone of South Africa's anti-money laundering regime.[3] The FIC Act introduces a regulatory framework of measures requiring certain categories of business (accountable institutions) inter alia an authorized user of an exchange, a collective investment scheme manager and a financial services provider to take steps regarding customer due diligence, record-keeping, reporting of information to the Financial Intelligence Centre, and internal compliance governance. The Financial Intelligence Centre uses this financial data reported to it and other available data to develop financial intelligence, which it is able to make available to the competent authorities, i.e., law enforcement agencies, South African Revenue Services, and supervisory bodies for follow-up with investigations or to take administrative action. POCA criminalizes activities in relation to the benefits of crime and delineates civil proceedings aimed at forfeiting the benefits of crime to the state.

26.2.2   *The Prevention and Combatting of Corrupt Activities Act, 2004 (PRECCA)*

The Prevention and Combating of Corrupt Activities Act is the primary law governing Anti-Bribery and Corruption prevention and enforcement in South Africa. It applies to organizations based in the country and those

---

[3] Van Jaarsveld, Izelde Louise (2011): Aspects of money laundering in South African law, University of South Africa, Pretoria, https://hdl.handle.net/10500/5091.

based outside but doing business in the country. The Prevention and Combating of Corrupt Activities Act 12 of 2004 intends[4]:

- to provide for the strengthening of measures to prevent and combat corruption and corrupt activities;
- to provide for the offence of corruption and offences relating to corrupt activities;
- to provide for investigative measures in respect of corruption and related corrupt activities;
- to provide for the establishment and endorsement of a Register in order to place certain restrictions on persons and enterprises convicted of corrupt activities relating to tenders and contracts;
- to place a duty on certain persons holding a position of authority to report certain corrupt transactions;
- to provide for extraterritorial jurisdiction in respect of the offence of corruption and offences relating to corrupt activities; and
- To provide for matters connected therewith.

26.2.3 The Protection of Constitutional Democracy Against Terrorist and Related Activities Act, 2004 (Amended in 2021)

The Protection of Constitutional Democracy against Terrorist and Related Activities Act of 2004 was enacted:

- To provide for measures to prevent and combat terrorist and related activities;
- to provide for an offence of terrorism and other offences associated or connected with terrorist activities; to provide for Convention offences;
- to give effect to international instruments dealing with terrorist and related activities;
- to provide for a mechanism to comply with United Nations Security Council Resolutions, which are binding on member States, in respect of terrorist and related activities;

---

[4] https://www.gov.za/af/documents/prevention-and-combating-corrupt-activities-act-0.

- to provide for measures to prevent and combat the financing of terrorist and related activities; to provide for investigative measures in respect of terrorist and related activities; and
- To provide for matters connected therewith.

In 2021, the Act was amended so as to:

- delete, amend and insert certain definitions for purposes of alignment with international instruments adopted upon the implementation of the Act;
- provide for offences related to terrorist training and the joining and establishment of terrorist organizations;
- provide for offences related to foreign travel and attempts to leave the Republic under certain circumstances;
- provide for offences in respect of the possession and distribution of publications with unlawful terrorism related content;
- provide for authorization to be obtained from the Director of Public Prosecutions in respect of the investigation and prosecution of certain offences;
- provide for the issuing of warrants for the search and cordoning off of vehicles, persons and premises;
- provide for a direction requiring the disclosure of a decryption key and the effect of a direction to disclose a decryption key;
- provide for the removal of, or making inaccessible, publications with unlawful terrorism related content; and
- Provide for matters connected therewith.

26.3   Cybersecurity Laws

South Africa well-developed financial infrastructure makes it an attractive target for cyber criminals who use the internet for extortion, fraud, child pornography, human trafficking, and selling illicit goods.[5]

[5] Karen Allen (2021): South Africa lays down the law on cybercrime, ISS Pretoria, https://issafrica.org/iss-today/south-africa-lays-down-the-law-on-cybercrime.

26.3.1   *The Protection of Personal Information Act 4 of 2013*

The Protection of Personal Information Act 4 of 2013 ("POPI"). It is a comprehensive piece of data protection legislation. POPI applies to the processing of personal information entered into a record by or for a responsible party by making use of automated or non-automated means, where the responsible party is domiciled in South Africa.[6] POPI Act promotes the protection of personal data processed by public and private bodies. It outlines the: rights of data subjects, regulates the cross-border flow of personal data, and introduces mandatory data breach reporting and notification obligations. POPI Act also creates a reporting duty on persons responsible for processing personal information, whereby they must report any unlawful access to personal information (a data breach) to the Information Regulator within a reasonable period of time.[7]

26.3.2   *The Cybercrimes and Cybersecurity Act (2021)*

In June 2021, the Cybercrimes and Cybersecurity Act (Act) was signed into law by South African President Cyril Ramaphosa, bringing the country's cybersecurity legislation in line with global standards. The Act defines cybercrime as including, but not limited to, acts such as: the unlawful access to a computer or device such as a USB drive or an external hard drive; the illegal interception of data; the unlawful acquisition, possession, receipt, or use of a password; and forgery, fraud, and extortion online. Malicious communications are also criminalized. It also describes how the South African authorities should conduct international investigations and how evidence must be collected, shared, and preserved for future prosecutions.

26.4   Cybersecurity in the Banking Industry

There are no specific laws or guidelines for cybersecurity governance of banks in South Africa. The Cybercrime and Cybersecurity does not

---

[6] Zaakir Mohamed (2020):Data protection and cybersecurity laws in South Africa, CMS, https://cms.law/en/int/expert-guides/cms-expert-guide-to-data-protection-and-cyber-security-laws/south-africa.

[7] Darryl Bernstein (2021): Africa: Implementation of Cybersecurity and Data Protection Law Urgent across Continent, https://www.bakermckenzie.com/en/insight/public ations/2021/06/africa-cybersecurity-data-protection-law.

provide governance guidelines. In the absence of specific guidelines, South African's banking sector should consider aligning with the G7 guidelines. The elements serve as the building blocks upon which an entity can design and implement its cybersecurity strategy and operating framework, informed by its approach to risk management and culture. The elements also provide steps in a dynamic process through which the entity can systematically re-evaluate its cybersecurity strategy and framework as the operational and threat environment evolves.[8] These element include:

- Establishing and maintaining a cybersecurity strategy and framework tailored to specific cyber risks and appropriately informed by international, national, and industry standards and guidelines;
- Defining and facilitating performance of roles and responsibilities for personnel implementing, managing, and overseeing the effectiveness of the cybersecurity strategy and framework to ensure accountability; and provide adequate resources, appropriate authority, and access to the governing authority;
- Identifying functions, activities, products, and services—including interconnections, dependencies, and third parties—prioritize their relative importance, and assess their respective cyber risks;
- Establishing systematic monitoring processes to rapidly detect cyber incidents and periodically evaluate the effectiveness of identified controls, including through network monitoring, testing, audits, and exercises;
- Timely (a) assessing the nature, scope, and impact of a cyber incident; (b) containing the incident and mitigate its impact; (c) notifying internal and external stakeholders (such as law enforcement, regulators, and other public authorities, as well as shareholders, third-party service providers, and customers as appropriate); and (d) coordinating joint response activities as needed;
- Resuming operations responsibly, while allowing for continued remediation, including by (a) eliminating harmful remnants of the incident; (b) restoring systems and data to normal and confirming normal state; (c) identifying and mitigating all vulnerabilities that

[8] G7 Fundamental Elements of Cybersecurity for the Financial Sector, https://assets.publishing.service.gov.uk/government/uploads/system/uploads/attachment_data/file/559186/G7_Fundamental_Elements_Oct_2016.pdf.

were exploited; (d) remediating vulnerabilities to prevent similar incidents; and (e) communicating appropriately internally and externally;

- Sharing technical information, such as threat indicators or details on how vulnerabilities were exploited, allows entities to remain up-to-date in their defenses and learn about emerging methods used by attackers;
- Reviewing the cybersecurity strategy and framework regularly and when events warrant—including its governance, risk and control assessment, monitoring, response, recovery, and information sharing components—to address changes in cyber risks, allocate resources, identify and remediate gaps, and incorporate lessons learned.

CHAPTER 27

AML/CFT Compliance and Audit

27.1 General

An independent AML audit is actually a test on a bank or financial institution's AML program. It is not a financial audit, but rather a test to see whether a firm has an appropriate AML program and is compliant thereof. It test the firm's AML Policy and Procedures; Customer Identification Procedure (CIP) review; the Evaluation of automated monitoring systems and management information systems. The 4 Pillars of an effective AML program are:

- The development of internal policies, procedures, and controls

To demonstrate a robust AML framework, a bank or financial institution must have detailed documentation in place. At a minimum, it must be able to provide its AML policy and procedures; as well as its AML business risk assessment (clearly analyzing the risks associated with the firm's customers, products, jurisdictions, delivery channels, and transactions, as well as explaining your mitigating controls). The auditor is looking to see whether the bank framework requirements and its day-to-day processes match the procedures as set forth. This will mean testing a sample of the bank client files and transaction monitoring systems.

© The Author(s), under exclusive license to Springer Nature Switzerland AG 2023
F. I. Lessambo, *Anti-Money Laundering, Counter Financing Terrorism and Cybersecurity in the Banking Industry*, Palgrave Macmillan Studies in Banking and Financial Institutions,
https://doi.org/10.1007/978-3-031-23484-2_27

- Designation of a compliance officer

The principal responsibility for a bank's ML/TF risk management lies with the board of directors. It is responsible for defining and overseeing a bank's AML/CFT policy and allocating operational responsibilities and resources. The bank senior management staff must be knowledgeable about the AML risks associated with the business and understand the necessary controls to have in place to mitigate these. The auditor may need to speak with the key stakeholders in the firm, especially the board and those senior managers that sit on any relevant risk or compliance committees, and the chief compliance officer, if any.

- An ongoing employee training program

Training is one of the most important ways to stress the importance of AML/CFT efforts, as well as educating employees about the appropriate steps to take while facing AML/CFT. To that end, the first step in designing an effective program is to identify the target employees. While all employees should be mandatorily trained on general AML requirements and guidance, a more targeted training program should be implemented for individuals who can directly impact the bank's ML efforts. Training should cover the aspects of the BSA that are relevant to the bank and its risk profile, and appropriate personnel includes those whose duties require knowledge or involve some aspect of BSA/AMLcompliance.[1]

- An independent audit function to test programs.

The independent testing helps inform the board of directors and senior management of weakness, or areas in need of enhancements or stronger controls. Independent testing should be conducted by the internal audit department. The person conducting the BSA/AML independent testing should report directly to the board of directors or to a designated board committee comprised primarily, or completely, of outside directors. The independent testing, including the frequency, should be commensurate

---

[1] FFIEC (2020): Bank Secrecy Act/ Anti-Money Laundering Examination Manual, pp. 1–43, https://www.ffiec.gov/press/pdf/FFIEC%20BSA-AML%20Exam%20Manual.pdf.

with the ML/TF and other illicit financial activity risk profile of the bank and the bank's overall risk management strategy. Risk-based independent testing programs vary depending on the bank's size or complexity, organizational structure, scope of activities, risk profile, quality of control functions, geographic diversity, and use of technology.

27.2   AML COMPLIANCE

AML Compliance Officer is an indispensable employee as they are fully responsible for the company's regulatory processes and reports. Banks must establish and maintain procedures reasonably designed to assure and monitor compliance with BSA regulatory requirements (BSA/AML compliance program). The BSA/AML compliance program must be written, approved by the board of directors, and noted in the board minutes. To achieve the purposes of the BSA, the BSA/AML compliance program should be commensurate with the bank's ML/TF and other illicit financial activity risk profile. The BSA/AML compliance program must provide for the following requirements:

- A system of internal controls to assure ongoing compliance.
- Independent testing for compliance to be conducted by bank personnel or by an outside party.
- Designation of an individual or individuals responsible for coordinating and monitoring day-to-day compliance (BSA compliance officer).
- Training for appropriate personnel.

The BSA/AML compliance program must also include appropriate risk-based procedures for conducting ongoing customer due diligence (CDD) and complying with beneficial ownership requirements for legal entity customers as set forth in regulations issued by Financial Crimes Enforcement Network (FinCEN).

27.3   CFT COMPLIANCE

Combating the Financing of Terrorism Compliance refers to the set of banking policies and standards used by financial institutions to adhere to the requirements of international Anti-Money Laundering laws. The use of innovative technology in the banking sector brings with it not only significant and potentially transformative benefits, but also risks of unintended consequences to the fight against terrorism financing compliance.[2] CFT compliance requires countries to implement FATF guidelines in developing their regulatory framework to prevent terrorist financing activities from occurring. CFT compliance is necessary to ensure better understanding of terrorist financing risks so that illicit organizations receiving dirty funds could be stopped. To that end, banks need to perform ongoing monitoring of customer accounts, their transactions and taking into account the overall risk they pose. By tracking down suspicious activities, illicit money trails can be found effectively to prevent terrorist organizations from getting the better of the legal financial system.

27.4   AML/CFT AUDIT

27.4.1   Internal AML/CFT Audit

One of the roles of the internal audit is to support the process of enforcing regulations. The system of internal controls, including the level and type, should be commensurate with the bank's size or complexity, and organizational structure.[3] Banks and financial institutions are required to maintain an adequately resourced and independent audit function to test compliance (including sample testing) with procedures. Put differently, a bank must establish policies for conducting audits of (i) the adequacy of the bank's AML/CFT policies and procedures in addressing identified risks, (ii) the effectiveness of bank staff in implementing the bank's policies and procedures; (iii) the effectiveness of compliance oversight and quality control including parameters of criteria for automatic alerts; and (iv) the effectiveness of the bank's training of relevant personnel.[4] Failing to do so can have undesirable consequences for an institution, including

---

[2] FAFT (2021): Opportunities and Challenges of New Technologies for AML/CFT Compliance, pp. 1–76, https://www.fatf-gafi.org/media/fatf/documents/reports/Opportunities-Challenges-of-New-Technologies-for-AML-CFT.pdf.

[3] FFIEC (2020): Bank Secrecy Act/ Anti-Money Laundering Examination Manual, pp. 1–43, https://www.ffiec.gov/press/pdf/FFIEC%20BSA-AML%20Exam%20Manual.pdf.

[4] BCBS (2020): Sound management of risks related to money laundering and financing of terrorism, pp. 1–62, https://www.bis.org/bcbs/publ/d505.pdf.

regulatory violations, penalties, monetary fines, and regulator involvement. The internal auditors must be able to perform its assignments on their own initiative in all areas and functions of the Regulated Entity and they must be free to report their findings and assessments internally through clear reporting lines. AML audits must identify deficiencies, gaps, and weaknesses that may exist in the content, controls, and operations of the AML program. While preserving independence, internal audit must work together with management and the relationship between the two needs to rest on mutual trust. This can be achieved by discussing findings and remediation plans during the course of the audit. The internal audit report is first presented to management, which is, in turn, requested to comment on the findings before it is presented to the Board of Directors or Audit Committee.[5]

27.4.2   External AML/CFT Audit

External auditors play an important role in evaluating banks' internal controls and procedures in the course of their financial audits, and in confirming that they are compliant with AML/CFT regulations and supervisory practice.[6] An external AML/CFT audit must be performed by a skilled, competent auditor knowledgeable in AML/CFT. It must encompass all the different components of an audit procedure such as audit scope, audit objectives, audit methodology, audit observations, gap analysis, and relevant recommendations. The external auditor must develop an understanding of the bank's money laundering, terrorist financing, and other illicit financial activity risk profile. Based on the bank's risk profile, the external auditor needs to develop an audit plan, assess the level of risk and select the procedures to be used. Many banks rely on technology to aid in BSA/AML compliance and, therefore, the scoping and planning process should include developing an understanding of the bank's information technology sources, systems, and

[5] Alicia Vella (2021): The role of Internal Audit within the AML Framework, https://www.mazars.com.mt/Home/Insights/Our-Articles/The-role-of-Internal-Audit-the-AML-Framework.

[6] BCBS (2020): Sound management of risks related to money laundering and financing of terrorism, p. 6, https://www.bis.org/bcbs/publ/d505.pdf.

processes used in the BSA/AML compliance program.[7] Compliance audit reports must be issued in a timely manner to the Board of Directors of a company to allow them to take appropriate actions to address deficiencies and areas of non-compliance. After completion, the audit report must be duly signed and dated by the audit professional or firm. It must be communicated, in a timely manner, to the Board of Directors of the bank or financial institution allow them to take appropriate actions to address deficiencies and areas of non-compliance. Whenever, recommendations or shortcomings have been identified, the bank must share the findings with the relevant employees who are directly involved in the deficiencies that need to be corrected, solicit the advice of these employees, especially Front-Line staff on how they feel the Program could work better. Additionally, the risk or AML/CFT committee must set deadlines and timeframes for the changes and list those who are responsible for getting the tasks completed. Finally, detailed records of the Audit must be kept.

27.5 The AML/CFT Compliance Index (AML/CFT CI)

The AML/CFT Compliance Index (AML/CFT CI) comprises seven components that serve to capture seven groupings of recommendations[8]:

- legal measures,
- institutional measures,
- preventive measures for financial institutions,
- preventive measures for DNBFPs,
- preventive measures for the informal sector,
- entity transparency, and
- international cooperation.

[7] FFIEC (2020): Bank Secrecy Act/ Anti-Money Laundering Examination Manual, pp. 1–43, https://www.ffiec.gov/press/pdf/FFIEC%20BSA-AML%20Exam%20Manual.pdf.

[8] Concepcion Verdugo Yepes (2011): Compliance with the AML/CFT International Standard: Lessons from a Cross-Country Analysis, IMF Working Paper, pp.1–76, https://www.imf.org/external/pubs/ft/wp/2011/wp11177.pdf.

27.5.1   Basel AML Index

The Basel AML Index is an independent annual ranking that assesses the risk of money laundering and terrorist financing (ML/TF) around the world.[9] The Basel AML Index is developed and maintained by the Basel Institute's International Centre for Asset Recovery. The Basel AML Index is an independent annual ranking that assesses risks of money laundering and terrorist financing (ML/TF) around the world. The Basel AML Index aims to provide a holistic picture of ML/TF risk. Risk, as measured by the Basel AML Index, is defined as a jurisdiction's vulnerability to ML/TF and its capacities to counter it. It is not intended as a measure of the actual amount of ML/TF activity in a given jurisdiction. The Basel AML Index provides risk scores based on data from 17 publicly available sources such as the Financial Action Task Force (FATF), Transparency International, the World Bank, and the World Economic Forum. The risk scores cover five domains (Fig. 27.1):

- Quality of ML/TF Framework,
- Bribery and Corruption,
- Financial Transparency and Standards,
- Public Transparency and Accountability,
- Legal and Political Risks.

The composite score is aggregated by analyzing more than a dozen indicators of countries' adherence to anti-money laundering and countering the financing of terrorism (AML/CFT) regulations, levels of corruption, financial standards, political disclosure and the rule of law—as well as, more recently, concrete metrics of effectiveness (Fig. 27.2).

The Basel AML (2021) score includes data from the Judicial Independence ranking of the World Economic Forum (WEF) Global Competitiveness Index as an indicator of Legal and Political Risks. The Judicial Independence data, which is published annually and covers around 70 percent of jurisdictions globally, have a weighting of 5 percent of the total AML risk score. It also includes the Trafficking in Persons (TIP) Report of the U.S. Department of State, which ranks around 160 governments according to their perceived efforts to acknowledge and combat human trafficking. This data are included in the category of Quality of

---

[9] BIS (2020): Basel AML Index, https://baselgovernance.org/basel-aml-index.

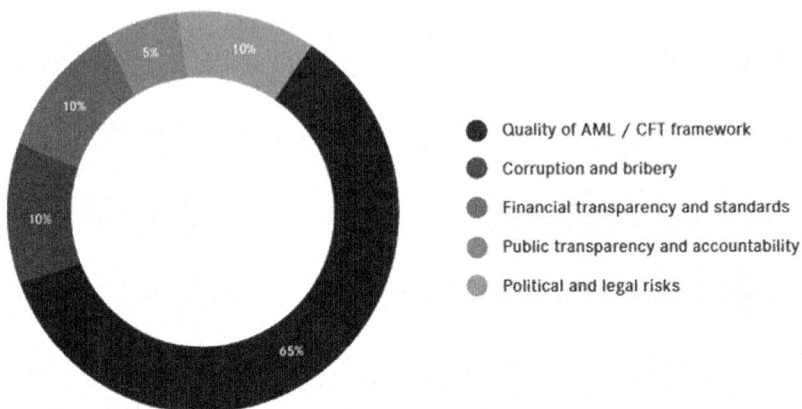

Fig. 27.1   Basel AML index (*Source* BIS [2020])

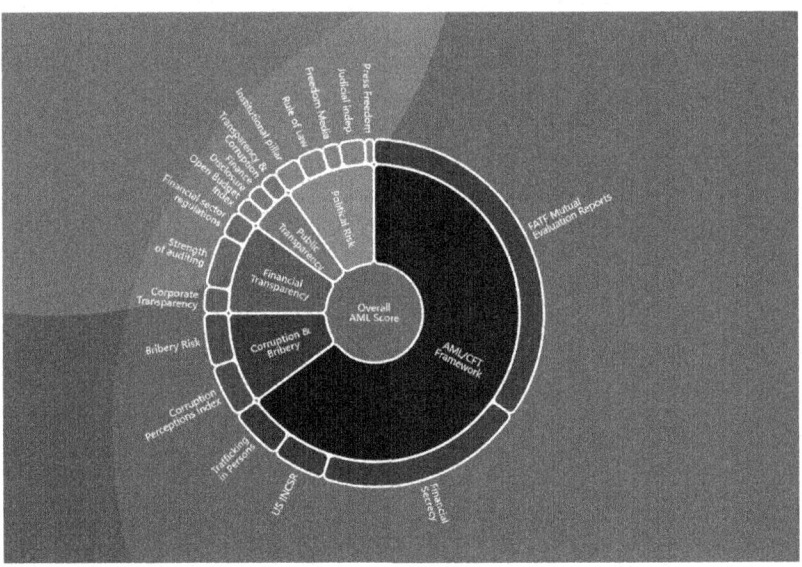

Fig. 27.2   BIS—Scaling & weighing indicators (*Source* BIS [2020]: Scaling and weighing indicators)

Fig. 27.3 Five worst countries in 2021 (*Source* BIS [2021])

AML/CFT Framework with a 5 percent weighting. The inclusion is justified by the fact that human trafficking is said to be the third largest source of income for organized crime groups after drug and arms trafficking, generating an estimated USD 150 billion in profits each year. The five worst countries in 2021 include Haiti, Democratic Republic of the Congo, Mauritania, Myanmar, and Mozambique. The five countries with the least fincrime compliance risk in 2021 index: include Andorra, Finland, Cook Island, Slovenia, and Norway (Fig. 27.3).[10]

27.5.2 *The Global Organized Crime Index*

The Global Initiative-TOC has developed the Global Organized Crime Index, a unique, data-driven analytical tool that evaluates 193 UN member states according to two metrics: according to their criminality on a score from 1 to 10 (lowest to highest organized crime levels), which in turn is based on their criminal markets score and criminal actors score; and according to their resilience to organized crime, from 1 to 10 (lowest

[10] BIS (2021): Basel AML Index 2021: An ounce of prevention worth a pound of effectiveness when it comes to countering criminals, championing compliance, https://www.acfcs.org/basel-aml-index-2021-an-ounce-of-prevention-and-being-less-effective-on-effectiveness/.

to highest resilience levels). By providing a consolidated hub of data and baseline evidence of the phenomenon in countries across the world, the Index aims to be a catalyst for further debate on transnational organized crime. Ultimately, the Index strives to inform policymakers and regional bodies so they can prioritize interventions based on a multi-faceted assessment of vulnerabilities and enhance national, regional, and global cooperation in countering organized crime.

CHAPTER 28

International and Regional Cooperation

28.1 GENERAL

The international community has made the fight against money laundering and the financing of terrorism a priority. Among the goals of this effort are: protecting the integrity and stability of the international financial system, cutting off the resources available to terrorists, and making it more difficult for those engaged in crime to profit from their criminal activities.[1] Effective cooperation and exchange of information among prudential supervisors and AML/CFT supervisors that are responsible for banks (hereinafter "supervisors") is essential to lessen ML/FT risk, to maintain the integrity of the banking system and to ensure the prudential soundness and stability of banks.[2]

---

[1] IMF (2022): Anti-Money Laundering/Combating the Financing of Terrorism—Topics, https://www.imf.org/external/np/leg/amlcft/eng/aml1.htm.

[2] BIS (2019): Basel Committee on Banking Supervision—Introduction of guidelines on interaction and cooperation between prudential and AML/CFT supervision, pp. 1–20, https://www.bis.org/bcbs/publ/d483.pdf.

© The Author(s), under exclusive license to Springer Nature   215
Switzerland AG 2023
F. I. Lessambo, *Anti-Money Laundering, Counter Financing Terrorism and Cybersecurity in the Banking Industry*, Palgrave Macmillan Studies in Banking and Financial Institutions,
https://doi.org/10.1007/978-3-031-23484-2_28

28.2   Cooperation and exchange of information in AML/CFT

Money launderers, terrorists, drug dealers, and human traffickers all operate within global networks, making it as sinister as it is ubiquitous.[3] The BIS provides guidelines to that end.

28.2.1   In the Authorization Process

The prudential supervisor should share with the AML/CFT supervisor appropriate information related to the application and receive information gathered or created in the exercise of the AML/CFT supervisor's functions, which is relevant in order to assess the application. He should consider the bank's envisaged risk mitigation system, internal control system, and adequacy of governance and organizational structures to properly manage ML/FT risks presented in the authorization process. When assessing the fitness and properness of shareholders including the ultimate beneficial owners and other persons that may exert significant influence, members of senior management, and members of the board of directors, at the time of authorization of a bank as well as performing ongoing assessment, the prudential supervisor must consult with the AML/CFT supervisor to obtain additional information, in order to ensure that the persons have a record of integrity and good repute, according to the essential criterion 7 of principle 5 in Core principles for effective banking supervision.

28.2.2   In the Ongoing Supervision

The prudential supervisor should take into account the impact of the ML/FT risks by collecting and considering all relevant information identified by the AML/CFT supervisors. These prudential assessments should pay particular attention to the potential ML/FT risks that could stem from the cross-border banking group structure. The information held by the AML/CFT supervisors could provide valuable insight for the exercise

---

[3] Navin Beekarry (2011): The International Anti-Money Laundering and Combating the Financing of Terrorism Regulatory Strategy: A Critical Analysis of Compliance Determinants in International Law, pp. 149–150, International Anti-Money Laundering Regulatory Strategy 31:137.

of prudential supervision. AML/CFT-related information in relation to a bank, its members of senior management, the board, as well as any other information, findings or concerns could indicate weaknesses in the bank's prudential risk components, such as risk management, internal controls and governance. To that end, (i) Prudential information about a bank's governance and risk management could be relevant for the AML/CFT supervision and (ii) Prudential information about the business model could be relevant for AML/CFT supervision.

28.2.3 Regarding Enforcement Actions

The sharing of information may depend on the type and severity of the supervisory action, the confidentiality requirements of the investigation, whether the international counterpart provides reciprocal assistance, and whether such sharing would prejudice the interests of the home jurisdiction of the prudential regulator.

28.2.4 Confidentiality Treatment

Supervisors should establish and maintain official channels to facilitate and structure ongoing dialogue, information exchange and cooperation between prudential and AML/CFT supervisors, and use those channels effectively to inform relevant stages of the supervisory process. Prudential and AML/CFT supervisors should exchange information periodically and when necessary as relevant for their respective tasks, taking into account the appropriate mechanisms.

28.3 COOPERATION AND EXCHANGE OF INFORMATION IN CYBERSECURITY

Cybersecurity is becoming a key part of the foreign policy agenda. For the last few years, cybersecurity has been a matter of concern for most organizations, independent of their size.[4] In October 2021, the United States

---

[4] Jaroslaw Sordyl (2020): Cooperation and exchange of information as an effective cybersecurity measure for organizations, https://securityboulevard.com/2020/03/cooperation-and-exchange-of-information-as-an-effective-cybersecurity-measure-for-organisations/.

convened the Counter Ransomware Initiative, which included representatives from 30 countries and the European Union to discuss the security threat posed by ransomware.[5] Majors developed jurisdictions or blocks have stress out the need for international cooperation: The EU identified "a need for closer cooperation at a global level to improve security standards, improve information, and promote a common global approach to network and information security issues …".[6] Likewise, U.S. Cybersecurity Strategy reaffirms the need to strengthen the capacity and interoperability of those allies and partners to improve our ability to optimize our combined skills, resources, capabilities, and perspectives against shared threats.[7]

28.3.1   The OECD Approach

The OECD has been at the forefront of facilitating international cooperation on digital security policy since the 1990s. The OECD focuses on the economic and social aspects of cybersecurity, as opposed to aspects that are purely technical, directly related to criminal law enforcement or national security. Its approach to digital security is grounded in risk management and focuses on identifying the most effective policy tools to address the economic and social challenges that often limit the ability of stakeholders to optimally manage digital security risk. In 2018, the OECD has launched the Global Forum on Digital Security for Prosperity holds international multi-stakeholder events gathering policymakers and experts from the private sector, the technical community, and civil society.

28.3.2   The International Telecommunications Union (ITU)

The International Telecommunications Union (ITU), a United Nations agency that is considered the "premier global forum through which

---

[5] Eugenia Lostri, James Andrew Lewis, Georgia Wood (2022): A Shared Responsibility: Public-Private Cooperation for Cybersecurity, Center for Strategic and International Studies, https://www.csis.org/analysis/shared-responsibility-public-private-cooperation-cybersecurity.

[6] Directive (EU) 2016/1148 of the European Parliament and of the Council of 6 July 2016 concerning measures for a high common level of security of network and information systems across the Union.

[7] White National Cybersecurity Strategy 2018.

parties work towards consensus on a wide range of issues affecting the future direction of the ICT industry" (ITU) launched the Global Cybersecurity Agenda, which is "a framework for international cooperation aimed at enhancing confidence and security in the information society." The ITU Global Cybersecurity Agenda identifies five strategic pillars: legal, technical, organizational, capacity-building, and cooperation.[8]

28.3.3 *The European Union Agency for Network and Information Security (ENISA)*

The European Union Agency for Network and Information Security (ENISA) is a center of network and information security expertise for the EU, its Member States, the private sector, and Europe's citizens. ENISA works with these groups to develop advice and recommendations on good practice in information security. It assists EU Member States in implementing relevant EU legislation and works to improve the resilience of Europe's critical information infrastructure and networks. ENISA seeks to enhance existing expertise in EU Member States by supporting the development of cross-border communities committed to improving network and information security throughout the E[9]U.

---

[8] Acayo, Grace (2017): International cooperation on cybersecurity matters, https://www.unodc.org/e4j/en/cybercrime/module-8/key-issues/international-cooperation-on-cybersecurity-matters.html.

[9] https://www.enisa.europa.eu/.

GLOSSARY OF TERMS

Account takeover (ATO) the fraudster gains access to a corporate email account, for example, by using stolen credentials and uses the account to commit fraud or obtain personally identifiable information.

Application is computer software designed to help a user perform specific tasks.

Business email compromise (BEC) in a BEC scam, the fraudster typically purports to be a senior executive within the company and asks an employee to make a payment—often with an element of urgency and/or secrecy.

Cash Deposits Sums of currency deposited in one or more accounts at a financial institution.

Compliance An action or state of adhering to a set of legislation, regulations, rules, policy, specifications, or understood norms.

Critical infrastructure The physical or virtual systems and assets that are vital to an organization or country. If these systems are compromised, the result would be catastrophic.

Customer Due Diligence (CDD) A set of internal controls that enable a financial institution to establish a customer's identity, predict with relative certainty the types of transactions in which the customer is likely to engage, and assess the extent to which the customer exposes it to a range of risks (i.e., money laundering and sanctions).

© The Editor(s) (if applicable) and The Author(s), under exclusive license to Springer Nature Switzerland AG 2023
F. I. Lessambo, *Anti-Money Laundering, Counter Financing Terrorism and Cybersecurity in the Banking Industry*, Palgrave Macmillan Studies in Banking and Financial Institutions,
https://doi.org/10.1007/978-3-031-23484-2

Cyberattack Any attempt to violate the security perimeter of a logical environment. An attack can focus on gathering information, damaging business processes, exploiting flaws, monitoring targets, interrupting business tasks, extracting value, causing damage to logical or physical assets, or using system resources to support attacks against other targets.

Cybersecurity The efforts to design, implement, and maintain security for an organization's network, which is connected to the Internet. It is a combination of logical/technical-, physical- and personnel-focused countermeasures, safeguards, and security controls.

Data security refers to the process of protecting data from unauthorized access and data corruption throughout its lifecycle. It includes data encryption, hashing, tokenization, and key management practices that protect data across all applications and platforms. Data security is narrower than cybersecurity.

DDoS (Distributed Denial of Service) Attack An attack which attempts to block access to and use of a resource. It is a violation of availability. DDOS (or DDoS) is a variation of the DoS attack (see DOS) and can include flooding attacks, connection exhaustion, and resource demand.

Denial of Service (DOS) A DOS attack works by sending traffic from unrelated sources toward a server on which an organization's website is hosted. It causes the server to overload and shut down, resulting in the organization losing its site temporarily.

Digitization is the conversion of data, information, text, pictures, sound, or other representations in analogue form into a digital form (i.e., binary code) that can be processed by computer.

Distributed Ledger Technology (DLT) refers to a type of technology protocol that enables simultaneous access, validation, and updating of an immutable ledger (digital record) distributed across multiple computers (and typically, across multiple entities or locations).

Domestic Transfer Electronic funds transfer in which the originator and beneficiary institutions are located in the same jurisdiction. A domestic transfer, therefore, refers to any chain of wire transfers that takes place entirely within the borders of a single jurisdiction, even though the actual system used to send the wire transfer may be located in another jurisdiction or online.

DOS (Denial of Service) An attack that attempts to block access to and use of a resource. It is a violation of availability. DOS (or DoS) attacks include flooding attacks, connection exhaustion, and resource demand. A flooding attack sends massive amounts of network traffic to the target overloading the ability of network devices and servers to handle the raw load.

Due Diligence The investigation and examination of a company or group conducted in the process of preparing for a business transaction. Due diligence should be completed before entering into any financial transaction or business relationship.

Electronic Money (E-Money) Electronic cash represents a series of monetary value units in some electronic format, such as being stored electronically online, on the hard drive of a device, or on the microchip of a plastic card.

Hacker A person who has knowledge and skill in analyzing program code or a computer system, modifying its functions or operations, and altering its abilities and capabilities. A hacker may be ethical and authorized (the original definition) or may be malicious and unauthorized (the altered but current use of the term)

Hacking is a criminal offence relating to unauthorized access to an automated data processing system?

Human Trafficking The trade of humans, most commonly for the purpose of sexual slavery, forced labor or commercial sexual exploitation. Trafficking occurs in almost every country in the world and is often cited as the second largest criminal enterprise in the world.

Internet of Things (IoT) The global network of all Internet-enabled devices and machines that are connected to the Internet and can collect, send, share, and act on data, using embedded sensors, processors, and communication hardware, without human interaction.

IPS (Intrusion Prevention System) A security tool that attempts to detect the attempt to compromise the security of a target and then prevent that attack from becoming successful. An IPS is considered a more active security tool as it attempts to proactively respond to potential threats.

Know Your Customer (KYC) Anti-money laundering policies and procedures used to determine the true identity of a customer and the type of activity that is "normal and expected," and to detect activity that is "unusual" for a particular customer.

Layering The second phase of the classic three-step money laundering process between placement and integration, layering involves distancing illegal proceeds from their source by creating complex levels of financial transactions designed to disguise the audit trail and to provide anonymity.

Malware Malware is a considerable threat to the banking sector. Malware infecting vulnerable end-user devices (such as computers and cell phones) can pose a risk to a bank's cybersecurity each time they connect with the network.

Monitoring An element of an institution's anti-money laundering program in which customer activity is reviewed for unusual or suspicious patterns, trends, or outlying transactions that do not fit a normal pattern.

Money Laundering The process of concealing or disguising the existence, source, movement, destination, or illegal application of illicitly-derived property or funds to make them appear legitimate. It usually involves a three part system: placement of funds into a financial system, layering of transactions to disguise the source, ownership and location of the funds, and integration of the funds into society in the form of holdings that appear legitimate. The definition of money laundering varies in each country where it is recognized as a crime.

PaaS (Platform-as-a-Service) A type of cloud computing service where the provider offers the customer the ability to operate custom code or applications. A PaaS operator determines which operating systems or execution environments are offered. It does not allow the customer to change operating systems, patch the OS or alter the virtual network space.

Pharming This technique is used by fraudsters to redirect users from an authentic website to a fake website. Hackers use it to steal the information required for online transactions. Therefore, this technique puts customers' data at risk and financial security.

Phishing is the collection of data by fraudulent, unfair or unlawful methods.

Ransomware is a method of cybercrime where files are encrypted and users are locked out, with the criminals demanding money to re-access the system.

Red Flag A warning signal that should bring attention to a potentially suspicious situation, transaction, or activity.

RegTech is a sub-set of FinTech that uses new technologies to comply with regulatory requirements more efficiently and effectively than existing capabilities.

Regulatory Agency A government entity responsible for supervising and overseeing one or more categories of financial institutions. The agency generally has authority to issue regulations, to conduct examinations, to impose fines and penalties, to curtail activities and, sometimes, to terminate charters of institutions under its jurisdiction.

Risk Appetite The amount of risk that a firm is willing to accept in pursuit of value or opportunity. A firm's risk appetite reflects its risk management approach and comfort level for undertaking business in situations in which there could be an elevated sanctions risk.

Smurfing A commonly used money laundering method, smurfing involves the use of multiple individuals and/or multiple transactions for making cash deposits, buying monetary instruments or bank drafts in amounts under the reporting threshold. The individuals hired to conduct the transactions are referred to as "smurfs."

Spoofing is a type of cyberattack wherein hackers will find a way to impersonate a banking website's URL with another website that looks and functions exactly in the same way as the original website.

Stripping Involves omitting or removing key information, such as the sender's name or the business name, from a payment message to avoid detection. It may happen with or without the knowledge of other participants in the transaction.

Terrorist Financing The process by which terrorists fund their operations in order to perform terrorist acts. There are two primary sources of financing for terrorist activities. The first involves financial support from countries, organizations, or individuals. The other involves a wide variety of revenue-generating activities, some illicit, including smuggling, and credit card fraud.

Virtual Currency A medium of exchange that operates in the digital space that can typically be converted into either a fiat (e.g., government issued currency) or it can be a substitute for real currency.

Vulnerability Any weakness in an asset or security protection which would allow for a threat to cause harm. It may be a flaw in coding, a mistake in configuration, a limitation of scope or capability, an error in architecture, design, or logic or a clever abuse of valid systems and their functions.

Wire Transfer Electronic transmission of funds among financial institutions on behalf of themselves or their customers. Wire transfers are financial vehicles covered by the regulatory requirements of many countries in the anti-money laundering effort.

BIBLIOGRAPHY

Acayo, Grace (2017): International Cooperation on Cybersecurity Matters, https://www.unodc.org/e4j/en/cybercrime/module-8/key-issues/internati onal-cooperation-on-cybersecurity-matters.html.

Adrian, Furma, Zappa, Francisco (202): The Privacy, Data Protection and Cyber-security Law Review: Argentina, *The Law Reviews*, https://thelawreviews.co.uk/title/the-privacy-data-protection-and-cybersecurity-law-review/argentina.

Allen, Karen (2021): South Africa Lays Down the Law on Cybercrime, ISS Pretoria, https://issafrica.org/iss-today/south-africa-lays-down-the-law-on-cybercrime.

Archon Secure (2022): Cyber Threats in the Banking Industry, https://www.arc honsecure.com/blog/banking-industry-cyber-threats.

Barberini, Dimitri (2022):Anti-Money Laundering Regulations in Italy, Sanc-tion Scanner, https://sanctionscanner.com/blog/anti-money-laundering-reg ulations-in-italy-411.

Beekarry, Navin (2011): The International Anti-Money Laundering and Combating the Financing of Terrorism Regulatory Strategy: A Critical Analysis of Compliance Determinants in International Law, *International Anti-Money Laundering Regulatory Strategy* 31: 137, 149–150.

Bernstein, Darryl (2021): Africa: Implementation of Cybersecurity and Data Protection Law Urgent across Continent, https://www.bakermckenzie.com/en/insight/publications/2021/06/africa-cybersecurity-data-protection-law.

© The Editor(s) (if applicable) and The Author(s), under exclusive license to Springer Nature Switzerland AG 2023
F. I. Lessambo, *Anti-Money Laundering, Counter Financing Terrorism and Cybersecurity in the Banking Industry*, Palgrave Macmillan Studies in Banking and Financial Institutions, https://doi.org/10.1007/978-3-031-23484-2

BIS (2003): The Joint- Forum- Initiatives by the BCBS, IAIS and IOSCO to Combat Money Laundering and the Financing of Terrorism, pp. 1–10, https://www.bis.org/publ/joint05.pdf.

BIS (2019): Basel Committee on Banking Supervision- Introduction of Guidelines on Interaction and Cooperation Between Prudential and AML/CFT Supervision, pp. 1–20, https://www.bis.org/bcbs/publ/d483.pdf.

BMI (2011): *Cyber-Sicherheitsstrategie für Deutschland: 2011.* Berlin, Germany: BMI.

Bowcut, Steven (2021): Cybersecurity in the Financial Services Industry; https://cybersecurityguide.org/industries/financial/.

Burns, C. (2019): Analysis from Encompass Shows 2019 Set to be Year of Record AML Fines. https://bit.ly/34uu5gv.

Caterina Beccarini e Claudia Biancotti (2018): Cybersecurity: The Contribution of the Bank of Italy and IVASS, pp. 15–16; http://www.bancadiitalia.it.

Clements, Julie (2021, April 28): Cyber Security in the Banking Industry—Top Trends to Know, https://www.managedoutsource.com/blog/cyber-security-in-banking-industry-top-trends-to-know/

Chadd, Katie (2020): The History of Cybercrime and Cybersecurity, 1940–2020.

Cotoc, Corina-Narcisa, Nitu, Maria, Scheau, Mircea Constantin (2021): Efficiency of Money Laundering Countermeasures: Case Studies from European Union Member States, *Risks* 9: 120. https://doi.org/10.3390/risks9060120.

Cybersecurity Ventures (2016): Hackerpocalypse: A Cybercrime Revelation. Retrieved on August 1, 2022 from: https://www.herjavecgroup.com/hackerpocalypse-cybercrime-report/. See also: OECD (2022): OECD work on digital security policy, https://www.oecd.org/digital/ieconomy/digital-security/oecd-work-on-digital-security-policy.pdf.

Day, Jessica (2022): Cybersecurity in Digital Banking: Everything You Need to Know, https://stefanini.com/en/trends/articles/cybersecurity-in-digital-banking-everything-you-need-to-know.

de Mello, José Luiz Homem, Binnie, Ricardo, do Val Fausto, Ana Cristina (2021): The New Regulatory Framework for AML in Brazil, International Bar Association, https://www.ibanet.org/article/D7273F5F-ABAF-4B44-90AB-16CF5095FBB6.

Hutten, Benjamin W. (2021): Compliance Lessons in Recent Office of Foreign Assets Control Enforcement, *Journal of Financial Compliance* 4(3): 210–221.

IMF (2016): Italy Report on the Observance of Standards and Codes (ROSC), p. 4, https://www.imf.org/external/pubs/ft/scr/2016/cr1644.pdf.

IMF (2021): The Global Cyber Threat, Finance & Development.

IMF (2022): Anti-Money Laundering/Combating the Financing of Terrorism—Topics, https://www.imf.org/external/np/leg/amlcft/eng/aml1.htm.

Jack, Franklin, Rivzi, Zain, Stacey, Gillian (2022): Filling the Gap: Scope of Canadian Anti-Money Laundering Laws Expanded, https://www.jdsupra.com/leg alnews/filling-the-gap-scope-of-canadian-anti-1511836/.

Jones, David (2021): Banks Outpace Other Industries in Cyber Investments, Defense Strategies: Report, https://www.cybersecuritydive.com/news/banks-cyber-security-investments/610045/.

Klick, J., Lau, S., Marzin, D. (2015): *Cyber-Security aus Sicht der Sicherheitspolitik*, Berlin, Germany: Freie Universität Berlin.

Kolmar, Chris (2022): 19 Money Laundering Statistics [2022] Facts About Money Laundering in the U.S., https://www.zippia.com/advice/money-lau ndering-statistics/.

Konstantin, Baranov, Tchoubykina, Elena (2020): Anti-Money Laundering Laws in Russia, https://seamless.legal/en/rus/publication/doing-business-in-rus sia-2020/banking-sector/the-anti-money-laundering-law.

Llanos-Small, Katie (2021): Old Infrastructure, New Services Create Fresh Bank Cybersecurity Risks, https://iupana.com/2019/05/06/cybersecurity-in-arg entina-banks-financial-services/?lang=en.

Lostri, Eugenia, Lewis, James Andrew, Wood, Georgia (2022): A Shared Responsibility: Public-Private Cooperation for Cybersecurity, Center for Strategic and International Studies, https://www.csis.org/analysis/shared-responsib ility-public-private-cooperation-cybersecurity.

Megaw, Nicholas (2021): Goldman Bets on UK Anti-money Laundering Start-up, *Financial Times*, https://www.ft.com/content/24152e93-a465-4159-9018-486120161d5a.

Nicolay, Rupert (2018): Keeping Ahead of Cybersecurity Challenges in Financial Services, https://cloudblogs.microsoft.com/industry-blog/financial-ser vices/2018/10/24/keeping-ahead-of-cybersecurity-challenges-in-financial-services/.

O'Driscoll, Aimee (2022): Spain Cyber Security and Cybercrime Statistics (2020–2022), https://www.comparitech.com/blog/information-security/spain-cyber-security-statistics/.

Otamend, Santiago (2018): State of Cybersecurity in the Banking Sector in Latin America and the Caribbean-FATF: Implementing Effective Legislative Frameworks to Combat Money Laundering in the Global Digital Economy.

Parraguez, Luisa (2017): The State of Cybersecurity in Mexico: An Overview, at: https://www.researchgate.net/publication/315728675.

Phadtare, Madhura (2019): Money Laundering Challenges in Saudi Arabia, https://regtechtimes.com/aml-certification-in-saudi-arabia/.

Reddy, Lokanadha, Bhargavi, V. (2018): Cyber Security Attacks in Banking Sector: Emerging Security Challenges and Threats, *American International Journal of Research in Humanities, Arts and Social Sciences*.

RSI Security (2021): Cyber Attacks on Banking Industry Organizations in 2021, https://blog.rsisecurity.com/cyber-attacks-on-banking-industry-organi zations-in-2021/.

Savona, E. U., Riccardi, M. (2015): From Illegal Markets to Legitimate Busi nesses: The Portfolio of Organized Crime in Europe. Trento. https://bit.ly/ 1Dli7W1.

Security at DB, https://corporates.db.com/in-focus/Focus-topics/cyber-sec urity/security-at-deutsche-bank.

Sordyl, Jaroslaw (2020): Cooperation and Exchange of Information as an Effective Cybersecurity Measure for Organizations, https://securityboul evard.com/2020/03/cooperation-and-exchange-of-information-as-an-effect ive-cybersecurity-measure-for-organisations/.

Vaissman, Carolina Uribe (2021): Data Protection and Cybersecurity Laws in Brazil, CMS, https://cms.law/en/int/expert-guides/cms-expert-guide-to-data-protection-and-cyber-security-laws/brazil.

Van Jaarsveld, Izelde Louise (2011): *Aspects of Money Laundering in South African Law*, Pretoria: University of South Africa, http://hdl.handle.net/ 10500/5091.

Vyacheslav, Khayryuzov (2021): The Privacy, Data Protection and Cybersecurity Law Review: Russia, *Law Review*, https://thelawreviews.co.uk/title/the-pri vacy-data-protection-and-cybersecurity-law-review/russia.

Wheeler, Jackie (2022): Guidance on Anti-Money Laundering (AML) in Banking and Finance for 2022, https://www.jumio.com/aml-guidance-banking-fin ance-2021/.

World Bank (2017): World Bank Toolkit on Combating Cybercrime.

World Bank (2017): Financial Sector's Cybersecurity: A Regulatory Digest, p. 28, https://thedocs.worldbank.org/en/doc/524901513362019919-013 0022017/original/FinSACCybersecDigestOct2017Dec2017.pdf.

Zaakir, Mohamed (2020): Data Protection and Cybersecurity Laws in South Africa, CMS, https://cms.law/en/int/expert-guides/cms-expert-guide-to-data-protection-and-cyber-security-laws/south-africa.

INDEX

A

Annunzio-Wylie Act, 60
Anti-Drug Abuse Act, 57, 59, 60
Argentina, 36, 189–192
Assistance and Access Act, 166
Australia, 42, 163, 164, 166, 167

B

Bank Secrecy Act (BSA), 6, 58, 59,
  63, 65–68, 75, 206–210
Brazil, 36, 179–182
Budapest Convention, 37

C

China, 2, 25, 125–128
ComplyAdvantage, 9
Consumer Data Rights (CDR),
  166–168
Council of Europe, 37, 86, 87, 172
Cybercrime, 23, 30, 36, 37, 39–42,
  44, 45, 47, 50, 77, 78, 86, 87,
  104, 109, 114, 140, 141, 161,
  181, 185, 191, 194, 200, 201

convention, 37, 38, 47, 86, 87

cooperation, 42, 47, 87, 191

Cyber insurance, 54

Cyber risk assessment, 54, 71

Cybersecurity, 11, 12, 14–18, 20, 21,
  25, 33, 36, 41, 43, 47, 49, 51,
  52, 54, 68, 69, 72–75, 77, 82,
  86, 88, 93, 95, 108–110, 113,
  118, 119, 121, 125, 127–129,
  133–137, 140, 145, 148, 149,
  153, 155, 159, 174, 180, 181,
  185, 190–192, 201–203,
  217–219

Act, 72, 93, 133, 201

Counteroffensive, 11

History, 12

risks, 51, 71, 72, 74, 125, 126,
  153, 192, 202, 203

© The Editor(s) (if applicable) and The Author(s), under exclusive   231
license to Springer Nature Switzerland AG 2023
F. I. Lessambo, *Anti-Money Laundering, Counter Financing Terrorism
and Cybersecurity in the Banking Industry*, Palgrave Macmillan
Studies in Banking and Financial Institutions,
https://doi.org/10.1007/978-3-031-23484-2

D

Data protection, 39, 40, 47, 74, 81, 88–90, 125, 127, 135, 146, 154, 159, 170, 174, 191, 194, 195, 201

Data Security Standard (DSS), 74

E

European Union (EU), 9, 68, 79–86, 88, 90, 92, 102, 104, 108, 109, 114, 118, 122, 141, 146, 152, 154, 175, 191, 218, 219

Exchange of information, 42, 123, 160, 215–217

F

Financial Action Task Force (FATF), 5, 7, 8, 33–36, 99, 100, 114, 120, 132, 144, 148, 174, 208, 211

Financial Action Task Force on Money Laundering in Latin America (GAFILAT), 36

Financial Crimes Enforcement Network (FinCEn), 6, 7, 31, 58, 75, 207

France, 99, 100, 102, 103, 105, 106

G

General Data Protection Regulation (GDPR), 81–83, 89, 90, 93, 98, 105, 113, 141, 154

Germany, 12, 43, 92–94, 96, 97

H

Human right safeguards, 39

I

International Association of Insurance Supervisors (IAIS), 8, 45

Immigration & Customs Enforcement (ICE), 78

International Criminal Police Organization (INTERPOL), 40

International Cyber Security Protection Alliance (ICSPA), 44, 45

International Money Laundering Information Network (IMoLIN), 34, 35

International Organization of Securities Commissions (IOSCO), 8, 45

International telecommunication union (ITU), 41

Internet Society (ISOC), 44

J

Japan, 42, 87, 131–135

M

Money laundering, 1–9, 33–36, 50, 57–65, 75, 79, 80, 84, 85, 91, 99–101, 107, 108, 114, 119–121, 126, 131–133, 137, 138, 140, 143–145, 147, 151, 152, 156, 157, 169, 170, 173, 179, 180, 183, 184, 186, 189, 190, 192, 193, 195–198, 209, 211, 215

Control Act, 57, 59

Cycle, 1, 2

international organizations, 35

mutual assistance, 38

Specialist, 9

Suppression Act, 61

N
National Defense Authorization Act
   (NDAA), 68
Network information security, 126

O
Organization for Economic
   Co-operation and Development
   (OECD), 33, 36, 43, 218

P
Payment Card Industry (PCI), 74
Personal Information Protection &
   Electronic Documents Act
   (PIPEDA), 160, 167
Privacy Act, 166
Protection of Personal Information
   Act, 201

S
Sarbanes-Oxley (SOX) act, 74
Saudi Arabia, 193–195
Second Payments Services Directive
   (PSD2), 81–83
Security

application, 22, 28, 30, 51, 105,
   108, 109
cloud, 19, 20, 28, 29, 128
information, 7, 11, 12, 26, 43, 52,
   54, 86, 88, 95, 96, 98, 109,
   118, 126–129, 141, 155, 157,
   160, 161, 165, 218, 219
network, 11, 25, 26, 29, 30, 51,
   54, 86, 88, 108, 109, 118,
   126, 128, 218, 219
Security of Critical Infrastructure
   (SOCI), 167
South Africa, 87, 197, 198, 200, 201
Spain, 113, 114, 118
Switzerland, 119–123

T
Turkey, 37, 173, 174, 176

U
United Kingdom (UK), 9, 42,
   151–155
United Nations Office of Drugs and
   Crime (UNODC), 42, 180
USA PATRIOT Act, 59, 65–67, 70,
   72

Printed by Printforce, United Kingdom